Hijacked

NAASR Working Papers

Series Editor: Brad Stoddard, McDaniel College in Westminster, Maryland.

NAASR Working Papers provides a venue for publishing the latest research carried out by scholars who understand religion to be an historical element of human cognition, practice, and organization. Whether monographs or multi-authored collections, the volumes published in this series all reflect timely, cutting edge work that takes seriously both the need for developing bold theories as well as rigorous testing and debate concerning the scope of our tools and the implications of our studies. NAASR Working Papers therefore assess the current state-of-the-art while charting new ways forward in the academic study of religion.

Published:
Constructing "Data" in Religious Studies: Examining the Architecture of the Academy
Edited by Leslie Dorrough Smith

Method Today: Redescribing Approaches to the Study of Religion
Edited by Brad Stoddard

"Religion" in Theory and Practice: Demystifying the Field for Burgeoning Academics
Russell T. McCutcheon

Forthcoming:
Imagining Smith: Mapping Methods in the Study of Religion
Edited by Barbara Krawcowicz

Jesus and Addiction to Origins: Toward an Anthropocentric Study of Religion
Willi Braun (edited by Russell T. McCutcheon)

Key Categories in the Study of Religion: Contexts and Critiques
Edited by Rebekka King

On the Subject of Religion: Charting the Fault Lines of a Field of Study
Edited by James Dennis LoRusso

Remembering J. Z. Smith
Edited by Emily D. Crews and Russell T. McCutcheon

Hijacked

A Critical Treatment of the Public Rhetoric of
Good and Bad Religion

Edited by
Leslie Dorrough Smith,
Steffen Führding, and
Adrian Hermann

SHEFFIELD UK   BRISTOL CT

Published by Equinox Publishing Ltd.

UK: Office 415, The Workstation, 15 Paternoster Row, Sheffield, South Yorkshire S1 2BX

USA: ISD, 70 Enterprise Drive, Bristol, CT 06010

www.equinoxpub.com

First published 2020

© Leslie Dorrough Smith, Steffen Führding, Adrian Hermann, and contributors 2020

All rights reserved. No part of this publication may be reproduced or transmitted in any form or by any means, electronic or mechanical, including photocopying, recording or any information storage or retrieval system, without prior permission in writing from the publishers.

ISBN-13 978 1 78179 726 6 (hardback)
         978 1 78179 727 3 (paperback)
         978 1 78179 728 0 (ePDF)

British Library Cataloguing-in-Publication Data

A catalogue record for this book is available from the British Library.

Library of Congress Cataloging-in-Publication Data

Names: Hijacked! A Critical Treatment of the Public Rhetoric of 'Good' and 'Bad' Religion (2017 : Bonn, Germany) | Smith, Leslie Dorrough, 1975- editor. | Führding, Steffen, 1981- editor. | Hermann, Adrian, editor.
Title: Hijacked : a critical treatment of the public rhetoric of good and bad religion / edited by Leslie Dorrough Smith, Steffen Führding, and Adrian Hermann.
Description: Sheffield, South Yorkshire ; Bristol, CT: Equinox Publishing Ltd., 2020. | Series: NAASR working papers | "A group of international scholars gathered in June 2017 at the University of Bonn to participate in a conference entitled Hijacked! A Critical Treatment of the Public Rhetoric of "Good" and "Bad" Religion. Their work together forms the content of this book." | Includes bibliographical references and index. | Summary: "Whether intentionally or not much of our public discourse on religion involves a subtle, but incredibly powerful, distinction between "good" and "bad" religion. The implications of these labeling practices are far-reaching, indeed, for such judgments manifest in terms such as "fundamentalist," "radical," and "extremist," words that are often the gauge by which governments worldwide determine everything from the parameters of religious freedom, to what constitutes an act of terrorism, to whether certain groups receive legal protections. Conversely, it is often surprising to see how different groups that may otherwise better typify the extremist profile remain unscathed by punitive governmental or social measures because of their pre-existing social popularity or perceived normalcy. This volume argues that public inquiry into religion is guided by unspoken value judgments, which are themselves the products of rarely-discussed political interests. Put differently, is quite easy for scholars to revoke or impart religious "credentials" to a group depending on whether that group's members behave as outside commentators think religious people should"— Provided by publisher.
Identifiers: LCCN 2019038751 (print) | LCCN 2019038752 (ebook) | ISBN 9781781797266 (hardback) | ISBN 9781781797273 (paperback) | ISBN 9781781797280 (ebook)
Subjects: LCSH: Religion—Public opinion—Congresses. | Religious fundamentalism—Public opinion—Congresses. | Religion—Study and teaching—Social aspects—Congresses. | Religion and sociology—Congresses. | Rhetoric—Social aspects—Congresses.
Classification: LCC BL60 .H475 2017 (print) | LCC BL60 (ebook) | DDC 201/.7—dc23
LC record available at https://lccn.loc.gov/2019038751
LC ebook record available at https://lccn.loc.gov/2019038752

Typeset by JS Typesetting Ltd, Porthcawl, Mid Glamorgan

Contents

Preface   vii
Leslie Dorrough Smith, Steffen Führding, and Adrian Hermann

Part I: The Public Rhetoric of Good and Bad Religion

Introduction to Part I   1
Leslie Dorrough Smith, Steffen Führding, and Adrian Hermann

1. Introduction: "And What Kind of Society Does That Create?"   3
   Russell T. McCutcheon
2. Good Muslim, Bad Muslim: Neo-Orientalism and the Study of Religion   12
   Aaron W. Hughes
3. Religious Studies and the Jargon of Authenticity   23
   Jason Ā. Josephson-Storm

Part II: Politics

Introduction to Part II   35
Leslie Dorrough Smith, Steffen Führding, and Adrian Hermann

4. Toward a Critique of Postsecular Rhetoric   37
   Naomi R. Goldenberg
5. The Political Utility of the Past: The Case of Greek Fire-Walking Rituals   48
   Vaia Touna
6. Privatized Publics and Scholarly Silos: Gender, Religion, and their Theoretical Fault Lines   56
   K. Merinda Simmons
7. What's Religious Freedom Got to Do With It? On the Niqab Affair in Canadian Politics   61
   Matt Sheedy

Part III: Media

Introduction to Part III   69
Leslie Dorrough Smith, Steffen Führding, and Adrian Hermann

8. The Strange and Familiar Spiritual Journey of Reza Aslan   71
   Martha Smith Roberts
9. The Journalist-Ethnographer, Religious Diversity, and the Euphemization of Social Relations   87
   Carmen Becker

10	Scopophilia and the Manufacture of "Good" Religion *Leslie Dorrough Smith*	98
11	Naturalizing the Transnational Capitalist Class: Reza Aslan's *Believer* and the Ideological Reproduction of an Emerging Social Formation *Craig Prentiss*	108
12	Authentic Religion—or, How to Be a Good Citizen *Steffen Führding*	118

Part IV: University

	Introduction to Part IV *Leslie Dorrough Smith, Steffen Führding, and Adrian Hermann*	127
13	'Bad Religion' on the University Campus: "Political Correctness" and the Future of the Insider/Outsider Problem in the Study of Religion *Adrian Hermann and Stefan Priester*	129
14	Studying Religion in a Post-Truth World *Stephanie Gripentrog*	150
15	The Good, the Bad, and the Non-Religion: The Good/Bad Rhetoric in Non-Religion Studies *Christopher R. Cotter*	154
16	The Campus as a 'Safe Space'? A Sociology of Knowledge Perspective on the New Student Protests *David Kaldewey*	169

Part V: Classroom

	Introduction to Part V *Leslie Dorrough Smith, Steffen Führding, and Adrian Hermann*	181
17	What Teaching New Religions Tells Us about the Discourse on 'Good' and 'Bad' Religion *David G. Robertson*	183
18	Unintentionally Constructing 'Good' and 'Bad' Religions in Teaching Classical European Social Theories at a Japanese University *Mitsutoshi Horii*	194
19	Good and Bad, Legitimate and Illegitimate Religion in Education *Wanda Alberts*	205
20	Benign Religion as Normal Religion *Suzanne Owen*	212
	Index	219

Preface

Leslie Dorrough Smith, Steffen Führding, and Adrian Hermann

As any news observer knows, staying up on current events today is often an act of navigating through various accounts of so-called religious extremism. Such news stories often begin when journalists report on an act of violence, polarizing rhetoric, or nationalist xenophobia performed in the name of a particular religion. Within such reporting it is not unusual to find scholars, pundits, and politicians who claim that such extremist acts betray the "real" version of that religion that otherwise operates innocently (and positively) outside of the media's eye. This more "authentic" religion is often deemed superior on the grounds that its more tolerant, diverse, and (generally speaking) progressive philosophies are indicative of some core that typifies the religion, depicting the more conservative and/or extreme variant as a hijacking or twisting of that positive core.

This is not merely one way of reporting the news; it is, in practice, one of only a few standard narrative forms on the subject. Americans have seen such narrative choices animated by their last two presidents, as debates over how to rhetorically classify terrorist violence performed by Muslims have centered on whether to include mention of the religion Islam in the label. President Barack Obama generally refused to refer to the Islamic State (also known as ISIS or ISIL) as a Muslim group on the grounds that "real" Muslims would not behave in such fashion. On the other hand, his successor, Donald Trump, has regularly referred to any sort of violence performed by Muslims as indicative of "radical Islamic terrorism," and promised in his inauguration speech to eradicate it "from the face of the Earth" (Holley 2017). Whether one prefers one method of labelling over another is, obviously, rooted in the specifics of one's own political aims. But there is no doubt that, whichever method one prefers, both reflect a general sense that it is quite possible to differentiate "good" from "bad" religion.

Indeed, much of our public discourse on religion involves this subtle, but incredibly powerful, distinction, one that manifests in a variety of adjectives, interpretive frames, and other rhetorical techniques that, on the surface, may appear quite neutral. However, these descriptors are hardly self-evident, but are the product of a series of politicized opinions and moral judgments, a fact that complicates the position of many public figures—from scholars to politicians to journalists—who claim that their use of this labelling is simply obvious or objective. In fact, many types of public experts frequently identify certain religious groups as "illegitimate," "twisted," "hijacked," or even "non-religious" when members of those groups do things that are actually quite common religious practices. These include things such as: failing to acknowledge the legitimacy of other religious or cultural groups; displaying what are usually considered sexist, racist, or other prejudicial behaviors; engaging in violence or other physical or political power plays to achieve their members' desired ends; and adopting beliefs or practices that compromise the popular sense that religion is categorically peaceful, loving, good, and helpful.

The implications of these labelling practices are far-reaching, indeed, for such judgments manifest in terms such as "fundamentalist," "radical," and "extremist," words that are often the gauge by which governments worldwide determine everything from the parameters of religious freedom, to what constitutes an act of terrorism, to whether certain groups receive legal protections. Conversely, it is often surprising to see how different groups that may otherwise better typify this extremist profile remain unscathed by punitive governmental or social measures because of their pre-existing social popularity or perceived normalcy, as evidenced by the sharp rise in (pro-Christian, anti-Muslim, anti-Semitic) white supremacist activity in the US after Trump's inauguration (SPLC 2018). Being able to identify this labelling practice at work (not to mention the dynamics that inform it) is thus of utmost importance, for it is quite common for a variety of social commentators to evoke or impart religious "credentials" to a group depending on whether that group's members behave as such observers and analysts think religions *should*.

The public inquiry into religion thus continues to be guided by these unspoken value judgments, which, although almost constantly in the limelight, are rarely discussed as political phenomena in and of themselves. In an effort to correct this, a group of international scholars gathered in June 2017 at the University of Bonn to participate in a conference entitled "Hijacked! A Critical Treatment of the Public Rhetoric of 'Good' and 'Bad' Religion." Their work together forms the content of this book. Those of us who organized the conference were interested in how an international group of scholars might, together, consider the rhetorical strategies that various social groups use to construct the category "religion" as a public, political tool. Our goals for the group included, among other things: analyzing the political interests that shape such good/bad perceptions; identifying the frequently unnoticed rhetorical practices that create this distinction between "good religion" and "bad religion"; and exploring new opportunities for critical analysis of this political dynamic that are more analytically sound.

The task of the conference participants was to underscore how such forms of political interest animate the good/bad religion dichotomy across four influential social realms that helped to structurally organize the conference: politics, the media, the university, and the classroom setting. The reader will find this same four-part structure reflected in Parts II–V of this book, with three foundational essays forming Part I.

Parts II–V each highlight a central case study (featuring an area of interest or specialty of the writer), along with a series of scholarly responses to that initial exemplar. As was true at the conference, so this book exemplifies how one can tap into the almost endless expanse of social life to find any number of examples, applications, and interesting moments of analysis that demonstrate the power of the good/bad religion dichotomy at work. Thus, while the reader will most certainly be intrigued with the sheer range of topics discussed (everything from Greek fire-walking to schoolchildren's textbooks to how we talk about "cults"), the larger principles we engage are applicable far outside of any one example. This is, we hope, a major contribution of this work: to demonstrate the ubiquity, power, and mechanics of the rhetoric of "good" and "bad" religion.

As the editors we want to thank the team at the Forum Internationale Wissenschaft of the University of Bonn for the excellent organization of the conference. Special thanks are due to Petra Tillessen, the main organizer on the ground, as well as to Sónia Lopes Belabbes, Raja Bernard, Mila Brill, Philipp Kuster, and Rafaela Eulberg. We also want to thank the German Research Foundation (DFG) for their financial support, and are equally grateful to Janet Joyce, Valerie Hall, and Sarah Lee at Equinox, as well as to the editor of the NAASR Working Papers, Brad Stoddard, for their interest in this project and for envisioning this volume as part of the new series. We also would like to thank Hamish Ironside for editing and Jill Sweet for typesetting this book.

Leslie Dorrough Smith is Associate Professor of Religious Studies and Director of the Women's and Gender Studies program at Avila University (Kansas City, MO, USA). She is author of *Righteous Rhetoric: Sex, Speech, and the Politics of Concerned Women for America* (Oxford, 2014), and *Compromising Positions: Sex Scandals, Politics, and American Christianity* (Oxford, 2020).

Steffen Führding, PhD, teaches at the Department for the Study of Religion at Leibniz University Hannover. He has published on the history of the study of religion and theoretical debates within the discipline, including the monograph *Jenseits von Religion* (transcript, 2015).

Adrian Hermann is Full Professor of Religion and Society and Director of the Department of Religion Studies at Forum Internationale Wissenschaft, University of Bonn. His work focuses on the global history of the concept of "religion," the use of non-fictional media in contemporary religious movements, and the religious history of the globalized world. He is the author of *Unterscheidungen der Religion* (Göttingen: Vandenhoeck und Ruprecht, 2015) and is currently working on a monograph on Philippine independent Catholicism around 1900.

References

Holley, Peter. 2017. "'Radical Islamic terrorism': Three words that separate Trump from most of Washington." *Washington Post*, March 1. Retrieved from www.washingtonpost.com/news/the-fix/wp/2017/02/28/radical-islamic-terrorism-three-words-that-separate-trump-from-most-of-washington/ (archived at www.webcitation.org/78aCGISfc).

SPLC. 2018. "The Year in Hate: Trump Buoyed White Supremacists in 2017, Sparking Backlash Among Black Nationalist Groups." February 21. Retrieved from www.splcenter.org/news/2018/02/21/year-hate-trump-buoyed-white-supremacists-2017-sparking-backlash-among-black-nationalist (archived at www.webcitation.org/78aAYuCTH).

Part I

The Public Rhetoric of Good and Bad Religion

Introduction to Part I

Leslie Dorrough Smith, Avila University
Steffen Führding, Leibniz University
Adrian Hermann, University of Bonn

This opening part of the book comprises three foundational essays, all of which display for the reader the weight of the issues that drive the chapters that follow. Although often addressing a series of disparate perspectives and/or data sets, all three of these essays direct us back to a most central point in this volume: those who report various types of information about religion (whether journalists, scholars, or other types of culture-critics) are, themselves, important points of data. They are not simply epiphenomenal to the process of producing knowledge.

The first essay (Chapter 1) is an introduction from *Russell T. McCutcheon*, who was one of a small group (including the editors/organizers) that originally began to brainstorm the concept of the conference on which this book is based. Anyone familiar with McCutcheon's work knows that his very substantial contribution to the field of Religious Studies lies largely with analyzing the political deployment of this good/bad religion distinction, and thus we start here with his own theoretical introduction to what is at stake when such categories emerge as the self-evident principles upon which supposedly rigorous scholarship on religion is grounded.

The second essay (Chapter 2) is written by *Aaron Hughes*, whose book *Islam and the Tyranny of Authenticity: An Inquiry into Disciplinary Apologetics* (Equinox, 2016) served as a model for all conference participants as we considered what shape rigorous analysis of this good/bad dichotomy might take. Hughes demonstrates how such rhetoric is highly operative in much of the subfield of Islamic religious studies, and brings to light that its primary function is to protect a specifically progressive view of Islam rather than generate and analyze historically critical data about the religion across time.

The third essay in this first part (Chapter 3), by *Jason Ā. Josephson-Storm*, responds to Hughes's contribution from the perspective of Buddhist studies, engaging with the insider/outsider problem in religious studies and questions of value-neutrality in the social sciences by challenging the often unstated view that insiders have privileged access as well as the claim that outsiders are necessarily more critical.

Chapter 1

Introduction: "And What Kind of Society Does That Create?"

Russell T. McCutcheon

He introduced himself as a doctor who had studied comparative religion at Georgetown with professors who were "the epitome of intellect and scholarship." He said that what he learned was that if you want to understand Islam, or anything, "you have to be sincere" and "you have to use your brain."

He looked around at the crowd.

"Because it's easy to demonize. You know, 'Everybody else is crazy and I'm just right'," he said sharply. "And what kind of society does that create? That's what ISIS does. That's what these zealots do. Do we want to be like that? As Americans, don't we want to be better than that? We better be better than that."

He glanced at his outline and made the point that of course Islam has its zealots, and he condemns them.

"But that's not what we're talking about," he said. "Because if you say, 'That's Islam,' then that's like me saying, 'Well, Christianity is David Koresh,'" he said, referring to the cult leader. (McCrummen 2017)[1]

This is from a newspaper account of Dr. Ayaz Virji—a 42 year-old rural health specialist who was born in Kenya but raised in Florida and who was then working in western Minnesota—speaking at a public forum on Islam, in Granite Falls, MN (population 3,000). As detailed in the article, back in November of 2016 his county had gone for then candidate Donald Trump in the US presidential election by six percentage points (a big spread in what was otherwise a close vote), leaving him and his family rethinking their move to the US's rural Midwest, what with the feeling in the air that "I think Islam hates us" (as candidate Trump had told CNN in a campaign interview on March 9, 2016; see Schleifer 2016). But, instead of leaving, he began speaking in public on Islam—*his* religion. The article, from which the above quotation was taken, provides a detailed description of his efforts and the locals' reactions.

I find this quotation rather interesting for the manner in which it, like the theme of the conference at Universität Bonn where earlier versions of the following chapters were first presented (in June of 2017), makes apparent the problems with essentializing any social identity (as if the actions of, say, the Branch Davidians should be understood as necessarily reflecting badly on all Christians)[2] while, *at the same time*, it demonstrates how we inevitably employ that very social strategy in our seemingly mundane, everyday acts of identification (inasmuch as the speaker presumes that there are "zealots," or what most simply refer to as extremists, who are in opposition to us—or, in this case, the group with which he himself identifies: Americans). The moral of this no doubt heart-felt talk seems to be that, instead of painting with a broad brush and demonizing all others, we must moderate those Othering strategies by painting with a rather finer brush so as to identify the "correct" outsiders; for, to answer his rhetorical question—"And what kind of society does that create?"—we might need to consider that a discourse on essential and uniform authenticity that can be corrupted and polluted (i.e., each identity has its limits, after all) may be a necessary device in the creation of any society with which an otherwise diverse collection of people is hoped to have some affinity and thus shared investments.

So, in reply to his question, we might say, "Show me a society and I'll demonstrate that it's more than likely created *in just this way.*"

For as scholars studying identity have long understood, we all need an Other; in other words, techniques that mark an affinity's boundaries seem to be among the socio-rhetorical mechanisms that we all use. Problems result, of course, when those who once might have felt that they enjoyed full standing in the group suddenly discover previously unapparent fracture points and gaps that suddenly turn them into traitors in someone else's midst. For example, a little later in the news story we read as follows:

> "I'll tell you. After the election, I was angry. And I was angry at my community for what they did. And I was ready to leave. OK? I was ready to go and say you know what? Not my job. People think I'm a terrorist? I'm outta here. Fine. Find somebody else. The reason I'm here is not because I want to—my faith is very personal to me. I'm here because who else is going to do this, if not me?"
>
> People were just sitting there, listening, not saying anything.
>
> He asked them to imagine how they would feel if he judged Christians the way some people judge Muslims.
>
> If he was dishonest, he said, he would pull out all the most violent Bible verses and say Christianity commands followers to kill.
>
> If he was unfair, he would call the Christian cross a "symbol of torture."
>
> The room was quiet.
>
> "How do you feel?" he asked.
>
> "Love thy neighbor? Do unto others?"
>
> "Why should I come to rural America and help people who think I'm a terrorist and say, 'Let's ban these people from coming here! Ban these doctors from coming here!'"

Judging by these claims and the rhetorical questions directed toward his initially silent audience, it seems to have been a charged but no less fascinating social occasion: for here a member who feels himself to have been cast out, at least in the authorized rhetoric of some in the group (i.e., recall Trump's claim: "I think Islam hates us") was working diligently either to remain or, perhaps better said, re-enter the group, noting his anger at what he characterizes as "my community." The eventual apologies from some in attendance suggests to us that we would be mistaken to assume that this community—whether his or not—was uniform in its views on the apparent Other in its midst.

But the question that, by the end of the article, still remains unanswered is whether the citizens of these small towns now see him (or, in fact, ever saw him) as a member of *their* community. As is evident from the apologies, some of them apparently felt chagrined or even saddened that Dr. Virji feels "more and more like a stranger in a rural Midwestern town." In fact, were he not a medical doctor, there's no telling how his presence may have played out; for given the scarcity of health professionals in much of rural America, the literal well-being of this one community (however its limits are defined) may be riding on its ability successfully to include at least this one apparently different member within its ranks.

So here we have a situation where two parties that are characterized by differences—the Muslim doctor and family on one side and some of the so-called "heartland of America" townspeople on the other (more than likely Christian and white in large part)—are challenged to try to find a similarity of sufficient significance to all parties for their co-participation in this imagined thing called a community to continue.

Now, as the late Jonathan Z. Smith noted long ago (e.g., see his book *Drudgery Divine* [1990], which, regardless its ostensible focus on the study of early forms of Christianity, I read as actually being an extended essay on how to engage in academically credible comparative work), every comparison requires a minimum of three elements: the two items being placed alongside each other, whether to be judged similar or different, and the "in terms of which" or the "with regard to" that structures the manner in which the two items are placed and thereby made to relate to one another. You and I are different, of course, in almost innumerable ways (i.e., How tall are you? When were you born? What's your favorite flavor of ice cream—if you eat ice cream, that is ...?) but should we instead be compared to one another in the light of our shared differences (i.e., similarities) that become apparent only once we are both compared to, say, a sponge, then perhaps our previously evident differences will pale in the light of the profound similarity that we, as two human beings (regardless which ice cream we each select), can suddenly be seen to share once that multicellular parazoan is placed on the table next to us (on comparison see Hughes 2017).

The lesson here is that an identity (i.e., shared traits sufficient to conclude that two things are similar enough for us to claim that they are the same) operates along a changeable continuum—a continuum which shifts and moves based on the fluid standard against which any two items are measured. For the sponge could have been a rock, or a horse, or, perhaps, a person with a sufficient number of heretofore unrecognized similarities *to just one of us*, such that our prior partnership (at least when we were compared to the sponge) dissolves, only to be replaced by one of us now being estranged from the other (along with the other's new partner).

The challenge of long term identifications—identities that seem to endure, such that people today routinely call themselves by family names that genealogists say can be traced back for generations, if not millennia—is managing those all too changeable standards and the varied situations that prompt those changes. For adjust them just a bit—i.e., make the simple modification of tracing my lineage though my mother rather than my father, for instance—and we might suddenly find ourselves on the outs with the group we'd once called our own. (Case in point: in my own case I'm of Scottish decent, or so one might conclude based upon my surname, but I'm told that I have more French in me than anything, while I'm supposedly neither and, instead, am Canadian, though I've worked in the US for 25 years, making me hardly the Canadian that I once took myself to be ...)

And so we return to the rhetorical role that ISIS and David Koresh played that evening in a public forum in Granite Falls. For they were both rather useful to the doctor in helping to modulate that continuum of virtually limitless similarities and differences that he simultaneously shares with his audience.

For if we entertain that Dr. Virji was, on that occasion, a social actor (with considerable symbolic capital, we can't forget, given that such towns badly need a local doctor, as already noted) trying *to do something with words* (in this case, to work his way back into a social group from which he felt newly alienated) then we can understand that the utility of "zealots" is not that it is an innocuous term that innocently names a stable thing somewhere out there in the world but, rather, that positing the existence of that uniform group of extreme Others helps to make evident a set of qualities whose commonality he sought to establish, thereby uniting all those gathered in that room on that one evening—himself included—by excluding all those others. For despite the apparent differences between himself and the locals—differences easily recognized by the locals, apparently, which may include a large number of observable traits and practices, to be sure (from skin color or language and accent to the food one eats, the holidays one celebrates, the sorts of names one has, and, in this case, the number of times a day one prays, let alone how and where one does it)—at one such talk, as reported by the *Twin Cities Pioneer Press*, he said:

> "Do I look like a terrorist?" he said smiling at them, and after talking for an hour about what "99.99 percent" of Muslims believe, he ended with a slideshow of family photos.
> "Look! We're normal!" he said. "That's our cat!"

Such references to the zealots, then work rhetorically much as did my above mention of the sponge: both are a rhetorically useful extreme instance in the light of which differences that were once apparent to each of us, about each of us, begin to disappear.

For normalcy, of course, is a negotiable judgment—in this case, it is claimed with regard to a number of overlapping, mundane traits whose otherwise unnoticed or unsignified commonality is accentuated only by drawing attention to the distance between, for instance, us both having cats, on the one hand, and the abhorrent atrocities that we've learned that members of the Islamic State have regularly practiced (from horrendous beheadings, burning, and drownings of prisoners to throwing people accused of homosexuality to their deaths from structures several stories high) or the distance between us and what we know that the Lord's Resistance Army (LRA), now operating in Uganda and southern Sudan, have done (a group using Christian symbols and identifiers, seeking to rule Uganda by, for instance, the rigid implementation of the Ten Commandments)[3]—another group that Dr. Virji brought up during one of his community talks.

Now, I myself likely share much that I consider to be consequential with the doctor and his family, so I don't wish my analysis to be taken as a criticism of his efforts; rather, despite probably wishing to live in his world, with a cat (or, better, with my dog, Izzy), and while I admit to having tremendous feelings of estrangement from the world as envisioned by either members of ISIS or the LRA, let alone the Branch Davidians, as a scholar I am nonetheless curious about how this sliding scale of identity works (in both the case of the local and familiar as well as the foreign and strange), for our daily lives are filled with experiences of objects and subjects that we take to have enduring identities—so how, if my above analysis is persuasive, does this even result? Or, to put it another way, I am now old enough to have seen a variety of once close, even self-evident and thus taken-for-granted social ties wither and, eventually, disappear. I could, for example, mention the time, in high school, when I witnessed my father call one of his younger but estranged sisters (with whom he'd been close, as a child, as members of families often are, but with whom there had been an ill-defined falling out some decades before, which seems to have involved the social upheaval provoked by what was then my mother's new presence and role in his family). He had called to let her know that he'd learned that her husband had recently died—the first time they had spoken in many years. Overhearing his side of the phone conversation, speaking to an aunt I'd never met (and still have not), I listened as he repeated his name on the phone, to her, and then identified himself as "your brother," since she'd clearly not known who this person was who was calling her. Looking back on that occasion—though I didn't have the words for it then—it made plain that identity is an historical phenomenon, that it changes over time and occasion, and that it thereby results from routine actions that, due to some social and thus historical disruption, may cease at some point to be routine. And the identity that previously resulted—i.e., the ease with which we once overlooked differences and were content with highlighting certain similarities that we happened to share—then ceases as well. So nurturing, even managing the contingent, sliding scale of similarity and difference—a management that's sometimes prone to crumble, as both the doctor's small town and my father's family make evident—takes effort, the sort of work that the good doctor decided to invest in that evening when he spoke—which brings me back to notions of essence and authenticity which I only hinted at earlier.

For if a social actor is able to successfully represent just this, and not that, collection of contingently shared traits (after all, had we assorted and grouped ourselves by means of eye color, birth order, or earning potential rather than, say, height, let alone gender, skin color, or national origins, then you and I would likely not be in the same group together) as *necessarily* shared, as *inevitably* common, and as *unquestionably* uniform (a representation that takes considerable rhetorical effort, of course), then two things follow: (i) we now have a way to assert that our group, inasmuch as it is a group, has a deep core, an immovable anchor, and a solid foundation—or, we might as well just call it a timeless and unchanging *essence*—and (ii) we now also have a way to chart, measure, and then characterize and value any deviations from this source, such that those we consider to be interlopers, despite their proclaimed affiliation, can be understood (at least by those claiming greater proximity to the supposed core) to be illegitimate, alienated outliers—in a word, *inauthentic*. (This wagon-circling is precisely what some in the town may have done to cause the alienation experienced by the doctor, such as when someone on the street one day, stopped him on the sidewalk to tell him that Jesus loves him.[4] But it was also what the doctor himself was doing rhetorically, with examples of the like-minded and like-interested Muslims he cited, in order to argue that the so-called extremists do not represent Islam.) And, should these unauthorized others persist in their claims of membership, those occupying the orthodox high ground—the other side in this social contest—can resort to what have by now become the familiar counterclaims that zealots have "hijacked the movement."

My hope is that by this point readers are willing to entertain that, as suggested earlier, all of these words, at that public forum, are doing something other than just neutrally describing realities on the ground; instead, they are actively, rhetorically, constituting the very ground on which group-building takes place. For such words as orthodox or fanatic, let alone zealot and hijack, are in fact shorthand devices that each name a specific way of managing all of those possible combinations and permutations of similarity and difference mentioned above.

Now, we've seen this term, hijack, used in this manner for quite some time; so a word that may have developed from the sense of robbing someone along the highway (the verb, to jack, meaning to hold up, as in rob—as well as raise or hoist [from which the word heist may also derive, in fact]) is now often used to name the act of stealing an identity rightly owned by someone else (though appropriation is the preferred term among scholars today, at least when those in power do it; when others do it's just called borrowing, influence, or syncretism), such as the November 19, 2015, *New York Times* headline, "Muslims Defend Islam From Being Hijacked by ISIS" (Bromwich 2015) or their March 15, 2017, headline, in their Women in the World section, "Camille Paglia Claims Feminism Has Been Hijacked by 'Upper-Middle Class Professional Women'" (WITW 2017). But, as I hope to be the case, in these apparently factual claims of authorized center and illegitimate periphery readers may now hear (if we think back to the doctor in rural Minnesota) a contest that is being played out, in which one among many possible positions (e.g., Paglia's view of what feminism ought to be or the doctor's sense of an Americana that everyone in that room in which some may feel equally invested) is making a move to constitute a particular (and, for sure, self-beneficial) normative center in opposition to an opposed alternative. It's what we might also call the metropole (i.e., mother city), against which a specific position is defined as the edge, as the boundary and limit, way out in the sticks, occupied by heathens (i.e., those living in the rural heath) and thus the people on the farthest reaches (i.e., Latin: *extremis*, from which we, of course, derive our modern English word extremist). Now, should those people on the margin not be content with their assigned place—i.e., not recognize *our* authority to assign to *them* their role in our identity drama—then, as already noted, we can assert that they've illegitimately grabbed what's not rightfully theirs, claiming that they've hijacked the movement.

Should my proposal be read by some as uncontroversial (i.e., that this sliding scale, along with the tactical assignment of center and boundary, is a necessary element in all efforts to order a space by establishing Self and Other), then what sets the following papers apart is that they are all written by scholars of religion—people whose disciplinary expertise is usually assumed to be limited to studying those things that we commonly classify as religions. But this is a field whose identity, as much as any other, is changeable; the following conference participants therefore seem to agree that limiting themselves only to studying whatever happens to be called religion is premised on a rather suspect (and dated) theory of religion as somehow special, unique, or distinct from everyday life (and thereby requiring unique methods for its study). Should one instead theorize religion as a fluid name that some (and not all, of course) of us give to certain collections of mundane claims, acts, and institutions that human beings devise and use for all too human purposes and effect, then one will not only draw upon common tools from across the human sciences in carrying out one's studies on religion (making the field cross-disciplinary) but—and this is the important part, I think—one will also see one's work in the academic study of religion as having relevance and application far beyond what for some were our field's traditional disciplinary walls. So in this volume we have a set of writers and researchers, trained in detailed work in this or that tradition, myth, or ritual, who nonetheless have something to say about how this culture-wide Self/Other process, and its various modulations, works in other domains, as exemplified in a surprisingly wide number of instances (from the university classroom itself to media and political discourse in which attempts are made to moderate the modern identities that we now inhabit). For if religion is claimed to be unique, as so many before us have argued and assumed (and as many still do to this day), then the alternate scholars of religion included in his volume, those who are more akin to identity theorists, have at their disposal in this one cultural domain much data to study—if, that is, we instead maintain an interest in how inherently changeable, historical situations are regularly dehistoricized, essentialized, and thereby authorized by social actors in practical situations where something is at stake. In a word, they no longer study the sacred (as did our predecessors and some peers) but, instead, taking a page from the tradition that follows Emile Durkheim's work, the routine procedures by which so-called sacred things are made, negotiated, and, yes, contested and unmade. So, for those interested in making this shift in how we study identity, in that domain commonly known as religion we find a tremendous number of useful examples of how claims of essence and authenticity—along with judgments of their illicit hijacking by those who would have it all work in some other fashion, for some other effect—are asserted, contested, and reasserted.

So although I started with reference to a rather specific, current dispute over American identity and the place of Islam (debates not limited to the US since they have long been seen all across Europe as well) I end at a very different place—but it is still referencing the same techniques; for this volume itself, not unlike the Minnesota doctor, represents a marginal position working to achieve its place in the larger scholarly community. The event in Germany where this volume originated brought together some prior friends and collaborators, to be sure, but it also added some newcomers to the mix, put them together into a set apart situation for three days, where they spoke, listened, and ate together, and what you hold in your hands is the result. Whether the shift that these authors implicitly invite you to make when you think about what it is that a scholar of religion does or studies, is, of course, up to each reader to decide. But to my way of thinking, as one who has long maintained that there was more in the world for a scholar of religion to study than just those things usually called religious, and as one who wasn't content with assuming our job was to find the implicitly religious in non-religious things (e.g., the religion of sports), it is rather exciting to think of the kind of group that this newer generation of international scholars might help us to create.[5]

Russell T. McCutcheon (University Research Professor and Chair of the Department of Religious Studies at the University of Alabama) is a former President of the North American Association for the Study of Religion (2015–2018) and a longtime contributor to debates on theory in the academic study of religion.

Notes

1   At the time of reviewing this introduction prior to publication, sometime after it was originally written, it was apparent that Dr. Virji remains in practice; see Goetz (2018) on the purpose and pushback he experienced.
2   While ISIS (or ISISL, i.e., the Islamic State of Iraq and the Levant) may be well known to current readers following international news, the name of David Koresh (1959–1993) may be rather unfamiliar to some; he was the leader (i.e., prophet) of the group, living outside the city of Waco, TX—a group that had splintered off from the Seventh Day Adventist Church (itself originating from the Millerite movement [founded by David Miller (1782–1849)], of the so-called mid-19th century Second Great Awakening). Koresh was accused by local authorities of statutory rape (i.e., having entered what the group knew as a spiritual marriage with a 12-year-old girl) and eventually was part of a violent and extended clash with the US's Bureau of Alcohol, Tobacco and Firearms (ATF), which began with heavily armed agents delivering a search warrant to also investigate illegal firearms at their so-called compound. An almost two-month standoff/siege followed the initial raid, on February 28, 1993 (when four ATF agents and 6 Davidians were killed in exchanges of gunfire), ending in an April 19 fire beginning around noon (the source of which were the Davidians themselves, FBI tapes revealed) that quickly consumed their entire facility and killed 80 people, including Koresh (believed to have been shot by a follower).
3   Learn more about the LRA, and its child soldiers led by the infamous Joseph Kony (b. 1961), at Al Jazeera (2014), or visit the New York Times archive (www.nytimes.com/

topic/organization/lords-resistance-army) for a variety of stories on the group, such as its kidnapping, between January and June 2017 alone, of 498 people (see Reuters 2016); or consult www.theresolve.org/the-lra-crisis/key-statistics for statistics concerning the death toll in light of the LRA's direct actions. Some may recall the 139 high school girls kidnapped by the LRA in October of 1996.

4   As reported in the story, this exchange prompted the doctor to wonder "what would happen if he said, 'Muhammad loves you'" in reply.

5   While I was able to play a small role in helping to conceptualize portions of the Bonn conference, I was not able to attend it. So I extend my thanks to the three organizers and editors for kindly inviting me to help set the table for the published version of its papers.

References

Al Jazeera. 2014. "Profile: The Lord's Resistance Army." *Al Jazeera*, May 6. Retrieved from www.aljazeera.com/news/africa/2011/10/2011101418364196576.html (archived at www.webcitation.org/6yQr5GBSL)

Bromwich, Jonah E. 2015. "Muslims Defend Islam From Being Hijacked by ISIS." *New York Times*, November 19. Retrieved from www.nytimes.com/2015/11/20/world/europe/muslims-defend-islam-from-being-hijacked-by-isis.html (archived at www.webcitation.org/6yQsU7YIl).

Hughes, Aaron. 2017. *Comparison: A Critical Primer*. Sheffield: Equinox Publishing.

Goetz, Kaomi. 2018. "Muslim Doctor Finds Purpose and Pushback in Rural Town." *Washington Post*, February 12. Retrieved from www.nextavenue.org/muslim-doctor-rural-town (archived at www.webcitation.org/78jzi2Oqf).

McCrummen, Stephanie. 2017. "In Minnesota Town That Voted Trump, a Muslim Doctor Tries to Understand His Neighbors." *Washington Post*, July 2. Retrieved from www.twincities.com/2017/07/02/in-a-midwestern-town-that-went-for-trump-a-muslim-doctor-tries-to-understand-his-neighbors (archived at www.webcitation.org/6yQqZXnxN).

Reuters. 2016. "Lord's Resistance Army Kidnappings Hit Six-Year High: Monitors." *Reuters*, July 20, 2016. Retrieved from www.reuters.com/article/us-uganda-rebels-idUSKCN1001CJ, archived at www.webcitation.org/6yQrZixYO

Schleifer, Theodore. 2016. "Donald Trump: 'I think Islam Hates Us'." *CNN*, March 9. Retrieved from www.cnn.com/2016/03/09/politics/donald-trump-islam-hates-us/index.html (archived at www.webcitation.org/6yQqiQ9Q6).

Smith, Jonathan Z. 1990. *Drudgery Divine: On the Comparison of Early Christianities and the Religions of Late Antiquity*. Chicago, IL: University of Chicago Press.

WITW. 2017. "Camille Paglia Claims Feminism Has Been Hijacked By 'Upper-Middle-Class Professional Women'." *New York Times*, March 15. Retrieved from http://nytlive.nytimes.com/womenintheworld/2017/03/15/camille-paglia-claims-feminism-has-been-hijacked-by-upper-middle-class-professional-women (archived at www.webcitation.org/6yQstgURI)

Chapter 2

Good Muslim, Bad Muslim: Neo-Orientalism and the Study of Religion

Aaron W. Hughes

While I will certainly talk about "good" and "bad" Muslims eventually, allow me to begin with a series of reflections that do not simply revolve around the academic study of Islam.[1] Indeed, my concern the more I think about it over the years has never really been about the study of Islam, or Islamic studies, than it has been about religious studies. I, thus, wish to lay the blame of the paucity of theorizing (or, at least, good theorizing) squarely at the foot of the academic study of religion, particularly the American Academy of Religion (AAR), which has the unfortunate tendency of forcing many of us to contort our discourses into something ecumenical or positive for the sake of membership in the so-called guild. The field of religious studies, through its organizations that are after all a reflection of it and of us, creates these contortions—what topics should be researched, what ones avoided, which subject we should gravitate towards, and those from which we should abstain—that are subsequently governed by institutional mechanisms, such as collegiality, book awards, fellowships, and so on.

I have articulated my position on this in several publications (Hughes 2007, 2012, 2015), especially as it pertains to the academic study of Islam as carried out in religious studies departments. I call this latter phenomenon, to distinguish it from more firmly grounded textual and historical work, "Islamic religious studies" (see, in particular, Hughes 2012: 3–7). So rather than rehearse my argument again here in the present context, I thought that it might be more interesting to push some of the boundaries that I have delineated in these previous works with the aim of addressing more explicitly the theme of our volume, to wit, "hijacking."

My earlier work has focused primarily on the study of Islam and the decidedly non-intellectual summersaults that many self-styled *academic* experts of that religion perform. Most of this could be reduced to the notion that Islam is a beautiful religion and that those who commit violence in its name are not really Muslims. From this admittedly simplistic formulation a host of formulations follow, the most common being to construct a good Islam, something that involves ignoring traditional topics and gravitating to various forms of presentism. While I do not necessarily think they are wrong to do so in order to try to correct the many half-truths that political sophists peddle, my main worry has always been with the type of religious studies that encourages such analyses and the concomitant fallout that this has had for a more critical study of religion in general and of

Islam in particular. In fact, I think we know the answer without having to ask the question.

I do not think that this is necessarily the Study of Islam's fault. In fact, I think that those who carry out said study have been hijacked, again to use the phrase that connects our musings in this volume, by the regnant discourses associated with the academic study of religion. For the study of any religion to pass muster in this day and age, there are certain narratives that must be adopted, preordained scripts to be followed, and specific conversations that must be entered. If you do not engage in these narrow and heavily proscribed discourses, the consequences are fairly obvious: one is described as too critical, too angry, too reductionist, too political or too ideological, or some combination thereof.

The academic study of religion would seem to be the culprit, in other words, and not necessarily the study of any specific religion. We all know the terms of reference into which the study of specific religions must be contorted—religion and peace studies, interfaith relations, religion and ecology, religion and women, as if the terms "religion" or "religions" offers the lifeline from as opposed to being the cause of our social, climatological, misogynistic, or other problems.

Indeed, if it is not clear already, I think it worth repeating in staccato speech. I have no problem with Islamic studies. My problem instead is with the academic study of religion. Here I think it important to clarify, if in fact the point needs clarification, that I have always but used scholars of Islam who abide in North American departments of religious studies as my segue into the more problematic and potentially nefarious if not actual self-destructive discourses associated with the academic study of religion. Much good work goes on in the field of Islamic studies, especially among those scholars who have either never heard of or who want no part in the academic study of religion because they know all too well its epistemological excesses.[2] Does this mean that they are theoretically sophisticated in social theory or the academic study of religion? No. Not at all. They do, however, possess a healthy dose of skepticism combined with an excellent knowledge of texts and historical contexts, things that many in religious studies lack.[3] Increasingly, it is these individuals—both in the study of Islam and in other subfields—with whom we, i.e., those of us who occupy the more critical wing of religious studies, must interact and convince of the merits of our analysis. While they may not know or be interested, for example, in the history or genealogy of the category of "religion" or other such "cutting edge" theoretical topics in religious studies, their skepticism and criticism of inherited religious narratives, not to mention their knowledge of the historical record, more than makes up for this (see, e.g., Crone and Cook 1977; Crone 1987; Powers 2011, 2014).

The AAR's big tent, and I think this is becoming increasingly clear to many of us, wants to hold under its flimsy canopy an ideal world that cannot possibly exist. Self-servingly it seeks to make religion the protagonist of our redemption, now defined along the secular lines of some scholarly imposed interfaith gathering. But who is interested in redemption? Who wants a field of study that reifies ideas at the expense of social actors? Or, who desires a field of study that thinks about normative and discrete religious traditions to the detriment of myriad and often overlapping social movements? Perhaps this big tent will be assailed and finally brought down by small-scale organizations, such as NAASR, such as the International Quranic Studies Association (IQSA), where groups of scholars with shared interests meet to talk about a specific problem using overlapping and non-gullible methodologies.

As an aside, let me briefly juxtapose the way Islam is carried out in the academic study of religion with how it is examined in other contexts. After the workshop in Bonn, of which the present volume is the end product, I went to another one in Florence devoted to the thorny issue of Islamic origins. Rather than dismiss this topic as "Orientalist" (as scholars of religions do) or rather than simply read later Muslim sources as transcripts of what actually happened, there is a growing group of scholars—none associated with the AAR, by the way—that have moved the discussion of Islamic origins into the late antique period, and connected the beginnings of that socio-religious movement to, among others, Manicheanisms, Syriac Christianities, South Arabian forms of Judaism, and in ways that are historically nuanced and that do not fall back on essentialist default positions. Yet, because this group is not interested in religious studies, our conversations were exceedingly technical, looking at Sabaic and Nabataean epigraphy and numismatics, for example, and wandering among the trees as opposed to surveying the forest. Again, it seems to me that individuals and groups like these are our natural conversation partners. However, and I think this is a big however, entrance to their intellectual world demands a certain level of textual and historical dexterity on our part. And, I hate to say this, but sometimes those of us in religious studies are not prepared to commit to that.

So, leaving that anecdote aside, but hopefully retaining the main issue or issues that it raised, what happened? Where and when did our field go astray and leave important conversations to other subgroups? How did we collectively arrive at a situation wherein we are actively encouraged to adjudicate—in the words of the Spaghetti Western, between "the good," "the bad," and "the ugly"? Are we hard-wired or structured this way given our field's collective origins in the ecumenicism of liberal Protestant Christianity? Is it because we threw the mundane and the social under the Paul Tillich express headed to the Hauptbahnhof of ultimate concerns? Or, as I have tried to articulate in a number of places have the aforementioned features or subfeatures simply picked up steam and been heavily augmented in the aftermath of the events of September 11, 2001, after which our field was determined to make religion a force for good in the world?

I know that a little has been written on September 11 and the academic study of religion. I think of Lincoln's important *Holy Terrors* (2006). But it strikes me that much more has to be crafted on how that fateful day hugely impacted the study of religion. How it forced us to further interiorize and spiritualize religion. How it cemented watertight categories based on the rhetoric of authenticity. And how it has defanged much critical work using the rhetoric of political correctness. I have to admit that as a Canadian, I am uncomfortably aware of "American exceptionalism." So while I am aware that 9/11 had a major influence on the study of religion in the United States, I also realize that things might, and probably should, be different elsewhere. But are they? So, with some of these issues in mind, in what follows I would like to address the theme or trope of "hijacking" in, I hope, ways that will help to structure our conversation. Whether we like it or not or indeed even whether we admit it or not—and I hope I am not too bold in enunciating this—all our scholarly acts are hijacked, in one way or another. Maybe this is just another way of saying that there is no such thing as "pure" scholarship. Or, even if there were, such scholarship *ipso facto* risks being co-opted for a host of political and/or ideological agendas.

Within this context, our organizers are to be congratulated for triangulating our proceedings into four distinct, yet mutually overlapping areas: politics, the media, the university, and the classroom. Each of these four theatres, if you will, potentially compromises us, pulls us in often competing directions, and forces us to make decisions that we might not otherwise have had to make. The classroom, for example, is the place where some of our most creative work ought to take place, and I am sure that for many here and elsewhere it performs precisely that type of venue. Yet, for a variety of reasons—and here I rely solely on my own experiences, such as very conservative Muslim students or Islamophobic North American ones, neo-conservative watchdog groups on campus, pro-Israeli and anti-Israeli student groups—we are hijacked.[4] Such students and/or student groups, including their non-student backers or handlers, even if we resist them or use them for so-called teaching moments, structure pedagogical expectations and often force us to go down roads we might otherwise be tempted to resist. I tried to get at this in the autobiographical introduction to *Islam and the Tyranny of Authenticity* (Hughes 2015: 8–11).

Our universities also set expectations for us. Colleagues and administrators encourage us to talk about religion in certain ways—ones in which we may not feel comfortable. As someone with an endowed chair in Jewish studies, my university president, for example, always invites me to events that involve the local Jewish community. Implicit with this is that I somehow have common ground with that community—on religion, on continuity, on Israel. But I don't. In fact, I increasingly feel out of sync with that community on so many levels. So, if we hold endowed chairs in particular religions or traditions—say, in Sikh studies, Islamic studies, or Hindu studies—we are often expected to talk about these religions and religious traditions in particular ways that do not offend students of said tradition and, even more importantly, the donors whose presumed beneficence makes this possible in the first place. We all know that donors have no interest in social theory, but in hearing about how great their religious civilization is and that you are doing a good job communicating that to students.

As for the media, I have written several studies where I have argued that the events of 9/11 suddenly recoded an entire field of study (e.g., Hughes 2012; Hughes 2015: 75–93). Prior to that date, Islamicists in North America were content to do what most humanists do: produce critical editions of texts, write histories of obscure groups and/or figures, and engage in what might otherwise be labelled as dry and esoteric scholarship. In the aftermath of 9/11 many scholars of Islam began to self-style themselves as media darlings. Their goal now was to portray

Islam in as positive a light as possible. This means, and this takes me to the title of my chapter, of saying what "real" or "authentic" Islam was/is and articulating the criteria whereby it could be distinguished from less real or less authentic expressions.

This hijacking, in other words, is much more institutional and structural than it is simply scholarly. This makes it much more insidious and difficult to address. It also means that its correction or realignment demands more than simply haranguing our less theoretically sophisticated colleagues in Islamic studies or any other subfield of religious studies.

In addition to the weight of institutional expectations and the assumptions built in to our endowed chairs, we would also have to throw into the mix: projects deemed fundable by external agencies, research thought to be publishable by blind peer review, and even just wanting camaraderie at scholarly conferences. To accommodate others, we bend ourselves and our scholarly acts in such ways—some slight, others perhaps less so—that reveal our basic human characteristics: we want to fit in. Even if we do not want to be part of a club that would have anyone like us as a member, we imagine ourselves as being part of clubs that never would even entertain the idea of accepting those not like us.

It is, to riff on the old anthropological maxim, "ideology all the way down, sahib." This does not mean that there exists some Archimedean point that offers us direct access to capital-T Truth. Nor does it mean that we flit about looking for whatever group or funding agency has the best receptions. On the contrary, it does mean that—to invoke J. Z. Smith, Bruce Lincoln, Russell McCutcheon, among others—that we be self-conscious, painfully self-conscious, about what we are doing, why we are doing it, and for whom we are doing it. But even that becomes different when we need connections that will help us advance both institutionally and in the field. Perhaps this is another way of saying that if I knew then what I know now I might have done things a little differently.

Let me just provide you with a personal narrative of how our research agendas are potentially hijacked. And, perhaps, just as tellingly the potential price of refusing to be hijacked in some ways. I am lucky enough to hold an endowed chair in Jewish Studies at a major research university—the Rabbi Philip S. Bernstein Chair, and perhaps the title of this chair says enough to you—even though I am a scholar of Islam. With that chair comes certain expectations, even though I am afraid that I could be charged with dereliction of duty, which wins me no favors in the local Jewish community, in fact quite the opposite. I also apply for funding from granting agencies—the usual suspects: the American Council of Learned Societies (ACLS), the National Endowment of the Humanities (NEH), the John Simon Guggenheim Foundation—where the peer review is single-blind, that is, reviewers know my identity, but I do not know theirs. And, when you have made a career out of being critical of entire fields of study, what do you think those reviewers say about my proposals, even ones that are not even provocative?

Perhaps this is another way of saying that the way to tenure-track positions, fellowships, success through the review process, and career advancement is to go along with the status quo. That status quo loves to replicate itself by instilling its values and concerns in others, and, of course, meting out punishment to those who transgress. Russell McCutcheon and I recently penned an article on collegiality in the academic study of religion and used as one of our "e.g.s" ASSR, the American Society for the Study of Religion, which functions as an honor society for scholars of religion based on election (Hughes and McCutcheon 2019). It is, in other words, the AAR's AAR. They meet once a year, in the Spring, on the college campus of one of its members and invite papers from other members around a common theme.

Some of ASSR's early past presidents include such noteworthy scholars in the history of our field: Erwin Goodenough, Mircea Eliade, Wilfred C. Smith, Joseph Campbell, Joseph Kitagawa, and Ninian Smart. Such names, not surprisingly, signal what is still largely the guiding hermeneutic of the organization (if not, some might claim, the field as a whole). According to their website (which I encourage everyone to look at), and I quote:

> New members of the ASSR are elected on an annual basis by vote of the society. They are nominated by current members of the ASSR, and chosen on the basis of their contributions to the field, their achievements and interest in the comparative study of religion, *and their record of collegial engagement*.[5]

Certainly "contributions to the field" and scholarly "achievements" are correctly noted as important qualifications for membership in a presumed elite professional association. Despite the fact that these two criteria are verifiable and relatively transparent, it is never entirely clear how one measures such "contributions" and/or "achievements." Are such criteria based on the number of books published, or some other metric (e.g., citations or impact on the field)?

As with all private clubs, gaining admission seems to occur when existing members nominate someone, who in turn must be ratified by a majority vote of the membership. We might stop to ask, as Russell and I do, what accounts for the absence of many seemingly qualified members or, rephrased, what accounts for members, whether mid-career or senior, who seem to have amassed what at first seems to be minimal publication records?

While those questions are perhaps unanswerable, our concern was less with such relative "quantifiable" data used to denote "contributions" and "achievements" than it was with the last stated criterion of membership, to wit, a "record of collegial engagement." This criterion seemingly has nothing to do with the manner in which we usually assess scholarship. Instead, it has everything to do with "getting along" with others, with being a team player, and, dare I say it, with not being too critical of others or the field's first principles. Moreover, it may well be the hidden reason why some are in the organization and others are not.

Russell and I then ask, as we must, just what type of intellectual heavy lifting does the phrase "collegial engagement" perform in organizations such as ASSR? It is, to be sure, a tricky business. We are encouraged to be team players and if we are somehow perceived to transgress the rules of the game, we risk marginalization or, in the case of pre-tenure, worse. This is why the Academy, I would suggest, is an inherently conservative and cautious institution that rewards conformity and is, and I say this from personal experience, fundamentally bothered by critique.

We should thus be aware of some of these structural and institutional forces that attempt to "hijack" us. If Bruce Lincoln is correct and scholarship is mythology with footnotes (1999: 208–210), then we are forced to confront what those footnotes are doing. Sure, they make us show our work, but, as we all know, footnotes are not necessarily objective, but are selective and conform to one's own intellectual agenda. Scholarship, to riff off of Lincoln, is further mythopoeia supported by mythology. It is what attunes us to certain conversations, but not others. It is what permits us to differentiate between our friends, viz., those with whom we agree or who agree with us, and our enemies, viz., those who do not.

In using this term "hijacking," then, I do not so much want to emphasize the illegality of the action. Unlike real hijacking, it is not a violent action committed by radical, fringe groups seeking to overthrow, at least symbolically, the political status quo. Here I think of the heyday of plane hijackings carried out by groups such as the Popular Front for the Liberation of Palestine (PFLP), the Japanese Red Army, or Croatian separatists. Rather, I use the term—and I assume in the same way the editors of this volume do—as forcing something to go to a different destination or use it for one's own purposes.

Unlike the heyday of plane hijackings in the 1970s and 1980s, our invocation of "hijacking" is of a distinctly different variety. Our situation now witnesses the inverse of the paradigm. Those doing the hijacking are no longer fringe groups trying to speak self-perceived truth to power. On the contrary, those doing the "hijacking" now have the power and are the ones calling the shots. They are the ones who determine what counts as valid scholarship and what does not. They are the ones who patrol borders as sentinels, determining who fits and who does not, and what goes where.

Like Lincoln's analysis of authority, the status quo is that which determines who gets to speak or be published in venues that are authority-conferring. He reminds us that authority is not an entity, but an effect based on the right speaker, the right stage, the right speech, and an audience that has been conditioned to respond with trust and reverence (Lincoln 1995: 11–12). At what point, however, does authority become coercion? At what point does it become "hijacking"?

It is thus incumbent upon us to understand the material conditions that have created authority, that structure it, and that disseminate it. For all of us are ultimately conditioned by authority. It is moreover an authority that is as fictive as it is real, and perhaps more institutional and thus pervasive than it is located in individuals.

Islam

Let me now try to concentrate some of the aforementioned comments in a case study of sorts.[6] Framed as a question: Why are we in religious studies so unwilling to revisit that which the status quo hands down to us? Why do we submit to its authority? I have tried to analyze some of the reasons earlier, but in the time that remains I would like to begin to look at the intellectual fallout as opposed to just the sociological or categorical problems associated with this.

I think we could begin with a fairly simple axiom of our field. Religious studies does not like violence. It does its best to extricate religion—its moods, its motivations, its intentions, and so on—from violent acts. Religious people do not murder physicians who terminate pregnancies nor they do fly planes into buildings nor occupy the land of Palestinians and burn down their olive trees. The field of which we all ostensibly are a part informs us that: "no. such actions are carried out by zealots, by the uneducated, by terrorists, by 'hijackers' of the beautiful traditions that we are supposed to study in the classroom."[7]

Rather than use such violent expressions to expand our conceptual understanding of religion or to push beyond Protestant-inspired clichés about what religion is or ought to be, we have instead simply decided to undermine the religious bona fides of such individuals and/or groups by marking them with the stain of "inauthenticity" (see Hughes 2017). Let me now move on to show how this works in Islam, the tradition that I am probably the most familiar with.

I have argued elsewhere that in ISIS's desire to create a caliphate in the areas of Iraq and the Levant—in addition to their charismatic appeal to other militant Islamist groups, such as Boko Haram in Nigeria and al-Shabaab in Somalia—they clearly perform what they consider to be normative religious identities (Hughes 2015: xi–xviii; Hughes 2017). Although many of us, both Muslim and non-Muslim, find this performance abhorrent, the religious motivations, protestations to the contrary, cannot be gainsaid. We can certainly try to undermine them, and many certainly have, but we have to ask ourselves: is it our goal to do this, to undermine the religious claims or motivations of those with whom we disagree and to uphold as courageous and beautiful those with whom we do agree?

Islamicist groups, including those who promote violence, construct identities for themselves in a manner that their actors regard to be fundamentally rooted in authoritative traditions that they perceive to go all the way back to Muhammad in the late antique period. For such actors, questions of whether or not they are "real" Muslims are absurd. Like any social group, they believe their beliefs and actions to be true and authentic.

So what are scholars of religion supposed to do? To hit the highlight of my title and to summarize my take on these issues, too many in the academic study of religion avoid such hard questions and instead resort to parroting time-honored clichés about what gets to count as authentic religious expression. In terms of Islam, the way most religionists talk about ISIS or Boko Haram or al-Shabaab or other such groups paradoxically deprives Muslims—all Muslims and not just members of these groups—of their agency. Here the figure of Edward Said is instrumental. While I love the work of Said, we always have to remember that his argument in *Orientalism* is primarily a literary argument that shows how the West—its literature, is arts, its scholarship—paints the East, particularly the Middle East. His argument, however, has been picked up by others and transformed—"hijacked," if you will—into a historiographic one.

One such example, and I think it only fitting to mention him in the present context, is Abraham Geiger. His *Was hat Mohammed aus dem Judenthume aufgenommen?*, an attempt to show parallels between rabbinic literature and the Qur'an, received a prize from the university hosting our conference, the University of Bonn, in 1833. Said makes no mention of Geiger nor does he make any mention of the rich German Orientalist tradition, much of which was produced by German-Jews like Geiger. Instead, Said focuses on the much more madcap Orientalist traditions of the French and the English (see my more general critique in Hughes 2015: 37–56).

Many are quite content to use the arguments in *Orientalism* and developed by Said's acolytes to expose the ideological underpinnings of Western category formation and to show how such categories have historically deprived Muslim actors of their agency. I have no qualms with this. However, I do have a problem when such individuals revert back to the very Western (read: Protestant) assumption about what gets to count as "good," "real," and "authentic" Islam and what does not. There is a real irony, in other words, when we see the reappearance of Orientalist assumptions emanate from the very same scholarly circles that, at least when it suits them, are willing to point out the political and ideological undertones of the representation of the Other, especially the Muslim Other.

Why do many professional religionists refuse to take the religious bona fides of groups like ISIS or Boko Haram or al-Shabaab seriously? This question may well be naïve because guiding the conversation, especially in the background, is how we imagine Islam in popular and public discourse, which must include the fear that groups like ISIS will somehow be made to transmute into *the* official representative of Islam. It is a delicate situation, to be sure. Yet, somewhere between the superficial claims of neo-cons who want to use groups like ISIS as a metonym for what they consider to be the "medieval" and inherently violent nature of Islam and the equally superficial liberal claim that Islam is fundamentally a religion of peace reside the real issues. It is up to us, as professional religionists, to sort through these claims no matter how uncomfortable they may make us, showing them for exactly what they are. With all the political baggage that surrounds the discussion, however, this becomes very difficult.

Conclusions

Our volume is premised on the notion that the rhetoric of "good" and "bad" religion performs certain types of political work. I think we could all, without too much difficulty, assent to this proposition. But after we do so, however, it seems to me that the real work begins and that it is incumbent upon us to proceed to investigate how all of this is done. That, of course, is precisely where the difficulty resides. We cannot simply say that so-and-so is responsible for it. Or that institutional pressure is exerted at a particular moment or through a particular agent or agency.

Where, then, do we search for the pressure points? When and by what means does our field exercise its authority? It is now up to us to ascertain how certain agendas are ultimately responsible for this "hijacking." I have tried to show here some of these fractures and others will inevitably add to and necessarily finesse our collective conversation. It does not matter in what tradition we work, or indeed if we work in no tradition. There are rules that we are expected to follow—pedagogically, institutionally, administratively, and, of course, intellectually.

Aaron W. Hughes is the Philip S. Bernstein Chair of Jewish Studies in the Dept. of Religion and Classics at the University of Rochester.

Notes

1. This paper was written for oral presentation. While I have added relevant footnotes and other citations, I have tried to maintain the oral character of the original iteration.
2. A good recent example of what I have in mind is the formation of the International Quranic Studies Association (IQSA) in 2012. This organization, not unlike NAASR, meets both prior to and concurrently with the AAR Annual Meeting.
3. See, for example, Tesei (2013–2014), Dye (2012), El-Badawi (2013), and Zellentin (2013).
4. Perhaps the most infamous of these is CampusWatch (www.campus-watch.org).
5. Online at www.assr-religion.org/membership.html (my emphasis).
6. Parts of this section rework Hughes 2017.
7. The most ludicrous example of this approach is perhaps best found in popularizers such as Karen Armstrong (e.g., 2014).

References

Armstrong, Karen. 2014. *Fields of Blood: Religion and the History of Violence*. New York: Knopf.
Crone, Patricia. 1987. *Meccan Trade and the Rise of Islam*. Princeton, NJ: Princeton University Press.
Crone, Patricia, and Michael Cook. 1977. *Hagarism: The Making of the Islamic World*. Cambridge: Cambridge University Press.
Dye, Guillaume. 2012. "Lieux saints communs, partagés ou confisqués: aux sources de quelques péricopes coraniques (Q 19: 16–33)." In Isabelle Dépret and Guillaume Dye (eds.), *Partage du sacré: Transferts, dévotions mixtes, rivalités interconfessionnelles*, 55–122. Brussels: EME and Intercommunications.
El-Badawi, Emran. 2013. *The Qurʾān and the Aramaic Gospel Traditions*. Abingdon: Routledge. https://doi.org/10.4324/9781315855981
Hughes, Aaron W. 2007. *Situating Islam: The Past and Future of an Academic Discipline*. London: Equinox Press.
Hughes, Aaron W. 2012. *Theorizing Islam: Disciplinary Deconstruction and Reconstruction*. Sheffield: Acumen.
Hughes, Aaron W. 2015. *Islam and the Tyranny of Authenticity: An Inquiry into Disciplinary Apologetics and Self-Deception*. Sheffield: Equinox.
Hughes, Aaron W. 2017. "ISIS: What's a Poor Religionist to Do." In Steven W. Ramey (ed.), *Fabricating Difference*, 77–91. Sheffield: Equinox.
Hughes, Aaron W. and Russell T. McCutcheon. 2019. "The Gatekeeping Rhetoric of Collegiality in the Study of Religion." In Leslie Dorrough Smith (ed.), *Constructing "Data" in Religious Studies: Examining the Architecture of the Academy*. Sheffield: Equinox.
Lincoln, Bruce. 1995. *Authority: Construction and Corrosion*. Chicago, IL: University of Chicago Press.

Lincoln, Bruce. 1999. *Theorizing Myth: Narrative, Ideology, and Scholarship.* Chicago, IL: University of Chicago Press.
Lincoln, Bruce. 2006. *Holy Terrors: Thinking about Religion after September 11,* 2nd edition. Chicago, IL: University of Chicago Press.
Powers, David S. 2011. *Muhammad Is Not the Father of Any of Your Men: The Making of the Last Prophet.* Philadelphia, PA: University of Pennsylvania Press.
Powers, David. S. 2014. *Zayd.* Philadelphia, PA: University of Pennsylvania Press. https://doi.org/10.9783/9780812209952
Tesei, Tomasso. 2013–2014. "The Prophecy of Ḏū-l-Qarnayn (Q 18:83–102) and the Origins of the Qurʾānic Corpus." *Miscellanea Arabica*: 273–290.
Zellentin, Holger. 2013. *The Qurʾān's Legal Culture: The Didascalia Apostolorum as a Point of Departure.* Tübingen: Mohr Siebeck.

Chapter 3

Religious Studies and the Jargon of Authenticity

Jason Ā. Josephson-Storm

The jargon of authenticity, which sells self-identity as something higher, projects the exchange formula onto that which imagines that it is not exchangeable.
—Theodor Adorno, *The Jargon of Authenticity*

In *Islam and the Tyranny of Authenticity* and the chapter included in this volume, Aaron Hughes criticizes standing presuppositions of the academic study of Islam. In so doing, he builds on an impressive body of previous scholarship and it is difficult in the space allotted to do justice to the extensive and important intervention of this extensive work.[1] Pressed to summarize, I would say that throughout his writings on the subject, Hughes's main contribution has been to explore the role theologically committed scholars have played in the construction of idealized notions of Islam. In particular, he argues that much of "Islamic religious studies" functions as a species of apologetics designed to anachronistically differentiate a supposedly authentic "good Islam" from a contemporary "bad," violent, political Islam that is discounted as not really Islamic. He specifically focuses his criticism on converts to Islam and other putative Muslim insiders and what he sees as their role in inventing an early Islam largely to meet contemporary progressive agendas. As he summarized elsewhere, these Muslim scholars of Islam "have largely invoked their authority to elevate their particular and idiosyncratic interpretations of Islam (e.g., liberal and egalitarian) over others and, in the process, deemed their version to be somehow more authentic and normative" (Hughes 2012: 2).

I am not a specialist in Islam, but like Hughes I have worked on the self-reflexive analysis of the academic study of religion (see Josephson 2012; Josephson-Storm 2017). In that respect, I would count myself as a fellow traveler in the critical analysis of our larger discipline and I have found his work vital, important, and stimulating.

But what I want to do here is show how the disciplinary logics of religious studies both support and in some cases undercut Hughes's broader characterization of the discipline. To telegraph my broader argument, first, while agreeing with Hughes that something very suspicious is going on in religious studies and our continual rehashing of insider/outsider polemics, I problematize the unstated assumptions of much of this discourse that insiders have privileged access to their own traditions, but I also challenge the claim that outsiders are necessarily more critical.

Second, the bulk of the response focuses on what I see as the underlying issue behind Hughes's critique—namely, the problem with value-neutrality in social sciences. I agree that religious studies has a problem with values. But I argue that the problem is not an excess of normativity or crypto-theology as Hughes seems to suggest, but rather, like many social sciences, we have misunderstood value-neutrality and forced our values underground. Moreover, I contend that we are regularly forced to select "authentic" examples of the traditions we study in a way that is basically unescapable.

Insiders, Outsiders, and the Standpoint of Critique

The most basic point of Theodor Adorno's attack on Heidegger and existentialism in *The Jargon of Authenticity* (*Jargon der Eigentlichkeit*, 1964) can be found in the work's title—references to authenticity have been repeated so much as to have become jargon. As Adorno (2007: 6) clarifies within: "While the jargon [of authenticity] overflows with the pretense of deep human emotion, it is just as standardized as the world that it officially negates." Paraphrased, Adorno suggests that the notion of an autonomous individual with their own self-actualizing "authentic" experience has become scripted, therefore calling into question the very individualism it purports to express.

By contrast, Aaron Hughes criticizes different, but no less rote, references to authenticity. As he puts it Chapter 2 of this volume, "too many in the academic study of religion […] resort to parroting time-honored clichés about what gets to count as authentic religious expression." But it is not merely the critique of repetition that Hughes and Adorno share, they also have in common a suspicion of routinized claims to speak from private experience.[2] As Hughes (2015: 5) argues it: "If one styles oneself as an insider, an outsider will necessarily lack some sort of metaphysical or intangible connection to the tradition in question." Here he is gesturing to a significant issue brought up by his work, and the conference as a whole: specifically the so-called insider/outsider problem in the academic study of religion. In brief, this long-standing debate involves competing notions of the function of scholarly explanation and a dispute about whether the interpretations of outsiders or insiders have privileged status.[3]

Although various older stratums of theorizing suggested that outsiders were likely to be less biased and see things that religious practitioners were likely to miss, the tide seems to have tipped in the other direction of late. Instead of allusions to outsider objectivity, one is more likely to encounter the oft-cited remark by Andrew Walls: "religion can best understand religion" (Walls 1980). Hughes criticizes this insider turn in the subfield, which he characterizes as scholarship "giving way to identity politics" (Hughes 2015: 10). In that respect, this shift is part of a broader trend that the sociologist Rogers Brubaker has referred to as "epistemological insiderism," which he defines as "the belief that identity qualifies or disqualifies one from writing with legitimacy and authority about a particular topic" (Brubaker 2017).

I would agree with Hughes and Brubaker insofar as various forms of unreflective "insiderism" have become disproportionately dominant across the academy. It seems scholars wary of appropriating the "other" are increasingly coming to study themselves.

But we can go elsewhere for theoretical resources to address this issue. In particular, feminist standpoint theory has formulated a useful self-critique to various kinds of insiderism. Originally, standpoint theory suggested that women, by virtue of being marginalized, had a better understanding of systems of oppression. This was eventually amplified into a version of the claim that knowledge was relative to a particular social standpoint or position (often understood in terms of gender). But especially after Audre Lorde famously criticized her fellow feminists for universalizing gender and ignoring the differences between the experiences of Black and white women in the United States, a number of feminist theorists have noted that various identity positions (esp. race, gender, class, culture) instead of being deconstructed were themselves being essentialized as sites of simultaneous subjugation and privileged theorizing (see Lorde 2007; Haraway 1988; Wylie 2003). On identifying this problem, one significant set of scholars has instead emphasized the fluidity and particularity of individual identity and criticized insider's claims to generalized knowledge of any given category.[4]

I think Hughes would agree with the challenge that this fluidity poses to claims of generalizable insider experience as he asserts that everyone is in some respect an outsider (Hughes 2015: 6). But he also levels a series of attacks on supposedly uncritical insiders. Hence, whether he is conscious of it or not he seems to be granting a common background assumption that identifies critique with outsiders and apologetics with insiders.

To explain, let me provide an extended example from Buddhist studies. The most obvious case of judgements about what constitutes good/bad or authentic/inauthentic Buddhism relates to discussions about the relationship between Buddhism and Japanese militarism in the build-up to the Second World War. Even scholars who have no connection to religious studies often reference the connection between Zen and nationalism to discredit what is often described as inauthentic, modern Buddhism.

But even scholars in religious studies who might have come across this issue in passing are unlikely to know that the historiography starts as an internal auto-critique of the Zen institution. This is true twice over. In the first case, the issue came to national attention because the Japanese Rinzai Zen priest and scholar Ichikawa Hakugen 市川白弦 (1902–1986) began criticizing the ideological relationship between institutional Zen Buddhism and Japanese imperialism in a range of publications starting in the 1950s and culminating in the influential work *Bukkyōsha no sensō sekinin* 仏教者の戦争責任 (Buddhists' responsibility for the war) (Ichikawa 1970). Crucially, part of Ichikawa's critique was focused on not just the problems of his own institution, but also confessing his own complicity.[5] Moreover, in 1997, the American scholar Brian Victoria published the controversial *Zen at War*. Not only was Victoria himself an ordained Sōtō Zen priest, but he acknowledges his debt to Ichikawa on the first page and largely recaps his predecessor's argument. That said, when this work became better known, a number of thinkers in Buddhist studies began to cordon off modern Japanese Zen as "not really Buddhist." In effect, it was scholars, often from secular or Christian backgrounds, who argued that Modern Buddhism, Japanese Zen Buddhism, or the Euro-American Buddhism had lost their way from true Buddhism.

I mention the example above because I think one of the minor issues that run through Hughes's work is that he too often presupposes that converts are uncritical and that scholarly outsiders have a greater aptitude to criticize religious institutions. But I would resist any too facile equation between a scholar's personal background and their capacity for critique.

In passing, I'll also note that more recent accounts of feminist standpoint theory provide a common-sense suggestion for the insider-outsider problem. As feminist philosopher Alison Wylie reformulated standpoint theory it now acknowledges that insiders and outsiders have epistemic privileges in different areas but that a full or complete picture is impossible from any one vantage (Wylie 2003). The implication of this for religious studies would be that the field needs both insiders and outsiders to form a complete picture.

The Impasses of Value-Neutrality in Religious Studies

Almost ever since religious studies (*Religionswissenschaft*) began attempting to differentiate itself from theology, it has been haunted by charges of normativity. Part of religious studies' claim to scientific/scholarly status was rooted in its capacity to adhere to some version of value-neutrality when carrying out its course of study. That the human sciences in general have aspired to notions of a neutrality drawn from the natural sciences is a separate problem. But basically, since the early twentieth century scholars of religion have often claimed to be able to compare different religions objectively and without personal bias, and this premise was key to asserting the discipline's putatively secular status as a social science.

That said, the whole attempt to formulate a value-free social science has been a mess from the beginning. The idea that social science should be value-free or ethically neutral presumes that there is a clear line separating facts from values and that as a consequence of this distinction scholars should adhere to facts and avoid values or other ethical norms. Again, this sounds straightforward or even admirable, but ever since David Hume argued for the distinction between "is" (facts) and "ought" (values) this distinction and its implications have been repeatedly challenged. Nietzsche would famously suggest that all facts are values, but you don't even have to go that far to run into problems. Philosophers that have granted a distinction between facts and values and argued for the existence of real facts have still frequently observed that values are necessarily involved in the interpretation of facts.

There is not space here to rehash the history of the debates around the purpose of the social sciences and the distinction between fact and value. But to hit two highlights, the German sociologist Max Weber is often regarded as the crucial figure in encouraging the ideal of value-neutrality (*Wertfreiheit*, lit.

value-freedom) in the social sciences. Yet, the main thrust of Weber's argument was not, as it is often misunderstood, the idea that all values should be expunged from social sciences, but instead that social scientists need to clearly distinguish between value-judgements and factual statements. Moreover, Weber argued that evaluative interests give scholarship its direction and relevance. It is powerful, subjective values that give scholars the "passion" for their topics and it is the topic's cultural relevance and value that produces its broader impact (Weber 1951: esp. 452–454). Values are unavoidably entangled in scholarship. To be clear, Weber granted the importance of values in selecting the subject of research, but he also warned scholars against allowing subjective values to determine scholarly conclusions.

The implication of Weber's initial argument for our field is that scholars who have dedicated their professional lives to the study of Islam, say, tend to be passionate about the subject regardless of whether they are converts, Muslims, or avowed atheists. The growth of Islamic studies after 9/11 is the result of broader cultural values and interests. So in all these respects, Weber would push against the implicit assumption that insiders are necessarily more biased in their subject matter and he would suggest that extricating the study of Islam from its cultural and political context without rendering it culturally irrelevant is harder than one might think. Values determine the *questions* we ask of our subject matter and this is probably a good thing, but Weber would also agree with Hughes that we should not let these values determine the *answers* we claim our sources provide. Weber would also encourage scholars to be as clear as possible where they are stating facts or making subjective value-judgements.

Weber did not have the last word on the subject. The American philosopher Hilary Putnam criticized Weber and his attempt to distinguish between fact and value. In *The Collapse of the Fact/Value Dichotomy*, Putnam argued that facts and values were often intrinsically entangled. He observed that science presupposed "epistemic values," such as "judgments of 'coherence,' 'plausibility,' 'reasonableness,' 'simplicity' and of what Dirac famously called the beauty of a hypothesis" (Putnam 2002: 31). In our field, academic book reviews often emphasize epistemic values, such as "originality," "significance," "accessibility," "clarity of organization," "breadth," and so on. All of these are normative judgements.

Even more relevant to the issue at hand, Putnam discusses "thick ethical concepts" which entangle fact and value at the most basic level. He refers to concepts like "cruel" (Putnam 2002: 34), when a student says "my professor is cruel." This statement includes both descriptive and evaluative elements. Descriptively it might refer to the professor's tendency to publicly point out errors of logic, but normatively the student is suggesting that a professor should change. The student's notion of what counts as cruelty therefore is likely to be deeply rooted in their sense of values and appropriate behavior. These values even have an impact on their sense of what counts as a cruel act or how cruelty is to be measured.

Closer to home, we might say that "violent" is similarly a thick ethical concept. The statement that "Christianity is violent" might be an objective description to the extent to which a scholar had carefully defined violent acts, stipulated what counted as membership in the Christian community, justified the representativeness of their sample and sample time period, and articulated a scale by which the relative violence of different religions could be compared, but it would still come off as a statement of normative force or downright ethical condemnation.

In sum, the problem is that most of our basic concepts in the humanities and social sciences express similar entanglements. "Real," "repressive," "traditional," "modern," "egalitarian," and even the term "religion" contain similar issues. To this I'd add that Hughes himself often deploys both epistemic values and thick ethical concepts in his own critiques, including such terms as "theoretically sophisticated," "historical dexterity," "problematic," "self-serving" and so on. But Hughes is not unusual in this respect—we have to admit that we have disciplinary norms which express values. To this one might add the observation that while some facts might be definitional or self-evident, normative judgements are generally involved in identifying what counts as a fact in the first place.

Accordingly, value neutrality has been difficult to sustain for a range of reasons. It is not just theologians who have run into problems. Indeed, the very notion that theological values can be clearly distinguished from non-theological values turns out to be hard to defend.

One of the problems is that scholars of religion keep making judgements (or being asked to do so), which in many respects echo theological distinctions between orthodoxy and heresy. Scholars do not need to make statements about authentic or good religions to run into trouble. By way of illustration, in the generalizations that underlie any kind of broader theorizing, scholars are required to adjudicate what counts as "real Islam" or "real Buddhism." This is an issue even when they avoid the phrase "real Islam" and the thick ethical concept it implies.

In this case values intrude because of the heterogeneity of the various "religions" and their own normative claims. For scholars to take any particular feature or doctrine as representative of a particular "religion" is generally to make an evaluative rather than merely empirical judgement. It has been hard for scholars to avoid blurring normative and empirical registers; by listing, for example, the "beliefs of Buddhism," which is in effect obscuring the difference between what Buddhists ought to believe and what they do believe. Even more basically, to compare Buddhism and Islam is often to take specific Buddhist and Muslim denominations in particular countries and at particular moments as representatives of whole "religions." In this respect, it does not matter if you are a secular scholar or a theologian, an insider or an outsider, because if you are going to write about Islam or Buddhism and not get too Deleuzian and refer to Islams or Buddhisms in the plural, then you are going to be selecting something as the authentic or real "religion" at least for the purposes of study and thus making a normative judgement.[6]

An alternative is often supposed to be restating the language of a scholar's sources. If a person says they are a Muslim, what ground does the scholar have to challenge their statement? This seems to make intuitive sense. Repeating the words of one's informant might seems to avoid the issue of normativity or normative definition. I'll grant that this strategy even works for some projects and research questions (even if it does not sidestep the basic entanglements of thick ethical concepts).

The problem is that there are many reasons why scholars might want to disagree with their sources. For instance, when Fukunaga Hōgen (福永法源, 1945–) claimed to be the reincarnation of both Jesus Christ and the Buddha and founded a Japanese religion focused on charging people for prophetic foot reading, it was not hard for scholars to assert that his movement was neither Christianity nor Buddhism despite his claims to the contrary, especially after he was arrested for fraudulently claiming to cure cancer with what amounted to foot rubs (Yonemoto 2000). Yet even if this was an easy decision to make, it rested in a normative verdict about what counts as "real" or "authentic" Christianity or Buddhism.

Similarly, the scholarly practice of repeating whatever an informant says merely outsources the theology. To take someone at their word that they speak for the "real Islam" is to acquiesce to the informant's own normative assertions and often to lend them scholarly authority. As Bruce Lincoln (1996: 227) argued in his famous "Theses on Method," when scholars simply repeat the truth claims of their subjects without interrogating them are just acting as cheerleaders.

I do not think that Hughes would disagree with me here, but he has a tendency to focus his critique of normativity on the crypto-theologies of putative insiders. But secular or outsider scholars are often just as normative. Either you take what your sources say at face value and essentially rubberstamp their theological statements or, in order to reject what your sources say, you come up with your own normative definition in order to do so.

To further expand on this issue, I'd like to provide one more extended example from Buddhist studies. In *Islam and the Tyranny of Authenticity*, Hughes (2015: 37-40) discusses a debate between two Buddhologists—Donald S. Lopez Jr. and Robert Thurman—over the proper portrayal of Tibetan Buddhism. Hughes largely sides with Lopez's criticism of Thurman as overly sympathetic toward an idealized Tibetan Buddhism. But the issue is that it is easy to reverse the critique, in other words to show how Lopez and company are perpetuating their own notions of Buddhist authenticity. I should say from the outset that it is not my intention in any sense to spare Robert Thurman from criticism. Rather, what I want to suggest is that there is a notion of Buddhist authenticity common to a significant stratum of Buddhist studies that is no less normative (and no less problematic) despite presenting itself as the secular or even critical position. It is my contention that portraying the issue as a conflict between secular social science and theology is too simplistic.

To explain, contemporary Buddhist philosophy can be roughly subdivided into two camps in regard to the issue of the relationship between Buddhism and science. On the one hand, there are thinkers like Eleanor Rosch, Francisco Varela, and James H. Austin, who argue that Buddhism anticipates the findings of psychology, neuroscience, or cognitive science. Most of these thinkers are themselves scientists. On the other hand, Buddhologists like Donald Lopez Jr. and David McMahan have gone to some pains to argue for the fundamental incompatibility between Buddhism and science. My point here is not to pick either side in this controversy, but rather to note the particular rhetorical strategies that Lopez and McMahan use to frame their arguments.

Both Lopez's *Buddhism and Science* (2008) and McMahan's *The Making of Buddhist Modernism* (2008) gain most of their rhetorical force by criticizing what they both refer to as "Buddhist modernism" which is generally presented as an inauthentic renovation of original Buddhism. To be fair, Lopez's monograph is sophisticated and he is self-conscious of the implications of his argument. In the work's conclusion he acknowledges the ways that the work might easily be construed as making a normative argument about what Buddhism should be. But McMahan's work exposes the Neo-Orientalist grounding assumptions of this whole canon of literature. Indeed, the book's main argument relies on adjudicating what counts as authentic or real Buddhism. McMahan makes this explicit when he argues that "what many Americans and Europeans often understand by the term 'Buddhism,' however, is actually a modern hybrid" (McMahan 2008: 5). As he elaborates over the course of his work, this inauthentic and hybrid religion owes more to Westernization and modernization than it does to original Buddhism. By contrast to this false Buddhist Modernism, McMahan describes a pure "traditional Buddhism" located in Asia. Thus, he is in effect producing a false binary between an idealized Asian tradition and its implicitly degenerate modern-hybrid form. Moreover, the very terms of McMahan's analysis suggest that what he is concerned with is Buddhist *Modernism* not modern *Buddhism*. In other words, Buddhist Modernism is not really Buddhism.

It is worth noting that the whole critique of Buddhist Modernism unconsciously recaps an older argument in Protestant theology known as the Fundamentalist-Modernist Conflict.[7] In brief, in this debate the fundamentalists charged their opponents with having lost the essence or core of Christianity by "modernizing" the faith to emphasize the religion's compatibility with science and secular culture. They accused Liberal Protestantism of being a de-Christianized or modernized Christianity. Its enemies charged what they saw as hybrid or inauthentic religion of having lost its cultural and historical roots. In sum, the attack on progressive Christianity was that it was not really Christianity but Christian modernism.

In effect, scholars of Buddhism like McMahan and company are making what was then the fundamentalist argument—modernized Buddhism is not Buddhism; the real Buddhism is the Buddha's historical Buddhism, which was necessarily incompatible with science (despite other scholar's arguments to the contrary). Without persecuting or defending either camp (indeed, elsewhere I have criticized claims that Buddha was a "neuroscientist"), I want to emphasize that this whole formulation is unconscious of its roots and entangled in larger issues about the role of normativity in the academy.

Conclusion

We cannot eliminate values from our research projects. The appeal to expunge theology from religious studies itself relies on values—such as secularism, laicity, or notions of the value of value-neutrality. Our basic scholarship relies on scholarly norms and thick ethical concepts and is necessarily entangled with the norms of those we study. Hence, even if we banished the theologians from our conferences we would have done nothing to eliminate the values and value judgements that run through our discipline.

This might seem dire. But I want to reiterate that the impasse I have been discussing is not singular to religious studies. It reflects in microcosm the problems with putatively value-free social science. So, what is to be done?

I agree with Hughes's critique of simplistic attempts to spare particular religions from critical scrutiny. I also agree that in many cases scholars are guilty of distorting their source material in service of unstated values. But it is clear that stressing the fact-value dichotomy does not actually get rid of values (nor would expunging values from our scholarship necessarily be a good thing). Indeed, the very critique of values and appeals to secularism or value-neutrality actually have their own normative force.

I argue that a key function of appeals to value-free social science is that they drive various motivations (political, theological, ethical) underground. It is the very assertion that social science should be apolitical that causes scholars to disguise their politics as factual statements. It is the notion that social scientific scholarship should be value-free that pressures scholars into hiding their ethical ideals or theological commitments. In summary, I argue that it is these self-same appeals to (secular) value-neutrality that produce crypto-theologies.

As an alternative, scholars should work to become conscious of their own values and make their motivations explicit. In part, this is because, like Putnam and others, I think that when values are explicitly stated they are then amenable to rationale inquiry and debate. Another implication of the entanglement of fact and value is that values often rest on specific claims of an empirical nature. In that respect, making values and their justifications explicit allows us to hold them up for scrutiny.

Finally, a key issue, at least for me, is not the fact that we make normative or value judgements, but rather I think we need to investigate what unstated normative judgements exist in specific areas of our field. In that respect, Aaron Hughes's work on the subfields of Islamic studies and Jewish studies has been invaluable.

Jason Ā. Josephson-Storm is Chair & Professor of Religion at Williams College. He received his PhD from Stanford University and has held visiting positions at Princeton University, École Française d'Extrême-Orient, France and Ruhr Universität, Germany. He is the author of *The Invention of Religion in Japan* (2012, winner of the Society for the Scientific Study of Religion, Book of the Year award), *The Myth of Disenchantment: Magic, Modernity and the Birth of the Human Sciences* (2017), and "Absolute Disruption: The Future of Theory after Postmodernism" (forthcoming).

Notes

1   See also Hughes (2007, 2012, 2014). He has also done similarly important work on Jewish studies, see Hughes (2013).

2   For Adorno, see for example Adorno (2007: 56).
3   For a fuller-survey of the discussion see the edited volume McCutcheon (1999).
4   Any follower of Marx or Freud would also be suspicious of our capacity for self-deception.
5   Ichikawa singled out for critique in particular his own article "Sensō kagaku Zen" (War, Science, and Zen, 1942), which argued that Japan was engaged in a "spiritual war" to establish lasting peace in Asia.
6   Moreover, as Hughes has rightly noted (citing Arnal and McCutcheon), even writing about plural "Islams" does not avoid the problem of coming up with a notion of Islam. It merely defers the issue to a question of the criteria for defining a member of the genus. (Hughes 2015: 123).
7   For this conflict in American Protestantism, see Marsden (2006).

References

Adorno, Theodor W. 2007. *The Jargon of Authenticity*. Translated by Knut Tarnowski and Frederic Will. London: Routledge.
Brubaker, Rogers. 2017. "The Uproar Over 'Transracialism'." *New York Times*, May 18. Retrieved from www.nytimes.com/2017/05/18/opinion/the-uproar-over-transracialism.html (archived at www.webcitation.org/78k2uiCXP).
Haraway, Donna. 1988. "Situated Knowledges: The Science Question in Feminism and the Privilege of Partial Perspective." *Feminist Studies* 14(3): 575–599. https://doi.org/10.2307/3178066
Hughes, Aaron W. 2007. *Situating Islam: The Past and Future of an Academic Discipline*. London: Equinox.
Hughes, Aaron W. 2012. *Theorizing Islam: Disciplinary Deconstruction and Reconstruction*. London: Equinox.
Hughes, Aaron W. 2013. *Abrahamic Religions: On the Uses and Abuses of History*. New York: Oxford University Press. https://doi.org/10.1093/acprof:oso/9780199934645.001.0001
Hughes, Aaron W. 2014. *Study of Judaism: Authenticity, Identity, Scholarship*. Albany: State University of New York Press.
Hughes, Aaron W. 2015. *Islam and the Tyranny of Authenticity: An Inquiry into Disciplinary Apologetics and Self-Deception*. London: Equinox.
Ichikawa Hakugen 市川白弦. 1970. *Bukkyōsha no sensō sekinin* 仏教者の戦争責任. Tokyo: Shunjūsha.
Josephson, Jason Ānanda. 2012. *The Invention of Religion in Japan*. Chicago, IL: University of Chicago Press.
Josephson-Storm, Jason Ā. 2017. *The Myth of Disenchantment: Magic, Modernity, and the Birth of the Human Sciences*. Chicago, IL: University of Chicago Press. https://doi.org/10.7208/chicago/9780226403533.001.0001
Lincoln, Bruce. 1996. "Theses on Method." *Method and Theory in the Study of Religion* 8(3): 225–227. https://doi.org/10.1163/157006896X00323
Lopez, Donald S. 2008. *Buddhism and Science*. Chicago, IL: University of Chicago Press.
Lorde, Audre. 2007. "The Master's Tools Will Never Dismantle the Master's House." In *Sister Outsider: Essays and Speeches*, 110–114. Berkeley, CA: Crossing Press.
Marsden, George M. 2006. *Fundamentalism and American Culture*. New York: Oxford University Press.
McCutcheon, Russell T. 1999. *The Insider/Outsider Problem in the Study of Religion: A Reader*. New York: Cassell.

McMahan, David L. 2008. *The Making of Buddhist Modernism*. Oxford: Oxford University Press. https://doi.org/10.1093/acprof:oso/9780195183276.001.0001
Putnam, Hilary. 2002. *The Collapse of the Fact/Value Dichotomy and Other Essays*. Cambridge, MA: Harvard University Press.
Victoria, Brian Daizen. 1997. *Zen at War*. New York: Weatherhill.
Walls, Andrew F. 1980. "A Bag of Needments for the Road: Geoffrey Parrinder and the Study of Religion in Britain." *Religion* 10(2): 141–150. https://doi.org/10.1016/0048-721X(80)90034-2
Weber, Max. 1951. "Der Sinn der 'Wertfreiheit' der soziologischen und ökonomischen Wissenschaften." In *Gesammelte Aufsätze zur Wissenschaftslehre*, 451–502. Tübingen: Mohr.
Wylie, Alison. 2003. "Why Standpoint Matters." In Robert Figueroa and Sandra G. Harding (eds.), *Science and Other Cultures*, 26–48. New York: Routledge.
Yonemoto Kazuhiro 米本和広. 2000. *Kyōso taiho : Karuto wa hito o sukūka* 教祖逮捕:「カルト」は人を救うか. Tokyo: Takarajimasha.

Part II

Politics

Introduction to Part II

Leslie Dorrough Smith, Avila University
Steffen Führding, Leibniz University
Adrian Hermann, University of Bonn

If it is common in polite company to shy away from conversations about politics and religion, then the next four chapters will strike the reader as anything but polite. They are, however, of vital importance, for as these essays will show, some of the most basic conceptualizations of order, social normativity, and law are inspired by the interests pursued by various religious groups and, by definition, those who stand outside of them. Such interests are neither unique nor limited to such groups, but are part of the larger social web of forces under which societies operate.

The realm of politics is the public place where such concerns are often worked out. We can see this in its most obvious form when politicians speak out against or in favor of certain religious groups; propose laws that, in the name of "tradition," or "family values," or "conscience," protect certain kinds of people (or, conversely, fail to protect others); or speak in the name of a vaguely rendered and religiously-inspired "morality" or "decency" that creates and sustains the law, even in cultures that have a legal separation of church and state. What often start out as ideological statements are usually closely tied to very physical ramifications, and so while we often casually think of politics and religion as a particular set of beliefs or attitudes, it is vital to remember that such things are what directly shape the boundaries of people's very lives, as several of the following essays demonstrate.

The anchoring essay in Part II comes from *Naomi Goldenberg* (Chapter 4), who introduces us to some of the theoretical considerations that exist when we consider how the power of nation-states intersects with the religious groups within them. Goldenberg argues that religion and nation-states are both forms of social control that often work hand in hand. While states generally delegitimize religious groups when they act in violent ways, there are some very interesting moments—namely, those that are deemed "private" and "familial" and which often disproportionately affect women and children—where such groups' controversial behaviors are considered outside the bounds of government sanction. She describes this as it pertains to the *metzitzah b'peh* (oral suction after circumcision), a practice of some ultra-orthodox Jewish groups.

Three additional contributions respond to Goldenberg, each considering where cultures manufacture the public lines of social legitimacy. First, *Vaia Touna* (Chapter 5) discusses the northern Greek tradition of fire-walking, a practice that the Greek Orthodox Church has attempted to officially ban as inconsistent with church tradition at the same time that it insists on the legitimacy of its own set of rituals. Since there is no division of church and state in the Greek context, this makes the rhetoric of "proper religion" and "proper citizen" all the more crucial.

Next, *K. Merinda Simmons* (Chapter 6) takes up Goldenberg's interest in the construction of the private realm as a place where violence in the name of religion is often permitted. In her essay, Simmons discusses how scholars of religion are often ready and willing to politically deconstruct the category of religion even as they fail to see the politics that underlie other categories, and considers how this plays out in the case of gender.

Finally, *Matt Sheedy* (Chapter 7) considers the recent controversy in Canadian politics over the practice of wearing the niqab. Sheedy shows how the lines of social, political, and religious legitimacy can shift dramatically over a single symbol—in this case, a garment worn by some Muslim women—and can itself become "all things to all people" depending on the cultural context in which it is presented.

Thus what we often call a "clash of values" in the public sphere might better be understood as a clash of interests, for religious speech uttered in the public realm has the power to make the concerns, preferences, and general interests of groups feel like something much more important, inviolable, and consequential when labelled "values." This elevation is no accident, indeed, for it comprises one of the most important social functions of religion: to authorize and legitimize the otherwise mundane social claims of particular groups.

Chapter 4

Toward a Critique of Postsecular Rhetoric

Naomi R. Goldenberg

> What counts as religious or secular in any given context is a function of different configurations of power.
> —William T. Cavanaugh, *The Myth of Religious Violence* (2009: 4)

We who study, write, teach, and talk about religion have an important task in the present historical moment in which a number of factors are contributing to a reassessment and realignment of categories such as nation, state, nation-state, the secular, and sovereignty in relation to religion. I suggest that our job at this juncture is to use the critical skills we have developed over years of reading, discussion and debate to encourage general audiences, students and colleagues to reflect more deeply and precisely about religion as a thoroughly political category. Approaching religion as politics by another name contrasts with the widespread postsecular narrative in which the term religion refers to a set-apart, yet paradoxically comprehensive, phenomenon that has been disparaged and underestimated but is now returning to effect major societal change.

I am using the term "political" capaciously as Roland Barthes employs it to "describe the whole of human relations in their real, social structure, in their power of making the world." Barthes analyses types of language that function as "depoliticized" speech—i.e. as discourses that disguise historical intention and contingency by being presented as having a "natural" or "eternal" ontology (1972: 142–143). An aura of unconditioned presence—an uninterrogated thereness—characterizes depoliticized idioms and vocabulary. He focuses on myth as one type of such language. I contend that in much of postsecular rhetoric, religion and cognate terms such as spirituality and sacredness operate similarly—that is, as denotations of phenomena that supposedly are of another order from that which is called politics or the secular. By refraining from questioning such depoliticizing rhetoric, theorists perpetuate misleading reifications of concepts that warrant close scrutiny. In this chapter, I will make a case for supporting a determined and sustained effort among religious studies scholars to deconstruct the foundational terms of the discipline with the aim of promoting more discerning and progressive trajectories of analysis.

Before proceeding any further with an argument that will subject several texts and authors to negative analysis and appraisal, I want to illustrate how problematizing the meaning of religion in a specific context can lead to constructive, significant insight. Mayanthi Fernando's posting on the website of "The Immanent

Frame" titled "Taking the Islamic in the Islamic State Seriously" provides an example (2017).

Fernando comments on Noah Salomon's book titled *For the Love of the Prophet: An Ethnography of Sudan's Islamic State* (2016). She admires the "dexterity" with which Salomon traces Sudan's history from a "secular colonial state" under British rule to a present-day "Islamic post-colonial one" (Fernando 2017). Despite her enthusiastic appreciation of the work, she questions the distinction that Salomon draws between these two formations of government. Fernando notes that Salomon agrees with much current scholarship that something called "the secular state" as a general term is not so much in the "business of separating religious from political life but of administering and managing religion which necessarily includes defining its proper form [...]" (ibid.). This description, she reasons, presents a contradiction. Since the British colonial state was 'secular' because it attempted to establish and manage a proper form of Islam that, among other things, marginalized Sufi orders; and since the present NIF (National Islamic Front) is termed a 'religious' state that also manages, defines, and administers 'religion' with special emphasis on controlling those same Sufi orders, isn't the NIF also 'secular'?

The point is not, she states, "that Sudan is not an Islamic state but a secular one." Instead, she suggests that Sudan ought to be thought of as both at once. Perhaps all modern states—be they 'secular', Islamic, or, 'religious'—are in the business of "managing religion." Fernando considers the possibility that the difference between the former British Sudanese state and the contemporary post-colonial Islamic one might lie in the "modality of sovereignty" practiced in each.

In her short but meaty posting, Fernando goes on to think about the use of poetry, fable, and literary traditions as tools of governance in Sudan. She wonders if such a "modality of sovereignty" that enlarges what she calls "political imagination" could be applied more widely. Her commentary shows that productive trajectories of theory can be opened up when the usual binary of religion and politics is set aside and what passes for religion in a particular place and governmental context is carefully and creatively analyzed.

I am experimenting with theory that would push religious studies out of habitual dualisms by locating foundational terms squarely within the purview of politics. To further this purpose, I suggest that religions ought to be thought of as vestigial states (cf. Goldenberg 2013a, 2013b, 2015, 2017, 2018). Key tenets of my argument are:

1   Religion is a rather recent category that has evolved as a type of strategy of governance. It is a classification that functions to manage groups by granting them particular powers and status in exchange for the acceptance of specific limitations. Often the institutions that are designated as religions once enjoyed a larger measure of sovereignty either over territory or population. Colonization and/or defeat in war are two factors that commonly reduce the scope of previous jurisdictions.

2   The label "religion" can function as a technology that serves the interests of dominant governments as well as marginalized competitors by referencing an enduring, stable, often theistic authority that can be cited as a foundation for changeable, mundane laws and institutional structures.

3   A vestigial state, aka a religion as per this hypothesis, tends to be imagined as a once and future government. The memory of former prominence is fostered as an animating principle along with the hope for a more complete restoration of a past system of governance in either this life or a future one. Thus, vestigial states tend to be restive and ambitious in varying degrees. Some focus on texts and teachings that are directed to limited domains such as the interior lives of individual selves, or the private realms of households and families. Others cite doctrines related to a renewed order of grander, more public scope to be established gradually or, perhaps, after a major catastrophe. Vestigial states can succeed in taking over the mechanisms of day to day procedures of dominant states as well as the control of ascendant philosophies of law and regulation. Israel serves as a contemporary example. In such instances, the descriptions of "dominant" and "vestigial" need to be reassessed.

4   Because vestigial—i.e. religious—governments model themselves on sovereignties and societies of the past, they support male leadership and advocate separate roles for men and women. Male authority tends to be idealized and mystified within religions and, with few exceptions, constitutes a primary characteristic of groups accorded the label. I have come to suspect that feminist goddess movements such as contemporary Wicca reinforce masculine hegemony by declaring themselves to be religions. This claim perpetuates the reification and naturalization of the category and thereby reinforces the impression that religion—that is largely synonymous with male supremacy—exists everywhere in one form or another. Because dominant governments consider the family to be an appropriate sphere of influence for religious institutions and ideologies, male authority over women and children is reinforced.

5   The dominant government keeps control of most forms of violence. Although a dominant state uses the vestigial ones it contains and authorizes to support its own legitimacy through such practices as referencing deities in foundational documents, on coinage, and in official ceremonies, the legalized administration of police and martial violence is not granted to 'religions' and remains a *sine qua non* of the power of a fully functioning state. Even in these neo-liberal times in which vestigial states called religions are being aggrandized by being placed in charge of jurisdictional spheres concerned with

social welfare and education, institutional authority over violence is franchised out only in limited circumstances.

Max Weber's observation about violence and government holds true. He writes:

> it is [...] the case that in the final analysis the modern state can be defined [...] by the specific means that are peculiar to it...namely, physical violence. [...] [W]e must say that the state is the form of human community that (successfully) lays claim to the monopoly of legitimate physical violence within a particular territory. [...] [A]ll other organizations or individuals can assert the right to use physical violence only insofar as the state permits them to do so. (Weber [1919] 2004: 33)

Expressed over a century ago, Weber's perception that legalized violence is the power that dominant states always reserve for themselves must be stressed in thinking about contemporary rhetorical binaries involving religion. Police and military violence as well as the violence in reserve that is necessary to enforce court decisions is a jealously guarded power of the state. If a group that is designated a religion employs violence, public rhetoric is quickly mustered to take away or modify the label 'religion'—perhaps by categorizing the violent group as an inauthentic expression of the truer, purer tradition. Current work by Aaron Hughes (2015, 2018) and Vaia Touna (2017) explores how assessments of the authenticity of traditions are rooted in political motivations.

Weber implies that the government monopoly on official, sanctioned violence does not preclude the dominant state from franchising out violence to other groups such as to the vestigial states that I am equating with religions—or, for that matter, to corporations with "private" security forces. In regard to religions, in some otherwise "secular" judicial systems such as those of the United Kingdom, domestic violence can be refereed by faith-based courts or tribunals. The cutting of the bodies of male and female children is another form of violence that dominant states sometimes allow groups it designates as religions to carry out. I will comment further on this practice with two examples in my conclusion.

Theorizing religions as vestigial states is an effort to bring the mechanisms of statecraft into clearer focus. It is a possible stepping stone to better thought that will undoubtedly supersede it to reach further. A crucial measure of insightful theory is how well it can illuminate the artificiality—i.e. the constructedness—of taken for granted tropes and categories of rhetoric that inhere in academic writing identified as postsecular.

The cornerstone of the work of authors who endorse various forms of postsecular theory is the tendency to treat religion as an ahistorical, non-contingent, consistent referent. Religion, or sometimes a cognate term such as "spirituality" (Braidotti 2014), is posited as a neglected source of valuable and inspirational values and practices of that which has been abjected from contemporary restricted and oppressive social or governmental orders. "Liberal" and "secular" are common adjectives for the grim, unsatisfying, and hyper-rational institutions and psychological conditions that are in need of the animation, inclusivity, and virtue embodied in whatever the postsecular theorist considers to be properly religious.

Although Jürgen Habermas's argument for the necessity of a return to the "unexamined semantic resource" of religion has been critiqued as too narrowly Christian and has been expanded to include other traditions, the idealization of religion that he first proposed remains foundational for postsecular thinking (Birnbaum 2015). In his incisive article titled "Why I Am Not a Postsecularist," Aamir Mufti describes the generosity shown toward non-Western forms of religion as a misguided corrective for colonialist prejudice (2013). Mufti introduces the term "ethnographic philanthropy" to describe the practice of applying critique and genealogical analysis to Western liberal colonial societies while exempting post-colonial ones from such scrutiny. He writes that an authenticity labelled religious in postcolonial societies is valorized as a good thing in part because it is akin to "the people." These post-colonial contexts are treated as exempt from the analytic habits of scholarship that historicize and explore political motives. Such critical practices are now widely thought of as appropriate only when applied to Western, liberal, secular societies. The gentler analytic approach to cultures and social groupings seen as more innocent is one way in which religion comes to be considered as good; while what is bad is synonymous with a broadly understood secular negativity that characterizes disenchanted modernity.

Mufti critiques the orientation of Talal Asad and Saba Mahmood, who have both authored work that is now canonical in religious studies scholarship (Mufti 2013: 8–12). He points out that Asad does not apply his genealogical method to Islam. Instead, Asad treats Islam as largely unified, intact "tradition" that contrasts to secular, liberal social arrangements, ideologies, and institutions that can be safely subjected to disaggregating analysis.

Mahmood's work in *Politics of Piety* (2010) supports the postsecular orthodox position that Mufti identifies. The book has been used to portray "Islam" as good and Western feminism—for which the writing of Judith Butler is a metonym—as bad. More specifically, Mahmood's text is cited to censure feminism for disparaging women who live in postcolonial situations and for failing to recognize the benefits of religious frameworks. Her fieldwork in Egypt among devout Muslim women in a particular Islamic movement is claimed to refute Butler's thinking about the concept of agency as a source of resistance in ideological systems (Mahmood 2006). The fact that some women have found a way to foster their self-worth and dignity by energetically cultivating "shyness," a quality that is highly valued in the milieu Mahmood researched, is supposedly an indictment of both Butler's work and of feminism as a whole. The reasoning is weak, but enduring. In the collection *Bodily Citations*, Butler tactfully agrees that the women Mahmood interviewed are asserting seemingly compliant "agency" in their competitive displays of shyness. She points out, however, that by doing so, they are "working the norm" in which they live as the only means by which innovation is possible (Butler 2006: 286). The intensification of shyness is itself a technique of agentic self-assertion that to some degree resists a prescribed meekness. "Ethnographic philanthropy" might explain why Mahmood's interpretation of assertive shyness has not received more robust critique.

Probably the most quoted, most reprinted essay in what can be considered a new postsecular feminist defense of religion is Joan Scott's "Secularism and Gender Equality" (2013). Scott concludes her article with a brief, even-handed recommendation to "insist [...] on a more nuanced and complex historical approach to the two supposedly antithetical concepts: the religious and the secular" (ibid.: 43). However, the body of her essay employs a partisan, simplified tone. A few paragraphs before the quotation above, Scott writes that her analysis "lets us take our distance from the emancipatory story secularism has learned to tell about itself" (ibid.: 42). The anthropomorphism is striking in its portrayal of secularism as some Scheherazade type figure that spins self-serving narratives. Her essay is rife with generalizations in which secularism is cast as the bad guy that has used an ahistorical entity termed religion as a scapegoat: problems in secular societies she says are obscured by "attributing all that is negative to religion" (ibid.: 42). Typically present in this type of work that scolds feminism and urges feminist theorists to back off "religion" is an aside that is included to give the impression of equanimity. Scott adds such a sentence. She declares that her call for a critical genealogy of secularism "assumes that, unlike secularism, religion is not affected by historical circumstances, not itself a 'modern' phenomenon, when, of course, it is" (ibid.: 42). She does not return to this thought or develop it further. Instead, her essay presents a holistic, unfairly criticized "religion" wearing a white hat while secularism is cast as a puffed-up, ignorant villain in black. A trope of religion-the-good/secularism-the-bad dominates her rhetoric.

The call for a chastened, revised feminism that ought to be respectful of religion is prevalent. Often the essays, books, and conferences that champion postsecular feminism focus on how capitalist secularism created a public/private split that is particularly disabling for women. It is argued that because religion is pushed into a private sphere, women who want to express religiosity in public are discouraged and scorned. Proponents of this position hold that secularists in general and feminist secularists in particular are promoting oppression by supporting the restriction of religion to the private sphere. An example of such scholarship is Linell Cady and Tracy Fessenden's popular edited collection *Religion, the Secular, and the Politics of Sexual Difference* (2013). Remarkably, none of the authors in the book connect the central tenet of their work about the linkage of religion with "the private" and "the personal" with the starting point and nexus of second wave feminism captured in the slogan—the personal is political. The understanding of the religious as political reinvigorates this basic feminist principle and enlarges its scope.

Some recent postsecular writing tentatively approaches a historical analysis of religion while paradoxically continuing to essentialize the term. In *Religious Difference in a Secular Age: A Minority Report* (2015), Saba Mahmood shows in detail how the category of "minority" was created in the Middle East and what effects of governance resulted. This foray into political history leads her to explain specific contexts in which family law became assigned to the jurisdiction of religion. She thus begins to trace the construction of religion as a regime of authority and regulation over variable social spheres. Nevertheless, this trajectory of deconstruction is not continued in her text. Instead, Mahmood sustains the pattern identified by Mufti of exempting religion from disaggregation.

The reification and decontextualization of religion in Mahmood's text is subtle and ambivalent. I interpret this nuance optimistically as an indication of the problem among postsecular theorists of maintaining a serious and informed discussion of power dynamics related to groups and governance that does not approach the deconstruction of "religion." A tone of apologetics for religion in general and Islam as a particular religion permeates Mahmood's writing. For example, in her chapter titled "Secularism, Family Law, and Gender Inequality," she observes that although "there is no doubt that Muslim and Christian family laws have been historically unjust to women in the Middle East [...] it is nonetheless, important to point out that gender inequalities enshrined in family law cannot be understood in religious terms alone" (Mahmood 2015: 132). This sentence briefly acknowledges some sexism in religion, but quickly moves off to place the lion's share of blame elsewhere. The chapter continues with an argument about how secular, capitalist Western practices have made the rather minimal oppression of women in Islam much worse. She writes that Ottoman marriage contracts were constrained in the "modern state." Such documents might in fact include a clause that gave a woman the right to divorce if her husband beat her "with enough force to leave marks"—a provision that Mahmood seems to suggest ought to be credited as progressive (ibid.: 132, n. 87).

Throughout her book, Mahmood writes as if religion, the noun, or religious, the adjective, references stable, consistent, and distinct phenomena. In her epilogue, she writes: "As a legal mandate, religious equality depends upon the agency of the sovereign state, which does not simply relegate religion to the private sphere but reorganizes it through its legal and political mechanisms" (Mahmood 2015: 211). Here religion appears as a thing in itself that is managed and moved around by the state. There is no reflection on how or when religion was created as an object to be manipulated. Toward the end of the chapter on family law, she hints at where she places religion in history: "The incorporation of premodern religious precepts into the legal structure of the modern state gives family law a primordial cast when in fact it represents a novel arrangement" (ibid.: 147). Thus, "religious precepts" described as "premodern" seem to have a location in an indistinct time long ago. Mahmood is uninfluenced by scholarship that positions religion as a modern category that is only anachronistically applied to ancient epochs. If she were to take note of such work, she might show some awareness of the problematic linking of religion with anything that could be called premodern.

In some parts of her text, she comes close to recognizing the contingent construction of religion, but does not sustain the insight. Of evangelical Christianity she writes that "it would be difficult to imagine this global force as 'religious' in any simple sense" (Mahmood 2015: 146). I wonder what this "simple sense" could be and what other factors might complicate the simplicity. Mahmood gives no indication of concern about such matters. She appears to know exactly what religion is in its essence and to assume that her readers share her confident presumption.

The unexamined premise that religion refers to something clear, simple, bounded, and definite is key to the postsecular rhetoric Mufti names. Challenging it is necessary both to sharpen thinking about national and global institutions and to avoid endorsing poorly thought-out directives. In her conclusion, Mahmood demonstrates how the reification of religion can lead to a vague, yet curiously authoritarian trajectory. Although the contemporary political context of Egypt is her particular focus, she closes her text with a call for bolder theory reaching beyond Middle Eastern specificity. She laments what she names a "collective incapacity to imagine a politics that does not treat the state as the arbiter of majority-minority relations." "Given this context," she suggests, "the ideal of interfaith equality might require not the bracketing of religious differences, but their ethical thematization as a necessary risk when the conceptual and political resources of the state have proved inadequate to the challenge this ideal sets before us" (Mahmood 2015: 213).

This proposition is both perplexing and disturbing. How can a capacity to imagine a new politics be fostered when basic uninterrogated components of the old politics—i.e. "interfaith equality," "religious differences"—are assumed to contain solutions? According to her, the "resources" of what she is calling "the state" are to be set aside, while "religious differences" that she positions as outside of the state ought to be allowed to flourish through some positive sounding process that constitutes "their ethical thematization." I assume that the "necessary risk" she favors involves increasing the sphere of influence of the ideologies and institutions that constitute "religious differences." Furthermore, any of "the conceptual and political resources of the state" presumably will not be permitted to constrain this aggrandizement because they have proven to be "inadequate." The plan seems to consist of ceding power to "religion" through diminishing "the state" because it is imaginatively and politically bankrupt. "The state" Mahmood disdains in her work is characterized with terms such as secular, capitalist, Western, and liberal. In contrast, she uses no adjectives for that which she refers to as religion. Since she offers no definition of religion and seems to recognize no need to approach concepts designated as religious critically, the prescription with which she ends her book does indeed constitute a risk.

Before sanctioning any such risk that would entail ceding more deference and power to religions, scholarship that historicizes and analyses terms and concepts pertaining to religion, religious differences, and religious freedom and their relationship to government should become much more familiar to a wider public. In the absence of awareness of the instability, temporality and thoroughly political character of these categories, appeals to religion can function to shield behavior that would otherwise be considered indefensible.

I conclude with two recent examples of defenses in US courts that draw on sentiment that accords with postsecular appreciation of religion and religious freedom. Both involve circumcision rituals—one type practiced on male infants, another practiced on female pre-adolescents.

In 2013 in New York City, Mayor Bill De Blasio made a campaign promise to discard the initiatives of his predecessor, Mayor Michael Bloomberg, to curtail *metzizah b-peh*—i.e. oral suction after circumcision—that is practiced among some ultra-orthodox Jewish groups. Although in 2012 eleven cases of herpes in male infants were traced back to the practice, Jewish groups would not agree to require parents to read and sign consent forms prior to the procedure. The forms explained that risks of oral suction include brain damage and death. (In fact, two of the 11 infants who had contracted herpes had suffered brain damage and two others had died.) Members of New York City's ultra-orthodox Jewish communities tend to be highly educated. Several doctors who clearly understand the risks to their offspring nevertheless support the practice (Otterman 2015).

In 2014, the De Blasio administration ceased support for Bloomberg's regulation to insist on the use of consent forms. The requirement was the subject of a lawsuit by ultra-orthodox groups on the grounds that the forms impeded religious freedom. In place of the consent forms, there was some agreement with rabbis and the health department to put in place a voluntary protocol that *mohelim* who practice oral suction be tested for herpes. The protocol was largely ignored. Since 2015 six babies in Brooklyn contracted herpes from oral suction. However, only two families would agree to identify the practitioners to the health department (Khan 2017). Because the ultra-orthodox are an important constituency for De Blasio, it is highly unlikely that oral suction will be curtailed or regulated further (New York Daily News 2017). The argument that religious freedom supersedes concerns for infants' health prevails in this situation.

A second example of how violence against children is being defended through invoking religious freedom is a case in Detroit. The headline of May 20, 2017 in the *Detroit Free Press* reads: "Religious Defense Planned in Landmark Detroit Genital Mutilation Case" (Baldas 2017a). Lawyers for two physicians and the wife of one of the physicians will use the First Amendment to the US Constitution to challenge a law forbidding the cutting of any part of a young girl's genitalia. The law has been unchallenged for 21 years.

All three defendants are members of the Dawoodi Bohra sect, an Indian-Muslim group with a mosque in Farmington Hills, Michigan. Mary Chartier, one of the defense lawyers, is arguing that what the doctors did to the girls does not constitute FGM. "And even if it did," she stated to the media, "it would be exempt because it would violate their [the defendants'] First Amendment rights. They believe that if they do not engage in this then they are not actively practicing their religion" (Baldas 2017a). Friends of Dr. Jumana Nagarwala, the lead defendant, have posted a $4.5 million bond, the largest unsecured bond in the history of Detroit's federal court, to gain her release after five months in jail. This sponsorship demonstrates strong support for the doctor's behavior (Baldas 2017b).

Both of these defenses of violence toward children in Michigan and New York on the basis of religious freedom are extreme uses of the First Amendment in the United States. Further research is necessary to establish whether a climate of opinion that allows harmful practices toward infants and children for religious reasons is gaining traction. If so, there would be one more reason why postsecular rhetoric about the virtues of the ill-defined yet protected category of religion ought to be vigorously challenged.

Naomi R. Goldenberg PhD (1976), Yale University, is Professor of Religious Studies in the Department of Classics and Religious Studies and former Director of Women's Studies at the University of Ottawa in Canada. Her publications include: *Resurrecting the Body: Feminism, Religion and Psychoanalysis* (Crossroad, 1993) and *Changing of the Gods: Feminism and the End of Traditional Religions* (Beacon, 1979). She has co-edited *Religion as a Category of Governance and Sovereignty* (Brill, 2015) with Trevor Stack and Timothy Fitzgerald and is completing *The End of Religion: Feminist Reappraisals of the State* (Taylor and Frances) with Kathleen McPhillips. Her book, *The Religious is Political: An Argument for Understanding Religions as Vestigial States* is in progress.

References

Baldas, Tresa. 2017a. "Religious Defense Planned in Landmark Detroit Mutilation Case." *Detroit Free Press*, May 21. Retrieved from https://eu.freep.com/story/news/2017/05/21/female-genital-mutilation-religious-freedom/319911001 (archived at www.webcitation.org/78hpxU3CG).

Baldas, Tresa. 2017b. "After 5 Months in Jail, Doctor in Genital Cutting Case Released on $4.5M Bond." *Detroit Free Press*, September 19. Retrieved from www.freep.com/story/news/2017/09/19/after-5-months-jail-doctor-free-bond-after-friends-put-u-4-5-million-bond-female-genital-cutting-cas/681265001 (archived at www.webcitation.org/78hqMYmdU).

Barthes, Roland. (1957) 1972. *Mythologies*, trans. Annette Lavers. New York: Hill and Wang.

Birnbaum, Maria. 2015. "Exclusive Pluralism: The Problems of Habermas' Postsecular Argument and the 'Making of' Religion'." In Trevor Stack, Naomi Goldenberg, and Timothy Fitzgerald (eds.), *Religion as a Category of Governance and Sovereignty*, 182–196. Leiden: Brill. https://doi.org/10.1163/9789004290594_009

Braidotti, Rosi. 2014. "The Residual Spirituality in Critical Theory: A Case for Affirmative Postsecular Politics." In Rosi Braidotti et al. (eds.), *Transformations of Religion and the Public Sphere: Postsecular Publics*, 249–272. New York: Palgrave Macmillan. https://doi.org/10.1057/9781137401144_14

Butler, Judith. 2006. "Afterword." In Ellen T. Armour and Susan M. St. Ville (eds.), *Bodily Citations: Religion and Judith Butler*, 276–291. New York: Columbia University Press.

Cady, Linell E. and Tracy Fessenden (eds.). 2013. *Religion, the Secular, and the Politics of Sexual Difference*. New York: Columbia University Press.

Cavanaugh, William T. 2009. *The Myth of Religious Violence: Secular Ideology and the Roots of Modern Conflict*. Oxford: Oxford University Press. https://doi.org/10.1093/acprof:oso/9780195385045.001.0001

Fernando, Mayanthi L. 2017. "Taking the Islamic in 'the Islamic state' Seriously." *The Immanent Frame*, April 13. Retrieved from https://tif.ssrc.org/2017/04/13/taking-the-islamic-in-the-islamic-state-seriously/ (archived at www.webcitation.org/78hbzpOwD).

Goldenberg, Naomi R. 2013a. "Theorizing Religions as Vestigial States in Relation to Gender and Law: Three Cases." *Journal of Feminist Studies in Religion* 29(1): 38–50. https://doi.org/10.2979/jfemistudreli.29.1.39

Goldenberg, Naomi R. 2013b. "Demythologizing Gender and Religion within Nation-States: Toward a Politics of Disbelief." In Niamh Reilly and Stacey Scriver (eds.), *Religion, Gender and the Public Sphere*, 248–256. New York: Routledge.

Goldenberg, Naomi R. 2015. "The Category of Religion in the Technology of Governance: An Argument for Understanding Religions as Vestigial States." In Trevor Stack, Naomi

Goldenberg, and Timothy Fitzgerald (eds.), *Religion as a Category of Governance and Sovereignty*, 280–292. Leiden: Brill. https://doi.org/10.1163/9789004290594_013

Goldenberg, Naomi R. 2017. "Queer Theory Meets Critical Religion: Are We Starting to Think Yet?" In Richard King (ed.), *Theory/Religion/Critique: Classic and Contemporary Approaches*, 531–543. New York: Columbia University Press. https://doi.org/10.7312/king14542-050

Goldenberg, Naomi R. 2018. "Forget About Defining 'It': Reflections on Thinking Differently in Religious Studies." In Brad Stoddard (ed.), *Method Today: Beyond Description and Hermeneutics in Religious Studies Scholarship*, 78–95, Bristol: Equinox.

Hughes, Aaron W. 2015. *Islam and the Tyranny of Authenticity: An Inquiry into Disciplinary Apologetics and Self-Deception*. Sheffield: Equinox

Hughes, Aaron W. 2018. "Religion without Religion: Integrating Islamic Origins into Religious Studies." *Journal of the American Academy of Religion* 85(4): 867–888. https://doi.org/10.1093/jaarel/lfx010

Khan, Shehab. 2017. "New York Orthodox Jewish Families to Identify Circumcisers Who Gave Babies Herpes." *The Independent*, April 21. Retrieved from www.independent.co.uk/news/world/americas/orthodox-jewish-circumcisers-babies-herpes-new-york-identify-williamsburg-brooklyn-a7695371.html (archived at www.webcitation.org/78hpaGIUo).

Mahmood, Saba. 2006. "Agency, Performativity, and the Feminist Subject." In Ellen T. Armour and Susan M. St. Ville (eds.), *Bodily Citations: Religion and Judith Butler*, 177–221. New York: Columbia University Press.

Mahmood, Saba. 2010. *Politics of Piety: Islamic Revival and the Feminist Subject*. Princeton, NJ: University of Princeton Press. https://doi.org/10.2307/j.ctvct00cf

Mahmood, Saba. 2015. *Religious Difference in a Secular Age: A Minority Report*. Princeton, NJ: University of Princeton Press. https://doi.org/10.2307/j.ctvc77k82

Mufti, Aamir. 2013. "Why I am Not a Postsecularist." *boundary 2* 40(1): 7–19. https://doi.org/10.1215/01903659-2072846

New York Daily News. 2017. "De Blasio's Responsibility to Baby Boys." *New York Daily News*, March 30. Retrieved from www.nydailynews.com/opinion/de-blasio-responsibility-baby-boys-article-1.3014272 (archived at www.webcitation.org/78hpfNFOv).

Otterman, Sharon. 2015. "Mayor de Blasio and Rabbis Near Accord on New Circumcision Rule." *New York Times*, January 14. Retrieved from www.nytimes.com/2015/01/15/nyregion/mayor-de-blasio-and-rabbis-near-accord-on-new-circumcision-rule.html (archived at www.webcitation.org/78hpUThRN).

Salomon, Noah. 2016. *For the Love of the Prophet: An Ethnography of Sudan's Islamic State*. Princeton, NJ: Princeton University Press. https://doi.org/10.23943/princeton/9780691165158.001.0001

Scott, Joan. 2013. "Secularism and Gender Equality." In Linell E. Cady and Tracy Fessenden (eds.), *Religion, the Secular, and the Politics of Sexual Difference*, 25–45. New York: Columbia University Press.

Touna, Vaia. 2017. *Fabrications of the Greek Past: Religion, Tradition, and the Making of Modern Identities*. Leiden: Brill. https://doi.org/10.1163/9789004348615

Weber, Max. [1919] 2004. "Politics as a Vocation." In David Owen and Tracy B. Strong (eds.), *The Vocation Lectures*, trans. by Rodney Livingstone, 32–94. Indianapolis: Hackett Publishing Co. Inc.

Chapter 5

The Political Utility of the Past: The Case of Greek Fire-Walking Rituals

Vaia Touna

Anastenaria, or fire-walking rituals (that is, the act of walking barefoot over a layer of hot embers) are described in scholarship as modern practices of religious communities of Orthodox Christians who are devoted to the Saints Constantine and Helen, and are believed by the participants to help purify, heal, and protect them throughout the year. Yet they are very much contested by the Church—making the classification of these practices, and their linkage to the past, a useful illustration of social management.

Until the nineteenth century the Anestanaria were located in what we know today as Bulgaria and Turkey, which were, then, parts of the Ottoman Empire. According to local tradition the origin of the Anastenaria lies in the village of Kosti, located today on the border between Bulgaria and Turkey, when as early as the thirteenth century a fire is said to have broken out in the village's church and the people of the village ran into the fire to save the icons from burning. This constitutes the origin tale that is told to this day. Of importance is the fact that the relation of the Anastenaria and the Orthodox Church has always been in tension. Early on clergy and bishops in the areas where the Anastenaria took place were very hostile to the practices, and the Anastenaria were persecuted with threats of excommunication; in fact, it is even reported that some were beaten and had their icons thrown into the fire.

After the collapse of the Ottoman empire and the formation of nation-states (and especially after the exchange of Greek/Turkish populations that followed the treaty of Lausanne in 1923), Greek refugees, who relocated to what is now modern Greece, brought with them these rituals—which are now mainly found in the northern part of Greece in the villages of Ayia Eleni and Kerkini in Serres, Meliki in Imathia, Laggada in Thessaloniki, and Mauroleki in Drama. It is said that out of fear of further persecutions from the local churches, fire-walking rituals were performed in private, until just after the Second World War. For in 1947 the Anastenaria at the village of Ayia Eleni (St. Helen) were performed in public for the first time, which opened a new circle of debates between the Church and the Anastaneria.[1] For example, that year the Bishop of Serres wrote the Holy Synod of the Orthodox Greek Church for advice as to how to handle the Anastenaria. The Synod replied: "be aware that this is a *pagan custom*, originating from the orgiastic feasts of Dionysus, and must therefore be abolished with the use of any spiritual means that the Church has at her disposition" (emphasis added).[2] Those debates between the church and the Anastenaria, which on some occasions even ended up in courts, resulted in many cases in the confiscation, by the church, of the icons used by the Anastenarides during their fire-walking rituals. (These icons were allowed back to the Anastenarides annually, but only during their three day festivities). Here, actual violence as well as discourses on good/bad religion marks not just the border between church/state or secular/religious but, as will be evident, those techniques are used by any dominant group over marginal groups in order to maintain and police those boundaries—case in point, the church in its ongoing contest with the fire-walkers.

Today, fire-walking rituals occur every year on May 21, when the Orthodox Greek Church commemorates Saints Constantine and Helen. The celebrations of the Anastenarides (the community of fire-walkers) commemorating the two saints lasts three days. During this time there are animal sacrifices, processions around the village with the participants holding αμανέτια (special scarves) and the χάρες (graces; that is, the icons) of the saints; and of course there is music, and dancing, all the while much of the village is filled with vendors and rides. On the third day the celebrations reach their peak, and it's the day of the fire-walking itself.

Although I'm from Greece myself, and my parents' village, where we would spend holidays and summers, is close to one of the "fire-walking" villages (that of Ayia Eleni), I had never visited the fire-walking rituals, which might tell you something about my growing up in Greece and my own cultural sensitivities. But on May 2009 I happened to visit the fire-walking rituals for the first time myself when serving as the local coordinator for the study abroad trip to Thessaloniki with Russell McCutcheon and students from the Department of Religious Studies of the University of Alabama. We arrived at the village of Ayia Eleni, in Serres (in northeastern Greece), around 5:00 p.m. (on the evening when the fire-walking would take place), and already there was a festive atmosphere. The village was filled with people eager to watch the fire-walkers. Passing through vendors and rides (for the event felt somewhat like a carnival at least for my American friends) we reached the κονάκι (konaki), a small, special house that every community of anastenarides (fire-walkers) owns. There participants gather, since early morning, to prepare for the ritual while dancing to the sounds of drum and lyre, all the while holding the special scarves and the large, framed icons of Constantine and Helen. People were crowded outside and all around the house to watch the fire-walkers dancing inside, while others would go inside another room of the house where there were framed pictures, most of them in black and white, which immediately pointed to the history of the community, the first fire-walkers, and also of the fire-walking rituals from years past. Next to the konaki was the Αγίασμα, a small structure with a well that contained holy water, as the sign outside the door indicated. Across from the konaki there was a grass field where the fire-walking was to take place. There, around dusk, men lit a large bonfire and waited about 90 minutes until the fire burned down. The men attending the fire then used long wooden poles to stir the fire to ensure that most of the wood burned down to embers. Meanwhile, the Anastenarides (those participating in the ritual that year) continued throughout the entire day to dance in the nearby konaki. Once the men, tending the fire, spread the coals evenly over the grass, creating a several meters long and a few meters wide circular patch, the anastenarides, dancing to the sounds of drum beats and lyre (some of them with bare feet—those, that is, who would walk on the fire), exited the konaki, some holding candles, and others the icons of the saints. They all formed a circle around the fire and, while they continued dancing and the music played, occasionally one by one they would quickly cross over the coals multiple times. Although it is the culmination of a long day, the fire-walking itself doesn't last more than half an hour. After the ritual ended with the fire-walkers leaving the field, some curious onlookers (who had previously formed a large ring around the entire event) went inside the field to feel for themselves the coals which, by then, had mostly cooled down.

The Anastanaria, as you might imagine, have been discussed and interpreted in many scholarly works and in various ways (e.g., Michael-Dede 1972, 1978a, 1978b, 1983; Danforth 1989; Xygalatas 2014). Of interest here is how Greek scholars tried to explain fire-walking (see Megas 1960, 1962, 1974; Diamantoglou 1953; Kakouri 1999). Not unlike the church, their narratives often focus on similarities and ignore differences, a process that McCutcheon, referencing Jonathan Z. Smith, characterizes as "an economy of signification."[3] That is, scholars tried to link the Anastenaria to the ancient Greek "religion" and its rituals, sometimes portraying them as survivals of Dionysian rituals, while other times as Bacchic, or Orphic cults, and the fire-walkers themselves have even been described both in the media and in various scholarly works as Maenads, or "Bacchant Christians." Yet other scholars, no less focused on past models to understand the modern practice, have linked them to the medieval Christian mystic movements, such as the Hesychasm (Megas 1974). As McCutcheon wrote, such efforts to find similarities are "[a]ll in the service of establishing limits in terms of which significance can be judged, thereby making comparisons, and thus meaning and identity, possible" (2005: 34).

The representation based on such similarity, though, that is perhaps most prominent in Greece about the Anastenaria (and which is supported both by scholars, the media, and the Greek Orthodox Church) is that they are—as already claimed by the Synod—paganistic survivals. This sort of portrait of Anastenaria as "pagan," and thereby related to rituals performed in honor of Dionysus, has been very popular since the nineteenth century, especially among theologians. For instance, in 1873 during the opening ceremony of the school year of the Phanar Greek Orthodox College (or as it is known in Greek, Η Μεγάλη του Γένους Σχολή [The Great School of the Nation]), Anastasios Hourmouziadis, a professor of theology, delivered a speech in the presence of Anthimos, the Ecumenical Patriarch of Constantinople at the time, discussing the case of the Anastenaria. He rather normatively concluded that those rituals were performed by people who were mentally ill and uneducated; he accused them of superstition, of participating in orgies and sacrifices to Aphrodite, all of which was evidence for him that they were not "in line with the practices of the Mother Church" (Hourmouziadis 1873: 1), and which therefore explains, at least to his satisfaction, why the clergy had rightly persecuted the Anastenaria. Yet, in the conclusion of that same essay, Hourmouziadis, although urging the Church to stop the performance of those rituals,[4] also sees the Anastenaria as proof that Greeks are the "genuine children of those immortal ancestors" (meaning the ancient Greeks). But, in order for Greeks to be their worthy descendants and to be perfected in their wisdom, the Holy Scriptures should be their building block since, as he writes, "every human wisdom will be proven to be fake without the divine light of the Christian faith" (ibid.: 29).[5] That modern Greek identity is understood to be the result of not just ancient Greek culture but also Orthodox Christianity is a view that is still very prominent today—not only among clergy, but also among many Greeks.

For example, a few days after I arrived in Greece on May of 2017 to conduct fieldwork research on the often unseen, collaborative relationships that lead to the production of knowledge about the past (such as between museum visitors and curators), I happened to hear in the news about the transfer of the relics of Saint Helen, mother of Constantine the Great, along with a section of the holy cross, from St. Marcus Basilica in the Vatican Museum in Italy (where they are permanently exhibited) to the Church of St. Barbara in Eagaleo, Athens (for a temporary exhibit until June 15). The transportation of the relics was fully covered by the media since, as it was reported, they were transferred to Athens on a special flight and were welcomed with honours usually paid only to visiting state leaders. Present at the welcoming ceremonies was the President of the Greek Republic, Prokopis Paulopoulos, the Archbishop of the Greek Orthodox Church, Ieronymos, as well as political and military dignitaries, along with ambassadors from ten other Orthodox countries. In a statement given to the newspaper "Proto Thema," the press representative of the Archbishop, Charis Konidaris, said the following in regards to the transfer of the relics:

> This event by itself brings to light the intellectual/spiritual and cultural identity of Europe. Europe can indeed serve its people only if its foundation continues to be the ancient Greek Literature, the Roman Law, and Christianity. Away from its Christian roots it is not the Europe its founders envisioned, that is, the Europe of Justice and Solidarity. (Charalampopoulou 2017; my translation)

The event itself and the statement are indicative not only of the position that the Orthodox Church still holds within Greek society but also the role it tries to play in the formation of its citizens' various identities (which includes the fire-walkers, of course). In fact, contests over the right and wrong way not only to be Christian but also to be a Greek are therefore at the heart of this. For here we have St. Helen, just one saint and thus, one ancient reference point; but on the other hand, we have authoritative references made to her by the Greek Orthodox Church as well as references (i.e., practices) of the Anastenaria, a group that occupies a rather curious and ambiguous position on the margins of modern Greek society. For example, although St. Helen plays an important role in the fire-walking rituals, the use of the icon of St. Helen by the fire-walkers is still not considered to be "in line with the practices of the Mother Church," as Hourmouziadis once wrote. In fact, it is not uncommon to hear from church officials even today that holding the icons and dancing on the fire is idolatrous or even satanic, while standing in line for hours to kiss what is supposed to be the relics of the same saint is not idolatrous but instead an act of "honorable worship." For even though the Orthodox Greek Church considers fire-walking rituals as representations of ancient Greek practices—a linkage that usually conveys authoritative significance—they have never been fully accepted by the Orthodox Church; apparently not everything from the ancient Greek past is to be valued in the same way. Discourses on good/bad religion are therefore evidence of competing interests in the present, of efforts to fabricate and maintain modern identities by resorting to what Russell McCutcheon calls the rhetoric of authenticity.

It is indeed important to observe, as already mentioned, that coercion has been one way by which the Orthodox Greek Church, the group known locally as the Church of Greece (Εκκλησία της Ελλάδας) tried to police another group which can be located at its margins, that is the Anasterarides, by confiscating their icons and with constant threats of excommunication. But it should be evident by now that social boundaries are also policed and thereby maintained by such items of discourse as the use of classifications, representations, and linkages with (or deviation from) an authoritative past. In my recently published book, *Fabrications of the Greek Past* (2017), I understand such techniques as among the many acts of identification that work together and which allow people to fabricate identities but also to maintain and police those identities. As such, these acts of identification have also the effect to maintain and police social boundaries. Fire-walking certainly may sound weird and extreme to some ears but it is no less extreme, for example, than people (sticking to Greek examples) who spend long hours on the Greek beaches every summer trying to change the color of their skin, sometimes with painful results, not to mention standing in line for many hours in order to "pay respect" to a couple of bones that are thought to belong to a saint. But the question is: what makes one practice so intriguing, bizarre, extreme, and the others not?

Certainly, classifying Anastenaria, as indicated at the opening of my response, as "religious communities of Orthodox Christians" and then representing them as "survivals of ancient Greek rituals" is doing a lot of conceptual and social work (work that we often overlook, as in when we just assume that this action of course is "ritual"; McCutcheon 2005: 34). What is particularly interesting about classifying those groups as "religious communities of Orthodox Christians" is that this classification operates within Greece as a self-evident distinction between the villages of Anastenaria and other villages in Greece, which they would not be characterized as such even though in many occasions life in villages revolves around a church/liturgical calendar.[6] For one, such classifications seem to, whether intentionally or not, domesticate those communities within the Greek culture so that their "otherness" gets naturalized and thereby minimized; but of course what gets to be naturalized in the "other" is the dominance of the Orthodox Christian Church itself.

What should not be overlooked is that those characterizations are unquestioned and taken to be self-evident descriptors that further "reproduce[s] divisions of power and ownership crucial to dominant socio-political arrangements" (McCutcheon 2005: 79). It allows people (scholars and the public in general) to set apart those communities as something special (whether to be praised as with those who study so-called folk life in Greece, or, criticized, as done by the church) within a nexus of relationships that constitute daily life.

With this in mind we should note that their link to the ancient Greek past can be seen both in a negative and positive way,[7] and each serves to manage or legitimize different interests in the present. Writing about claims of authenticity, McCutcheon writes: "debates over issues of authenticity thus do not correspond to some stable standard but, instead, are part of a systematic discourse linked explicitly to practical, political interests, regardless what those interests happen to be" (2005: 88). It seems that references to the ancient Greek past function in similar ways. On the one hand, they allow social actors in the present to authorize modern Greek identity, since these communities of people who were once refugees (i.e., the 1923 exchange of populations) are now seen by some as the carriers of authentic ancient Greek customs. On the other hand, to consider the Anastenaria as "survivals" of ancient Greek religion or as "paganistic," or even "religious communities of Orthodox Christians," keeps them in the margins of what is considered to be genuine and authentic Orthodox Christianity (which the Orthodox Greek Church certainly claims to represent).

So I propose the example of the Greek fire-walkers, and their various (past and present) representations, as a case study in the Church's efforts (one among many, of course) to maintain its authoritative and central position within Greek society. It does this by establishing itself as the proper interpreter and guardian not only of what it means to be Orthodox Christian but Greek as well—as an instance where coercion and rhetoric about the past work hand-in-hand as forms of social boundary maintenance. For, as Aaron Hughes (2015: 41) writes:

> The act of representation is, by nature, political. It is premised on the selection of criteria that are believed to coincide with preconceived notions of what is "right" and "proper" on the one hand, and what is "wrong" and "improper" on the other. The latter are marginalized, while the former traits are emphasized as somehow being essential to the representative act. [...] The important thing to note is that the binaries of right-wrong and proper-improper are relative, not surprisingly reflecting the needs and desires of those doing the representing.

Vaia Touna is Assistant Professor in the Department of Religious Studies at the University of Alabama, Tuscaloosa. She is author of *Fabrications of the Greek Past: Religion, Tradition, and the Making of Modern Identities* (Brill, 2017). Her research focuses on the sociology of religion, acts of identification and social formation, as well as methodological issues concerning the study of religion and the past in general.

Notes

1   On the debates between the clergy and those defending the Anastenaria, Xygalatas (2011: 67–68) writes: "Both sides used theological arguments. One group, based on the

ideas of Anastasios Hourmouziadis and his followers, condemned the Anastenaria as idolatrous, while others considered them as Satanic or anti-Christian [...]. They argued that firewalking is presented as a miracle. They defined miracles as the suspension of nature's laws and pointed out that they can occur only by divine authority [...]. Since the Church, which they considered to be the exclusive interpreter of divine will, was opposed to fire-walking, then it had to be work of the Devil. Church officials were also concerned about the financial aspects of the issue. They insisted that only the Church had the right to make a profit from religious relics. They claimed that the monopoly of the Church was legally established in a Greek public law enacted in 1940, which stated that 'private icon producing income must be confiscated and taken to the nearest church' [...]. Many ethnologists, on the other hand, claimed that the Anastenaria now constituted a Christianized ritual performed by pious Christians, one of the many pagan elements that the Christian Church had incorporated into its worship [...]. Other poised out the importance of the Anastenaria as evidence for the continuity of Greek civilization." See also Xygalatas (2014).

2   Archive of the Holy Synod of the Church of Greece (ΑΙΣΕΕ 1531/778–26/6/1947).

3   "Defined minimally as a story with a beginning, a middle, and an end, narrative structure results from the skill of ignoring countless historical moments, overlooking events, and marginalizing interactions, all in the effort to frame, exclude, isolate, and they raise yet others to a level of significance they could not have possessed if they were left merely as part of the continual background noise that surrounds us all. Narratives of careers, lives, and social groups therefore result from what Jonathan Z. Smith has aptly termed an economy of signification" (McCutcheon 2005: 34).

4   Though he advises doing so without violence, since, as he wrote, "the persecution and the whip and the fire and the ax and all the other cruelty had further strengthened and reinforced them" (Hourmouziadis 1873: 29) but, instead, through the healthy teachings of the Christian scriptures so that the Greek Christians would stop holding onto the customs of mythology.

5   It should be noted, though, that Hourmouziadis wrote at a time when the formation of nation-states in Europe had reached its peak and the newly founded Greek state, following German Romanticism, and its idea of the "folk spirit," was trying to find its one distinct identity in the authorized remote past, especially defined against European scholars, like the Austrian historian Jakob Philipp Fallmerayer, who contested in his work the claim that contemporary Greeks had any racial relation to the ancient Greeks. As Xygalatas observes (rightly, I think) in his study of these rituals, the "need for national unity and self-awareness was more than urgent in the newly founded Greek state, and Greek scholars saw in the German model an opportunity to show that the modern inhabitants of Greece were the direct descendants of ancient Greeks and beneficiaries of their cultural heritage" (Xygalatas 2014: 23)—a need that is still very prominent among modern Greeks.

6   Having links to a village myself I remember how, while growing up, we would always go from the city to the village to celebrate such holidays as Christmas, Easter, and August 15 (the Assumption of Mary); in fact, many Greeks would do the same if they have familial/ancestral links to a village, and those who don't would probably lament not having one. Yet, no one would suggest that villages are "religious communities" in the way the Anastenaria are commonly described.

7   See McCutcheon (2005: 73) on the idea of repression/concession.

References

Charalampopoulou, Ismene. 2017. "Με λαμπρότητα στην Αθήνα απο τη Βενετία τα λείψανα της Αγίας Ελένης." Retrieved from www.protothema.gr/greece/article/679369/me-labrotita-stin-athina-apo-ti-venetia-ta-leipsana-tis-agias-elenis (archived at: www.webcitation.org/78hcy9Gfo).

Danforth, Loring M. 1989. *Firewalking and Religious Healing: The Anastenaria of Greece and the American Firewalking Movement.* Princeton, NJ: Princeton University Press. https://doi.org/10.1515/9781400884360

Diamantoglou, M. J. 1953. "La Pyrobatie en Grece." *Revue Metaphysique* 23: 9–19.

Hourmouziadis, Anastasios. 1873. *Περί των Αναστεναρίων και Άλλων τινών Εθίμων και Προλήψεων.* Ανατολικός Αστήρ: Κωνσταντινούπολη.

Hughes, Aaron. 2015. *Islam and the Tyranny of Authenticity: An Inquiry into Disciplinary Apologetics and Self-Deception.* Sheffield: Equinox.

Kakouri, K. 1999. *Διονυσιακά: Εκ της σημερινής λαϊκής λατρείας των Θρακών.* Αθήνα: Ιδεοθέτρον.

McCutcheon, Russell T. 2005. *Religion and the Domestication of Dissent: Or, How to Live in a Less Than Perfect Nation.* London: Routledge.

Megas, Georgios A. 1960. "Αναστενάρια και Έθιμα της Τυρινής Δευτέρας εις το Κωστή και τα Πέριξ Αυτού Χωρία της Ανατολικής Θράκης." *Λαογραφία* 19: 472–534. Αθήνα: Σακελλαρίου.

Megas, G. A. 1962. "Αναστενάρια του 1962 εις την Αγίαν Ελένην των Σερρών." *Λαογραφία* 20: 552–557. Αθήνα: Σακελλαρίου.

Megas, G. A. 1974. "Η Έννοια και ο Χαρακτήρ των Αναστεναρίων." *Λαογραφία* 19: 3–18. Αθήνα: Σακελλαρίου.

Michael-Dede, M. 1972. "Το Αναστενάρι. Ψυχολογική και Κοινωνιολογική Θεώρηση." *Θρακικά* 46: 23–178.

Michael-Dede, Maria. 1978a. "Τα Τραγούδια και οι Χοροί των Αναστενάρηδων." *Θρακικά* 48: 75–129.

Michael-Dede, Maria. 1978b. "Σκέψεις για το Αναστενάρι από Έρευνα στην Ανατολική Ρωμυλία." *Δ' Συμπόσιο Λαογραφίας του Βορειοελλαδικού Χώρου ('Ηπειρος-Μακεδονία-Θράκη), Ιωάννινα, 10-12 Οκτωβρίου 1979. Πρακτικά,* 205–223. Θεσσαλονίκη: Ίδρυμα Μελετών Χερσονήσου του Αίμου.

Touna, Vaia. 2017. *Fabrications of the Greek Past: Religion, Tradition, and the Making of Modern Identities.* Leiden: Brill. https://doi.org/10.1163/9789004348615

Xygalatas, Dimitris. 2011. "Ethnography, Historiography, and the Making of History in the Tradition of the Anastenaria." *History and Anthropology* 22(1): 57–74. https://doi.org/10.1080/02757206.2011.546855

Xygalatas, Dimitris. 2014. *The Burning Saints: Cognition and Culture in the Fire-Walking Rituals of the Anastenaria.* New York: Routledge. https://doi.org/10.4324/9781315728711

Chapter 6

Privatized Publics and Scholarly Silos: Gender, Religion, and their Theoretical Fault Lines

K. Merinda Simmons

The discussions providing the occasion for this piece occurred at the international *Hijacked!* conference that brought together scholars to talk about public rhetorics of "good" and "bad" religion. While there, we talked a great deal about what the good/bad religion paradigm emphasizes and also what it masks—what it leaves unchecked or undertheorized. One such blind spot—and I would suggest this is true for broader scholarly discourses on religion, not just the modalities deemed good or bad, but certainly in those cases too—is how often tropes related to gender go unchecked. Scholars of religion who are interested in social theory should consider what we normalize in our own studies when something called gender is understood as a perhaps interesting but ultimately unnecessary accessory to the real work of studying various traditions or rituals...or even the politics of classification writ large. The elements of phenomena called religion and the discourses thereof are just as co-constitutive as they are contingent, after all. I fear at times we focus solely on the latter at the expense of the former. We do so at our peril, especially if keeping in mind William T. Cavanaugh's (2009: 4) claim that serves fittingly as Naomi Goldenberg's epigraph in her chapter: "what counts as religious or secular in any given context is a function of different configurations of power."

As one way in to pressing the interlocking nature of religion-related contingencies, this brief response will take up a larger theme Goldenberg mentions—that of "how violence usually marks the border between the state and religion." I am interested in the concept of sanctioned exceptions being made in actions or violences deemed "private" and delegitimizing moves made against those deemed "public." One of the emphases in gender and queer theories over the past couple of decades has been on the utility of violence (itself understood in a variety of ways) as a policing mechanism that controls and reclassifies boundary cases that threaten the seeming stability of the concepts/groups in question. The story that Judith Butler has told in a few contexts[1] about a boy who was killed for his gait makes the point in striking and tragic fashion. She talks of a young man who walked with a "swish," moving his hips back and forth in a way deemed discernably feminine. A few other boys see him, antagonize him, attack him, and ultimately throw him over a bridge, killing him. The question for Butler regarding why someone would be killed for a style of walk leads to broader questions about the anxiety at work in gender norms and their complicity. When physical safety is contingent upon keeping in line with established norms, what, she asks, is the relationship between complying and being coerced to perform those roles?[2]

So we might think, then, about how something called "gender" (this certainly works, too, for anything—secularity, religion, and qualitative forms of the same) comes to be manufactured and policed through the limits and transgressions of the category articulated in legislation regarding what genders count, what they get to do, with whom, where, and by what means.

There are plenty of case studies from which one might draw to talk about how we fashion and police boundaries around concepts that we use to organize the world. Recent controversies over so-called "bathroom bills" in the US that patrol trans people and the perceived threat thereof by spelling out a relationship between gender identity and biological sex are low-hanging fruit, for example. They offer a simple occasion to consider a few issues at stake: (1) the operative sex/gender binary that continues to govern in normative discourse surrounding bodies and what we deem important about them; (2) how safety and threat come to be determined in relation to the arbitrary boundaries often used to identify what becomes understood as gender; (3) how "private" spaces are fodder for public policy. Of course, bound to come up is the fact that where and how and when and around whom one does or does not perform essential bodily functions has always been a product of unavoidably public sets of social relations. Shitting, like fucking, or thinking, or—some would say (based on conversation at this symposium about *Believer*, Reza Aslan's once-popular, now-former television series)—believing, has never lived in an exclusive domain of irretrievably private performance. I have written elsewhere (Simmons 2015) about how the axiom about the personal being political becomes inoculated when we use it to tout experiential authority (stories of personal lives gaining importance or legitimacy by being called political, which gives rise to stories of personal lives as ends in themselves). Instead, the utility of thinking of the personal as political comes in recasting the colloquially private/interior/experiential as unavoidably situated politically and as fashioned by the contextual dynamics in which it is situated. This is what allows Eazy-E to assert in NWA's classic "Fuck the Police," "They put out my picture with silence / 'Cause my identity by itself causes violence."

Or, to put it another way and riffing off of a slogan popular among progressives in the US, politicians *can't* get their laws off our bodies. Those laws are the only ways we came to talk about bodies as things that "matter" in the first place. In the case of legislation regarding who gets to use what washroom—and in other examples that come quickly to mind—the "private" realm is exactly what's being legislated rather than granted some kind of exception, even if at times in the name of protecting the legibly normative (in the case of the bathroom bills, cis-gendered subjects) inside that same space. So what kinds of logics and/or dynamics make "privacy" a safe word for identifications of religion and not for those of gender?

I will just offer a brief illustration by way of anecdote. A telling scene played out at the airport gate in Birmingham, Alabama as I set out for the *Hijacked!* symposium in Bonn. With no invitation to do so, a man—"just call me Jimbo"—begins flirting forcefully with the woman sitting a couple chairs down from me. Her name is Emily. He looks to be at least thirty years her senior, and he is on his way with some friends to a pickle ball tournament. I find out what pickle ball is (a sort of tennis/paddleball/badminton hybrid, from what I gather) when he and one of those friends begin playing it right in front of the gate agents. One can, of course, imagine this showy demonstration (one that included animated voices, along with mild lunging and jumping) being not at all okay with the gate agents and security personnel, were its participants not white and English-speaking. The very ability to take up that kind of physical space in a crowded airport gate is indicative of vast amounts of privilege in a context where strict behavioral and spatial rules apply.

Before their game, Jimbo's conversation with Emily includes a couple of declarations—that (upon learning she hails from Mississippi) "interesting, good-looking women are always in the wrong place" and that she needs to visit him (somewhere in New England). He tells her this multiple times, demanding an answer. She chuckles politely but is clearly uncomfortable. He gives her his number. He watches her, making sure she enters it in her phone. "Now text me your contact information!" Cue Emily's invocation of her not-present boyfriend. Now she has created rhetorical distance through an invisible masculine figure that demands social deference where her own uneasy shifting and attempts at deflection cannot. The pickle ball game ensues, with his jumping back and forth not three feet in front of Emily. People even clap. They are charmed at the affable display. Later, Emily sits in the row in front of me on the plane. Jimbo's friend and pickle ball compatriot, headed to the washroom, stops at her row. "He's harmless. You gotta know he's harmless," he tells her. Emily chuckles again, still polite, still uncomfortable. "Oh yeah, totally, I know. I mean, he's a little forward ... but ..." "Harmless," Jimbo's friend interrupts. She nods, reassuring him. She waits to get off the plane.

There is quite a lot going on in this scene. There were group dynamics that created the scene to begin with: Emily was outnumbered. Jimbo had friends with him and was performing with and in front of them. There are also apparently circumstances under which TSA agents do not mind a friendly pickle ball rivalry as people disembark from a plane. Etc. However, I am most interested in the work done in the pickle ball partner calling Jimbo "harmless." In identifying him as such, the very concept and prospect of harm is raised by the dismissal or rejection of it as a possibility. So if violence marks borders and is used to police them, does the reference to (and rejection of) a hypothetical violence do that same work? In rhetorically performing otherwise to the imagined male who would harass and harm, Jimbo is able to inhabit that same space without negative consequence. If Judith Butler is right, and our performances of an ideal reveal the illusory and contingent nature of that same ideal (like the notion of masculine virility inside a heteronormative system), the policing becomes all the more necessary. "Harmlessness" must be uttered in order to keep up and running the very system by which he might do harm. In this instance, power is situated by virtue of the ability to speak its name, to deny rhetorically one's own access to it.

Rather than suggesting that we might identify good versus bad misogynies, I instead want to suggest that academic work makes similar moves to Jimbo's friend when the scholars writing it identify their intent on doing good, on their own harmlessness as a kindly end in itself, instead of talking about how such moves are often complicit in the very logic structures and the same epistemologies they seek to critique. I am not necessarily suggesting an aloof distance, as I do not think that is consistently sustainable—sometimes you catch yourself talking to strangers at airport gates. But nor am I suggesting the brand of identity politics that Aaron Hughes rightly critiques in his book, *Islam and the Tyranny of Authenticity: An Inquiry into Disciplinary Apologetics and Self-Deception* (Equinox, 2016). The self-referential nature of Jimbo is not far removed from Donald Trump's confession to Billy Bush that when he gets near beautiful women he has to kiss them. Self-awareness on its own is not enough, no more for scholars than for politicians or pickle ball players. It must be accompanied by thoroughgoing efforts to put our money where our mouths are intellectually as we chant "classification matters." This requires that scholars in religious studies come to terms with the implications of deconstructing "religion" as a classifying tool, all the while making for it a special case by leaving alone other tropes used to organize social life like race, class, gender, sexuality, nation, and so forth. A call for scholarly self-reflexivity must include our own willingness to take stock of the choices we make as theorists about what norms to critique and what norms to leave undisturbed. Otherwise, we are no more critical than Jimbo is harmless.

K. Merinda Simmons is Professor of Religious Studies at the University of Alabama. Her books include *Race and New Modernisms* (co-authored with James A. Crank, Bloomsbury, 2019), *The Trouble with Post-Blackness* (co-edited with Houston A. Baker, Jr., Columbia University Press, 2015), *Changing the Subject: Writing Women across the African Diaspora* (Ohio State University Press, 2014), and *Race and Displacement* (co-edited with Maha Marouan, University of Alabama Press, 2013). She is currently working on a monograph entitled *Sourcing Slave Religion: Theorizing Experience in the Archive*, as well as a co-authored (with Craig Martin) book entitled *Gender: A Critical Primer* (under contract with Equinox Publishing). She is the editor of the book series *Concepts in the Study of Religion: Critical Primers*.

Notes

1 See www.youtube.com/watch?v=DLnv322X4tY and www.youtube.com/watch?v=k0HZaPkF6qE. The latter is part of a longer discussion with Sunaura Taylor, an artist and activist for disability and animal rights, included in the film *Examined Life* (2008).

2 Butler's book *The Psychic Life of Power* (1997) is instructive here, as well. In it, she explains how one's "own" subject formation is a product of external power dynamics, which shape not only subjectivity but also a subject's attempts at and capacities for self-reflexivity. Such an approach challenges typical understandings of power being internalized by an already-existing self, as well as a concept of an "inner life" used to fuel conscience.

References

Butler, Judith. 1997. *The Psychic Life of Power: Theories in Subjection.* Stanford, CA: Stanford University Press.

Cavanaugh, William T. 2009. *The Myth of Religious Violence: Secular Ideology and the Roots of Modern Conflict.* Oxford: Oxford University Press. https://doi.org/10.1093/acprof:oso/9780195385045.001.0001

Hughes, Aaron. 2016. *Islam and the Tyranny of Authenticity: An Inquiry into Disciplinary Apologetics and Self-Deception.* Sheffield: Equinox.

Simmons, Merinda K. 2015. "'Well Isn't That Special?': What We Talk about When We Talk about Identity." In Monica R. Miller (ed.), *Claiming Identity in the Study of Religion: Social and Rhetorical Techniques Examined*, 19–27. Sheffield: Equinox.

Chapter 7

What's Religious Freedom Got to Do With It? On the Niqab Affair in Canadian Politics

Matt Sheedy

On March 10, 2015, former Canadian Prime Minister Stephen Harper gave a speech in the House of Commons on his government's desire to ban the wearing of the niqab in oath taking ceremonies for Canadian citizenship, stating:

> We don't allow people to [...] cover their faces during citizenship ceremonies. And why would Canadians, contrary to our own values, embrace a practice at that time that is not transparent, that is not open and, frankly, is rooted in a culture that is anti-women. Mr. Speaker, that is unacceptable to Canadians, unacceptable to Canadian women [...]. (CBC 2015)

Harper was responding to a Federal Court decision from January 2015, put forward by Zunera Ishaq, who challenged and effectively overturned the Conservative government's 2011 niqab ban (Payton 2011). What followed Harper's speech in the House of Commons was the most heavily publicized single-issue controversy in Canadian politics in recent memory as the niqab took center-stage throughout the federal election campaign of 2015 (Fatah 2015).

Commenting on Harper's speech, Justin Trudeau, then-leader of the Liberal Party of Canada, spoke in Toronto in response to the proposed niqab ban:

> You can dislike the niqab. You can hold it up it is a symbol of oppression. You can try to convince your fellow citizens that it is a choice they ought not to make. This is a free country. Those are your rights. But those who would use the state's power to restrict women's religious freedom and freedom of expression indulge the very same repressive impulse that they profess to condemn. It is a cruel joke to claim you are liberating people from oppression by dictating in law what they can and cannot wear. But what's even worse than what they're saying is what they really mean. We all know what is going on here. It is nothing less than an attempt to play on people's fears and foster prejudice, directly toward the Muslim faith. This is not the spirit of Canadian liberty, my friends. (Wherry 2015)

While media pundits praised Trudeau for his defense of Ishaq, niqab-wearing women, and Muslims in general, his rhetoric nonetheless appealed to the same conceptual logic as Harper's—namely, that of secular liberal ideology[1]—despite the many differences in their interpretations and corresponding policies.[2] For while Trudeau does not classify the niqab as "anti-women" or contrary to "Canadian values," by foregrounding religious freedom and freedom of expression as the ultimate arbiter in this affair, the niqab remains a *de facto* object of estrangement that only becomes legible once it is assimilated under these purportedly higher Canadian—and by extension Euro-Western—values.³ In this sense, the political discourse about the niqab in Canada, where the rhetoric of its' two main political parties can be said to reflect a dominant or normative representation, helped to shape the range of acceptable meanings of this culturally 'foreign' object,⁴ thus limiting the intelligibility of other possible interpretations.⁵ In this way, representations of the niqab were largely determined by etic norms and thus functioned as a symbolic vector for how people interpret the proper boundaries of political rights, such as freedom of choice, and values, such as multicultural inclusion. Not surprisingly, Ishaq's own rhetoric appealed to this idea of religious freedom, which many commentators, including scholars,⁶ sought to defend in the face of overwhelmingly negative perceptions of the niqab in public opinion polls.

The niqab affair in Canadian politics offers a striking example of the good/bad religion paradigm that Aaron Hughes seeks to challenge in *Islam and the Tyranny of Authenticity* (2015) inasmuch as it foregrounds the ideological nature of such classifications, while also providing a possible limit-test for what cannot be assimilated (for the time being?) as an example of 'good religion.' More specifically, it highlights the political nature of 'religion' as a contested category by focusing on an object deemed to be 'religious' coming into contact with a culture that has yet to construct a publically recognizable discourse about it *from an insider's point of view*. In this sense, considering the niqab's yet-to-be or liminal status can help to problematize the good/bad religion paradigm by revealing how religious identities are always contingent on the relational dynamics between insiders and outsiders, working and responding within the ideological prisms in which they reside.

Goldenberg's Vestigial States

In her essay "Toward a Critique of Postsecular Rhetoric" (Chapter 4, this volume), Naomi Goldenberg argues that religion should be thought of as a political category, and theorized in its relationship to other categories such as "nation, state, nation-state, the secular, and sovereignty." Moreover, she makes the case that scholars of religion should aim to "deconstruct the foundational terms of the discipline" in their work rather than fall back upon simplistic binaries like the good/bad religion paradigm.

Goldenberg takes her lead from Mayanthi Fernando's short article "Taking the Islamic in the Islamic State Seriously," where Fernando argues that all modern states are both religious and secular, albeit to varying degrees. This observation is meant to shift our focus from adjudicating over whether or not a modern state, be it Sudan or Canada, is *really* religious or secular toward thinking about how such states *manage religion*. This process of regulation is what Fernando (2017) describes as a "modality of sovereignty," which, on my reading, is meant to foreground how sites of authority influence the construction of religious identities, and thus how we perceive them, talk about them, and so forth.

While space does not allow me to comment at any length on Goldenberg's treatment of post-secularism, suffice it to say that I am in agreement with James A. Beckford that the concept has been used in so many different ways that it has failed to provide any clear analytic utility (Beckford 2012). For Goldenberg, post-secularism represents a theoretical turn that has failed to effectively historicize and contextualize 'religion' by placing too much emphasis on the role of colonialism and secularism, while paying scant attention to how local theologies also construct religious identities in ways that cannot be reduced to Western influence alone.[7] This is evident in the work of Saba Mahmood and Joan Wallach Scott, both of whom Goldenberg notes have done a decent job in tracing genealogies of Western liberal constructions of religion and the secular, while falling short in their critiques of post-colonial societies, especially when it comes to the role of Islamic ideologies in shaping the lives of women. This concern has some parallels with Hughes's critique of "Islamic religious studies," which he characterizes as a form of apologetics that elides the academics' task of re-describing insiders' narratives through the use of critical analytic categories, such as discourse analysis and redaction criticism (Hughes 2015). While Mahmood and Scott do not engage in apologetics in favor of any particular theology, Goldenberg's critique seems to suggest that their lack of engagement with the role of local theologies places too much blame on outside forces, which can have the effect (on my reading at least) of letting 'religion' off the hook. Without going into the particulars of either Goldenberg or Hughes's analysis, I find myself in general agreement with their concern over how much of contemporary scholarship continues to re-inscribe the binary construction of good/bad, authentic/inauthentic religion.

One detail that interests me about Goldenberg's theory of religions as "vestigial states" relates to how modern nation-states will draw on aspects of their "previous sovereignties" (e.g., by appealing to Judeo-Christian civilization) in order to legitimize themselves in the present. The question of violence is central here to the formulation of good/bad religion since the state's monopoly on violence has the power to label any 'religion' that is deemed violent as inauthentic. This includes perceived modes of violence, which I want to think about in relation to the various uses of symbolic discourse, of which the niqab is a prime example. Given that it is still extremely rare in a Euro-Western context, the niqab lacks an identifiable constituency or social formation that could speak about its uses in terms that are more recognizable in Muslim majority states, such as Pakistan and Saudi Arabia, and thus reflects a limit or boundary marker of what might be considered a 'reasonable accommodation' under law.[8] In this sense, niqab-wearing women must rely in large part on "previous sovereignties" such as freedom of choice as a justification for this practice, while at the same time failing to effectively meet the benchmark of 'good religion', as evidenced by the overwhelmingly negative views of the niqab in public opinion polls.

The Niqab and "Previous Sovereignties"

The niqab affair in Canada presents an instance of a minority practice that was deemed "anti-women" by one faction of state authority and successfully contested by a competing faction of that same authority through a discourse of religious freedom, as represented by Stephen Harper and Justin Trudeau respectively. Complicating matters further, throughout this affair the niqab stood in for a whole host of sign-symbols that are familiar in Orientalist and Islamophobic discourses (Green 2015; Sheehi 2011), such as "creeping" sharia law and the specter of terrorism, and was reliant on the support of hijab-wearing women who, while divided on the niqab question themselves (Clarke 2013), represent the closest constituency to this tiny minority.

In the midst of this affair, polling data for the 2015 Canadian election campaign suggested that a majority of Canadians were opposed to the niqab in general (and not just in citizenship ceremonies), as evidenced in the following report from the Angus Reid Institute: "In contrast to the majority of Canadians who support woman wearing the Hijab and a Nun's Habit—73 per cent and 88 per cent respectively—seven out of ten (73%) oppose Muslim woman wearing a Niqab in public—a veil that covers the face, showing only the eyes" (Angus Reid Institute 2014).

Here it is worth reflecting on a critical insight that Michael Warner brings to bear, when he writes: "Public opinion is understood as belonging to a public rather than to scattered individuals. Opinion polls in this sense are a performative genre. They do not measure something that already exists as public opinion but when they are reported as such, they are public opinion" (Warner 2014: 161). In addition to these and other problems, including sample size, the types of questions asked, and the mediation of such results, we might also ask what kind of "opinion" can there be in the absence of a discernable counter-public of niqab-wearing women? Are hijab-wearing women a viable proxy for niqabis, and if so how can they articulate a difference that they themselves do not embody and, at least in some cases, oppose for their own political-theological reasons? In this sense, the niqab affair offers a unique instance of how social formations are constructed ideologically, both through the previous sovereignties of the state as well as through minority or subaltern representations.

Wikipedia describes Zunera Ishaq as a "Canadian Sunni Muslim woman living in Mississauga, Ontario," that follows the Hanafi School of thought, who has worn the niqab since her teenage years in Lahore, Pakistan. If one reads on a little further down the page they will discover that she grew up in a home that was 'liberal' and that her father, who was a psychology professor, "insisted she understand the implications [of wearing the niqab] before making the choice" (Wikipedia 2017). "This was not something my husband asked for, as journalists now think—I didn't know my husband at the time. My sisters made the same decision. No one compelled them to wear the veil. They just felt more comfortable" (Fisk 2015).

There is a certain irony here when we consider the construction of public opinion surrounding the niqab in relation to Ishaq's own performative gesture, which included several public appearances on television and in newspaper articles, where she talked of her environmentalism, her love of Canadian winters, playing in the snow with her boys, and her volunteer work at women's shelters. While all of this may be 'true' and even plausibly verifiable in relation to the public record about life, the claim that she represents all niqab-wearing women is clearly absurd. If polls are to be trusted, the general public did not appear to be sympathetic to her 'choice,' and Trudeau's appeal to this higher Canadian value seems almost insignificant in light of the fact that this affair all but vanished from public attention after the federal election in October 2015.[9]

In their essay "Sex in Public," Laruen Berlant and Michael Warner interrogate dimensions of queer culture as a type of counterpublic, which was formed on the margins and has since gained partial legitimacy though narrow and limited forms of recognition. As they write:

> Queer culture has found it necessary to develop this knowledge in mobile sites of drag, youth culture, music, dance, parades, flaunting, and cruising—sites whose mobility makes them possible but also renders them hard to recognize as world making because they are so fragile and ephemeral. (Berlant and Warner 1998: 561)

Since this essay was first published in 1998, the reception of queer publics has shifted toward a more recognizable liberal subject, partially assimilated within an already existing matrix of marriage and equality rights, with the specter of more radical subjects slipping and spilling in the mainstream. While Warner and Berlant aim to uphold a tension between the movement for equality and respectability amongst LGBTQ Americans, on the one hand, and the radical space of queer subcultures that continue to push the limits of normativity,[10] on the other, their underlying thesis is that queer agency—however limited, circumscribed, and constrained—was forged in the margins of these counterpublics, creating common languages, kinship, and community, eventually leading to a recognizable "public" connected to symbols of authority and power. I see no such counter-public for niqab-wearing women in the Euro-West, whose visibility is often read as invisibility—inherently private, known only to initiates, and, paradoxically, both non-political and hyper-political at the same time.

I'll end here with a provisional thought or two: if vestigial states are dependent upon "previous sovereignties" as Goldenberg suggests, and if 'authentic' religion is constructed around a publically recognizable discourse that we might broadly characterize in our present Euro-Western constellation as 'liberal' or 'neo-liberal ideology,' what can limit cases such as the niqab tell us about the social construction of good/bad religion? Not unlike like Hughes's interest in Jewish and Islamic heresiology, as discussed in this volume, one fruitful avenue that may help us to uncover the construction of good/bad religion an example like the niqab, which is always mediated through a variety of proxies (e.g. national values, religious accommodation, or other hijab wearing women), thus making it clear how the strange is always made familiar and therefore 'good' (or potentially good) on someone else terms.

Matt Sheedy is Visiting Assistant Professor in North American Studies at the University of Bonn, Germany, and lecturer in the Department of Religion at the University of Manitoba. His research interests include representations of Muslims, Christians, atheists, and Indigenous people in North American popular and political culture. He is currently finishing up a book that focuses on Jürgen Habermas's theory of religion in the public sphere, and working on a longer-term project on the discourses on Islam and Islamophobia among popular atheist groups.

Notes

1. For treatments of secular liberal ideology see Cavanaugh (2009), Fernando (2014), and Shakman Hurd (2008).
2. One striking policy difference can be seen with the two parties' positions on Syrian refugees. Whereas the Harper government was criticized for prioritizing Christian and other non-Muslim minority claimants, Trudeau pledged and, once elected, followed through on admitting fifty thousand Syrian refugees without these sectarian restrictions. Cf. Procaylo (2015).
3. Here I refer to "estrangement" in Bruce Lincoln's (1994) sense of the term, which he contrasts with "discourses of affinity" that work by creating positive affective associations between people, objects, and ideas (e.g., linking Jesus or Mohammad with peace, or the American flag with liberty).
4. These include, for example, the idea that the niqab reflects a practice that is bound to tradition, culture, and orthodoxy and is thus coerced (by both tradition and by men), and therefore cannot be freely chosen in a way that reflects more familiar (Protestant) values, such as individualism, intellectual inquiry, freedom of expression, etc.
5. Here I am thinking of emic views on the niqab that reflect the complexities of cultural practices, theological norms, political views, socio-economic status, etc., in ever-changing configurations.
6. The most comprehensive study of niqab-wearing women in Canada to date is Lynda Clarke's "Women in Niqab Speak: A Study of the Niqab in Canada" (2013).
7. Hughes (2015: 37–54) offers a similar type of critique of post-colonial theory and its failure to account for how local theologies play a role in shaping violent ideologies, which, he argues, should be understood as no less 'Islamic' than more liberal varieties.
8. Similarly, debates on whether Sikh men in Canada should be allowed to carry a kirpan (ceremonial dagger) have continued intermittently for several decades now, and offers an interesting analogue with the niqab inasmuch as it also affects a very small percentage of citizens.
9. I place this term in scare quotes given the difficulty of measuring success by means of Trudeau's electoral victory, the need to consider the multiple variables involved, and the impossibility of reducing this issue to a single metric. More recent attempts by the government of Quebec to ban the niqab in a variety of public spaces under Bill 62 reveals the on-going ambiguity of its public reception and shows little movement in its representation and status as an object of estrangement. Since the summer of 2017 there have been several attempts by the government of Québec to ban the niqab from various public spaces such as buses, schools, and hospitals. See Sheedy (2019).
10. For some critical analysis of the mainstreaming of queer issues, or what some have referred to as "queer liberalism," see Eng (2010), Dugan (2004), and Puar (2017).

References

Angus Reid Institute. 2014. "Most Canadians View Muslim Community as a Partner, Not a Problem in the Fight Against Radicalization." November 24. Retrieved from http://angusreid.org/homegrown-terrorism-radicalization-canada-overblown-serious-threat/ (archived at www.webcitation.org/78jbHi2XD).

Beckford, James A. 2012. "SSSR Presidential Address Public Religions and the Postsecular: Critical Reflections," *Journal for the Scientific Study of Religion* 51(1): 1–19. https://doi.org/10.1111/j.1468-5906.2011.01625.x

Berlant, Lauren and Michael Warner. 1998. "Sex in Public." *Critical Inquiry* 24(2): 547–566. https://doi.org/10.1086/448884

Cavanaugh, William T. 2009. *The Myth of Religious Violence: Secular Ideology and the Roots of Modern Conflict*. Oxford, UK: Oxford University Press. https://doi.org/10.1093/acprof:oso/9780195385045.001.0001

CBC. 2015. "Niqab Ban for Public Servants Would Be Considered: Stephen Harper." CBC News: Politics, October 7. Retrieved from www.cbc.ca/news/politics/stephen-harper-niqab-ban-public-servants-1.3258943 (archived at https://web.archive.org/web/20151206170154/http://www.cbc.ca/news/politics/stephen-harper-niqab-ban-public-servants-1.3258943).

Clarke, Lynda. 2013. "Women in Niqab Speak: A Study of the Niqab in Canada." Retrieved from http://ccmw.com/wp-content/uploads/2013/10/WEB_EN_WiNiqab_FINAL.pdf.

Dugan, Lisa. 2004. *The Twilight of Equality: Neoliberalism, Cultural Politics, and the Attack on Democracy*. Boston, MA: Beacon Press.

Eng, David. 2010. *The Feeling of Kinship: Queer Liberalism and the Racialization of Intimacy*. Durham, NC: Duke University Press. https://doi.org/10.1215/9780822392828

Fatah, Sonya. 2015. "A Veil Ban, 'Barbaric Practices', and Canada's Election." *Al Jazeera: Politics*, October 18. Retrieved from www.aljazeera.com/indepth/features/2015/10/veil-ban-barbaric-practices-canada-election-151018130250880.html (archived at www.webcitation.org/78jPAIzGZ).

Fernando, Mayanthi L. 2014. *The Republic Unsettled: Muslim French and the Contradictions of Secularism*. Durham, NC: Duke University Press. https://doi.org/10.1215/9780822376286

Fernando, Mayanthi L. 2017. "Taking the Islamic in 'the Islamic state' Seriously." *The Immanent Frame*, April 13. Retrieved from https://tif.ssrc.org/2017/04/13/taking-the-islamic-in-the-islamic-state-seriously/ (archived at www.webcitation.org/78hbzpOwD).

Fisk, Robert. 2015. "Niqab Row: Canada's Government Challenges Ruling Zunera Ishaq Can Wear Veil while Taking Oath of Citizenship." Retrieved from www.independent.co.uk/news/world/americas/niqab-row-canadas-government-challenges-ruling-zunera-ishaq-can-wear-veil-while-taking-oath-of-a6674151.html (archived at www.webcitation.org/78jazgQSp).

Green, Todd H. 2015. *The Fear of Islam: An Introduction to Islamophobia in the West*. Minneapolis, MN: Fortress Press. https://doi.org/10.2307/j.ctt12878h3

Hughes, Aaron W. 2015. *Islam and the Tyranny of Authenticity: An Inquiry into Disciplinary Apologetics and Self-Deception*. Sheffield: Equinox.

Lincoln, Bruce. 1994. *Discourse and the Construction of Society: Comparative Studies of Myth, Ritual, and Classification*. New York: Oxford University Press.

Payton, Laura. 2011. "Face Veils Banned for Citizenship Oaths." *CBC News: Politics*, December 12. Retrieved from www.cbc.ca/news/politics/stephen-harper-niqab-ban-public-servants-1.3258943 (archived at https://web.archive.org/web/20160930191704/http://www.cbc.ca/news/politics/face-veils-banned-for-citizenship-oaths-1.1048750).

Procaylo, Nick. 2015. "Targeted for Extermination: Harper Says Prioritizing Christian and Religious Minority Refugees Isn't Discriminatory." *The National Post*, October 10. Retrieved from http://nationalpost.com/news/politics/targeted-for-extermination-harper-says-prioritizing-christian-and-religious-minority-refugees-isnt-discriminatory (archived at www.webcitation.org/78jNcrkkZ).

Puar, Jasbir. 2017. *Terrorist Assemblages: Homonationalism in Queer Times*, 10th anniversary expanded edition. Durham, NC: Duke University Press. https://doi.org/10.1215/9780822371755

Shakman Hurd, Elizabeth. 2008. *The Politics of Secularism in International Relations*. Princeton, NJ: Princeton University Press.

Sheedy, Matt. 2019. "Québec's Ban on Religious Symbols 4.0." *Sightings*, April 11. Retrieved from https://divinity.uchicago.edu/sightings/quebec's-ban-religious-symbols-40 (archived at www.webcitation.org/78w6whZym).

Sheehi Stephan. 2011. *Islamophobia: The Ideological Campaign against Muslims*. Atlanta, GA: Clarity Press, Inc.

Warner, Michael. 2014. *Publics and Counterpublics*. New York: Zone Books.

Wherry, Aaron. 2015. "Justin Trudeau and the Niqab: What Justin Trudeau Says and What the Federal Court Said." *Maclean's*, March 10. Retrieved from www.macleans.ca/politics/justin-trudeau-and-the-niqab (archived at http://www.webcitation.org/78jZV1iIa).

Wikipedia. 2017. "Zunera Ishaq." Retrieved from https://en.wikipedia.org/wiki/Zunera_Ishaq (accessed December 10, 2017).

Part III

Media

Introduction to Part III

Leslie Dorrough Smith, AVILA UNIVERSITY
Steffen Führding, LEIBNIZ UNIVERSITY
Adrian Hermann, UNIVERSITY OF BONN

The modern mass media (including newspapers, TV, movies, radio, and the internet) are particularly influential social arenas in which public opinion is formed and disseminated in plural societies. They are not merely passive mirrors of society reporting neutrally on events. Rather, they are among the most important and effective discourse producers. In other words, mass media do not simply reproduce discourses, but they also create them, influence their trajectories, and have an impact on the other discursive areas within their reach, such as politics and science.

The contributions in this section deal with the representation of religion in the media and the analysis of the rhetoric of good/bad religion. The anchoring essay comes from *Martha Smith Roberts* (Chapter 8), who presents the CNN series *Believer*, hosted by Reza Aslan, as a paradigmatic example for a specific liberal progressive discussion of religion in North American mass media. Roberts delivers a detailed description of the series (considering content, form, as well as marketing and genre of the series). She points out that *Believer*, rather than interjecting a critical examination of religion into the mass media, instead reinforces a series of popular perennialist ideas that are intellectually problematic. This happens primarily by portraying religion as a personal, "authentic," universal element of human experience.

The following four chapters take Roberts's considerations as a starting point and offer their critiques of different aspects of the show or compare the show with other productions.

Carmen Becker's response (Chapter 9) focuses on the construction of academic/scholarly authority in *Believer* and compares it to a German production called "Mosque Report." She uses Pierre Bourdieu's notion of symbolic power as the theoretical framework for her analysis. Becker's focus lies with the role played by the German series's protagonists as ethnographers of sorts, who, in this role, claim a privileged access to "authentic" knowledge about the religious people they discuss. Becker argues that this approach is used in order to generate hegemonic knowledge about the concept of religious diversity even as each episode otherwise attempts to portray the footage it shares on religion as neutral and unmediated.

In her analysis of *Believer*, Leslie Dorrough Smith (Chapter 10) draws on the work of feminist film theorist Laura Mulvey. In the 1970s, Mulvey used the term "scopophilia" to describe how filmmakers construct visually pleasing experiences for heterosexual men by framing images of women in certain ways that result in their sexual objectification. After an introduction to Mulvey's core arguments, Smith applies this perspective to Aslan's production. Smith states that part of the scopophilia involved in watching shows like *Believer* (and people like Aslan, more specifically) comes not from being exposed to something new, but from the feelings of control and domestication that the audience can vicariously assert as they imagine Aslan as the show's protagonist.

In Chapter 11, *Craig Prentiss* situates *Believer* as an ideological artifact of a social formation emerging from globalized capitalism. He draws on the theoretical considerations of Louis Althusser formulated in his famous essay "Ideology and Ideological State Apparatuses" and argues that *Believer* promotes and naturalizes an individual, deregulated spiritual religion that fits the demands of a transnational capitalist class. More specifically, Prentiss shows how *Believer* celebrates the notion that religion is the outcome of renegade individualists who can freely choose their religious paths outside of the hand of social constraints. The outcome is the marketing of a kind of "good" religion that does the work of naturalizing the conditions that have made such a transnational class possible.

In the last essay of Part III, *Steffen Führding* (Chapter 12) compares *Believer* with a German documentary called *Was glaubst du denn? (What Do You Believe In?)*. This documentary differs from the series in some regards. It fully relies on an insider approach that is not interrupted by an (academic) expert-presenter like Aslan. *What Do You Believe In?* does not present an exotic other, but apparently "normal" young people living their religion in a pluralistic society. Führding argues that this form of representation helps to legitimize and authorize a specific populist image of religion as "real," and thus as "authentic" and "good," while subtly allowing the audience to delegitimize other forms of religion that do not directly manufacture "good citizens" who secure the stability of the community.

Chapter 8

The Strange and Familiar Spiritual Journey of Reza Aslan

Martha Smith Roberts

CNN's hour-long "spiritual adventure series," *Believer*, starring and hosted by Reza Aslan, aired Sunday nights, right after *Finding Jesus*. Premiering March 5, 2017, the show's first season had six episodes examining the Aghori sect of Hinduism, an apocalyptic cult in Hawaii, Haitian voodoo, Santa Muerte in Mexico City, Haredi Judaism, and Scientology, respectively.[1] In each episode, Aslan led viewers on a participatory journey into the strange beliefs and practices of exotic others to find familiar, recognizable religious impulses. As an attempt to find universal human expressions of religion, *Believer* is an example of one of the ways in which religion is often depicted in American media. This particular genre of religious media, which includes the spiritual adventure series, relies on a sharp distinction between good and bad religion to construct a perennial religion that reflects Western individualism and pluralism. In this essay, I will be describing the representations of religion in *Believer* and examining some of the ways in which the trope of good and bad religion is utilized in the show. Drawing information from *Believer*'s first (and now only) season, I will discuss the marketing and genre of the series, as well as the form and content of the episodes. My role is primarily descriptive. In the following chapters of this volume, respondents will offer their critiques of the show's visual elements, connections to global capitalist ideologies, and comparisons to German series that do similar work.

Marketing Believer: Personal and Exotic

As the title intimates, the notion that there is a universal form of religious experience that can be found in diverse individual *beliefs* is the raison d'être of the series. The idea that the strange and familiar can be bridged through authentic experiences of the other also characterizes the marketing and media campaign surrounding the premiere of *Believer*. Taking viewers into the dangerous and exotic world of "cannibals, doomsday fanaticals, and new age radicals," Reza Aslan uncovers the "good" religion that exists at the core of even the most foreign of traditions.[2] The series offers viewers the opportunity to experience the exotic even as it reinforces a comfortable perennialism in which authentic religion is firmly located in the realm of the personal. Before the series aired, CNN began fashioning a dichotomy of good and bad religion that hinged upon these very notions of personal faith and authentic experience. *Believer*'s marketing campaign, which includes a supplementary website, audience participation, teaser trailers, and promos, lays the groundwork for the ways in which religion will be dealt with in the series.

Much of the media surrounding the series is flashy and technological, heavy with the post-production polish that CNN is known for. The series has a website full of supplemental materials meant to contextualize episodes and provide further information. Alongside the trailers and promos on the site, CNN posts short videos and essays, as well as a video series called "Reza Explains …" in which Aslan answers questions such as, "what is a cult?," "what is Scientology?," and "what do Hindus really believe?" These materials contain explanations of key terms, beliefs, and practices that viewers may not be familiar with. There is also a *Believer* blog site that addresses broader religious issues and includes online quizzes that test viewers' knowledge of "Christianity" or "the world's religions," respectively. Viewers are thus invited and encouraged to participate in this spiritual adventure outside of simply watching *Believer*, and interactive possibilities alongside the series abound. These materials reveal the assumed gaps in public knowledge of religion, and they provide information to connect the viewers' personal experiences to those beliefs that lie outside of them. Much like the website materials, a participatory advertising campaign for the series focused on bridging the strange and familiar by way of the universality of authentic personal religious experiences.

Beginning in February, the month before the series aired, CNN asked their viewers to share their own stories about faith by submitting their answers to the question "What do you believe?"[3] This marketing campaign foreshadowed the individualistic, experience-oriented quest of *Believer*. CNN summarizes the results of their inquiry on their website:

> Each of the nearly 7.5 billion people on this planet is a complex product of our upbringing, culture, and an inestimable number of other factors. But nothing informs how we live quite like what we believe. On the CNN Original Series "Believer," Reza Aslan traveled the globe and immersed himself in the world's most fascinating faiths with that in mind. And in the process, CNN went on a related journey, seeking answers to one question: What do you believe? Since February, more than 600 members of our global audience have shared with us what they believe and how they came to realize it—from chance encounters to life-changing tragedies to supernatural visions. For many others, their quest for understanding continues, with no end in sight. Here's what we learned from your stories.[4]

The website posted personal testimonies from Christians, Buddhists, agnostics, and more, to evidence a shared concept of "belief." For CNN, the variety of viewers' beliefs attested to the universality of religious experience. This kind of personal religious experience was also the defining feature of "good" religion that the show would build upon. Personal testimony, the confession of viewers' private beliefs, was essential to this campaign. Viewers were asked to take on the roles of expert and novice as they offered their answers and read those of others.

This form of contact and exchange of ideas, even those that one may not agree with, was used in the series itself, as Aslan encountered a wide variety of beliefs that were framed as thoroughly unfamiliar, but not necessarily bad.

CNN's report summarizes the six major "findings" about participants: "You've been passionate from a young age," "You know everything can change in an instant," "You think actions speak louder than words," "You find strength in believing (or not)," "You seek beyond major religions," and "You believe the search for meaning never ends."[5] Each of these statements is supported by several personal testimonies from viewers in the form of quotes, links to full statements, and audio clips. However, even as CNN presents their findings as universal truths, their evidence strives to show the diversity of the exotic other. Evidence of "seeking beyond major religions," for example, includes statements from converts to Yoruba and Norse Paganism; the evidence for "finding strength in belief" comes from Christian and Wiccan respondents, among others. CNN firmly locates *Believer* in the realm of a perennialist worldview, where all good religion, no matter how exotic, shares common forms. In order to produce the "good believer" as normative religion, CNN relies on a contrasting construction of "bad" religion that is positioned as outside of viewers' experiences and their empathetic reach. We see this most clearly in the visual advertising for the series.

The official promotional trailers, teasers, and bumpers for the show all expand on the ideas of personal experience and journey, yet they add even more of the exotic other into the mix. *Believer*'s main trailer illustrates the carefully produced version of strange, "bad" religion. The promo begins with a black screen and a chorus of voices that sing a deep and bluesy melody while hands clap to the rhythm.[6] Over this melodic, gospel-inspired backdrop, we see an image of Aslan sitting in lotus position in an outdoor temple in India. Quickly, other images follow, an evangelical service in Haiti, a Santa Muerte gathering, people dancing with hands over their heads in a variety of settings, and an accented female voice that says, "it's what you feel in your heart." Aslan is featured holding a Santa Muerte figure and saying, "I don't know how to describe it, but I kind of feel this connection." As we move through scenes from the upcoming season's episodes, it quickly becomes apparent that the show will feature experiences that lie outside of mainstream American religious culture. A flashy variety of images follow: nudity, mass worship services, hippy cult-types, voodoo priestesses, possession, fire rituals, painted-faced gurus, and Scientology buildings. We are also shown images of individuals professing their beliefs to the camera, one after another: A Haitian man says, "I believe in voodoo," a thin, shirtless, bearded man dances around a room and yells, "I am the messiah, I am the king." Another man says, "The spirits of voodoo are demons." And another, "It's like I was looking into outer space." And viewers see Aslan *participating* in it all and saying, "definitely one of the most extraordinary experiences of my life." CNN's narrator then closes the ad by inviting the audience to "Join the spiritually curious journey: *Believer*."[7] The ads ends with an image of Aslan, wearing all white and sitting barefoot and cross-legged, superimposed to appear to be floating over a grassy meadow; there is no doubt that he is the guide for this spiritual journey.

The notion of individual experience is joined with an exoticizing experiential framework in each of these advertisements. Alongside the exotic images, viewers are always shown Aslan participating: in rituals, ceremonies, dances, auditing, meditation, and more. Another promo invites viewers to "Meet the true believers...the religious rebels... They are cannibals, doomsday fanatics, and new age radicals. Become a guest of the gurus and the priests of voodoo. Hear the prayers to the dead and the cries of the possessed. Join the spiritually curious journey. *Believer*."[8] In these promos we see the confessional and personal fused with the exotic other. These "true believers" are not presented as traditional religious faithful. Gurus, radicals, fanatics, and cannibals are the exotic hook meant to pull the viewer in. There is nothing boring or normal about these images or words. The intent is clear: the show will take the viewer into unknown, dangerous territory—into bad religion. And Aslan will serve as the guide, crossing boundaries in their stead. The invitation at the end, to "join the spiritually curious journey" reminds viewers that this will be an experiential, participatory quest.

Producing Media Representations of Religion: Spiritual Adventure as Documentary Series

If this line of advertising seems familiar (to an American audience), it may be that one is recalling Oprah Winfrey's *Belief*, which aired on the Oprah Winfrey Network (OWN) in October of 2015.[9] The *Oprah.com* description of the series reveals a few of the similarities:

> Seven billion people, searching for connection, redemption, meaning. Oprah Winfrey presents the seven-night event, "Belief," a groundbreaking television event exploring humankind's ongoing search to connect with something greater than ourselves. Journeying to the far reaches of the world, and to places cameras have rarely been, "Belief" searches the origins of diverse faiths and the heart of what really matters. From the epic to the intimate, webbed throughout each hour are stories of people on spiritual journeys, taking them to sacred spaces.[10]

Belief was a seven-night miniseries that not only had a very similar title, but also similarly experience-centered content and a central question of "What do you believe?" *Belief* also ran a marketing campaign that solicited viewer feedback to that very question, presaging CNN's later campaign.

These parallels are not coincidental; they illustrate the characteristics of a genre of religion media that relies on a particular conception of good and bad religion. In *Belief*, viewers have not one guide, but many. Episodes are thematic and include a variety of traditions and individuals ("33 stories of faith and no faith"[11]) that fall under topics such as, "The Seekers," "Love's Story," and "Acts of Faith."[12] The religious journey as authentic self-discovery is the centrepiece of good religion. As a *Washington Post* piece by Diana Butler Bass noted, Oprah's *Belief* has an important lesson for viewers: "The age of top-down religion is over. That age is being replaced by an age in which even people who faithfully maintain distinctive religious identities are engaging in do-it-yourself spiritual journeys that often lead in remarkably similar directions of love, healing and justice toward a God (or gods) close at hand."[13] Bass correctly identifies the taxonomic work of this genre; hierarchy and institutions are often represented as bad religion, or more specifically, without individual experience and pluralist aims, these features of religion seem inauthentic or irrelevant to contemporary life.

Belief, like *Believer*, focuses on the universal individual experience of religion as authentic. I bring this up not as a diversion from *Believer*, but rather to illustrate that the show is part of a larger tradition of what Aaron Hughes might call "apologetic, theory-light" media representations of religion that fall broadly into a category of the "documentary series" genre, and that share a liberal humanist conception of good religion. These two recent examples have precedents in a number of series that seek to educate the public, including *Religions of the World*, a fourteen-part BBC series narrated by Ben Kingsley in 1998; *Around the World in 80 Faiths*, an eight-part BBC series hosted by Anglican vicar Peter Owen-Jones in 2009; and *Sacred Journeys*, a six-part PBS series from 2014 featuring Bruce Feiler accompanying American pilgrims on sacred journeys.[14] These are just a few examples of the documentary series genre of religious media.[15]

In fact, we might also recall *The Long Search*, a 1977 BBC production, as another moment in a history of media representations of religion through documentary series. *The Long Search* was a thirteen-episode series hosted by Ronald Eyre that examined world religions in locations around the globe, including Egypt, Japan, Sri Lanka, the US, and South Africa.[16] It has been utilized in college world religions courses for decades, sometimes in conjunction with the companion volume authored by Ninian Smart.[17] In the final episode of the series, Eyre reflects on the big questions the series raised, like "do you believe in god?" and "what is religion?"[18] His answers lean toward the personal and the perennial, much as we see in both *Believer* and *Belief*. Eyre uses the "mountain metaphor" to describe the fact that religions have similar goals, but different ascents to the top. This tendency to over-simplify with comparisons and to look for universal meaning in religious journeys and individual experiences is thus part of a longer tradition of a modern television genre.

Eyre's description of the intention behind *The Long Search* could also very well be a description for *Believer*. In 1978, he said:

> A small group of people, hiding behind no eminent front man, had the nerve to ask the question, "Is it possible for a moment to look through somebody else's eyes, share somebody else's feelings, pierce, just for a moment, that secret place where the deepest animating concerns lie hidden?" [...] [Then, having asked this], to take a camera around the world in search of an answer. That is what the *Long Search* is [...].[19]

The genre of the spiritual adventure documentary series has a lineage. Producers of series like these do face a challenge in presenting religion to a mass audience. Which traditions are included? How are they presented? How can complex religious traditions fit into an hour-long show? This is where Aaron Hughes observations about "noble lies" are helpful. As he notes in his introduction, drawing upon Jonathan Z. Smith, there is a lying inherent in generalizing, simplifying, or making discernible for an audience. There is a danger that follows, of "misrepresenting complexity [...] in the service of correcting negative stereotypes and of self-aggrandizement."[20] The documentary series genre utilizes the trope of good and bad religion as a way to simplify and generalize; it also misrepresents the complexity of religious phenomena in service of a participatory pluralist worldview.

So what are some of the ways in which *Believer* makes religion discernible for its audience? What are the narratives? And what do they privilege? The title and the ad campaigns offer the first clues, and when seen in light of the larger tradition of the genre, an emphasis on individuality, diversity, lived religion, and experience emerges. The tropes of "discovery" and "journey" are also intimately connected to this form. The documentary series genre, based in "experiential journeys that teach," thus provides the framework for the content and narrative arc of each episode. And while the contents of the religious traditions vary, the perennial message does not. Over and over again, Aslan finds what he is looking for: true believers that practice good religion.

The Episode: Perennialism as Form and Content

The documentary series genre takes a particularly polished form on CNN, a 24-hour news network offering a variety of programming that ranges from traditional newsrooms to feature films.[21] CNN also features other "adventure series" in its line-up, though only *Believer* is classified as "spiritual." The most successful was *Parts Unknown*, a food-centered adventure series, in which Anthony Bourdain traveled the world to sample unique and obscure cuisine (that show won four Emmys). *Believer* gives viewers a tour of religions along those same lines—unique, exotic groups serve as the entry point into folksy, personal experiences of the host in a variety of new settings. In fact, several reviewers and commentators have compared *Believer*'s first season to *Parts Unknown*, including Aslan himself, who told *Vogue* that *Believer* is "a show about religion in the same way that Anthony Bourdain's show is a show about food. It's not *really* about food, and it's not *really* about religion."[22] Aslan and Bourdain both take viewers on journeys into the unfamiliar. As Aslan was promoting *Believer* on talk shows and in interviews, he often referenced *Parts Unknown* as a way to communicate the goals of *Believer* to new viewers. "I often say Anthony Bourdain's show is not about food. It's about cultures, it's about other worlds—it's just that he uses food as a vehicle to open up these other worlds," and "that's really what this is about, it's about getting a window into another culture through the lens of their religious experience."[23] For Aslan, religion functions as a category, as cuisine does for Bourdain, to better understand some of the nuances of human culture.

However, Aslan has another objective as well, one that merges anthropological and theological aims:

> My goal has always been, not just with this show, but with everything I do, to subvert your expectations, to get you to think differently about groups that you

think are foreign, or exotic, or fearsome, to help you break through the outer shell of a person's religion, and to get to know their beliefs, so that you recognize how similar those beliefs are to your own.[24]

His perennialism is the heart of the series. Beyond the description and analysis of these traditions, Aslan wants to lead viewers to a new understanding of the similarity of all religions. He is very clear about his essentialist intentions:

> I think that's what is really going to be eye-opening, is people are going to realize that there's not that much that separates us—that we may use different myths and metaphors, we may use different languages, but when expressing the issues of ultimate concern, oftentimes we all come up with the same answers, the same ideas, the same hopes and aspirations, the same struggles.[25]

What is unspoken here is, of course, that Aslan does not present all religious traditions as exemplary of the same human struggle. Good and bad religion are often quite clearly differentiated. The strange and exotic that he uses as hooks for each episode remain just as negative at the end. The bad religion represented by oppressive caste systems, deadly cults, or ultra conservative traditions is simply not a part of the good religion that he wants viewers to identify with as real, true, religious experience.

The spiritual adventure portrayed in *Believer* is a combination of spectacle and emotional connection—exotic and personal at the same time. Each episode covers one topic from several vantage points, ultimately letting Aslan's own experience guide the viewer into a universal-humanist interpretation of the deeper meaning of the tradition. Aslan admittedly plays with categories of familiar and strange, often making the strange even stranger before reinforcing a safe, familiar perennialism—good religion stands in stark contrast to the bad, strange other. This contrast is an essential part of the production:

> My goal in every one of these episodes is to take you on really the same journey that I myself went on, to confront you with something that seems so beyond your experience, so outside your comfort zone, that you can't help but to think: This has nothing to do with me. Whether it's an Aghori drinking his own urine, or a Voodoo ceremony in which I'm ingesting different kinds of animal blood, or it's simply me being audited—in every experience, near top of the show, you're confronted with something that you might recoil against, that's quintessentially other to you. But I guess what I hope, is that, as you follow me along, as you start to understand the sentiment behind these actions, as you start to break through the specific symbols or metaphors or rituals or myths or beliefs, that each one of these religious groups holds dear, you start to recognize the connection we have.[26]

Aslan's format is reminiscent of a technique common in religious studies, "making the strange familiar and the familiar strange."[27] This should be expected. Aslan, a well-known author and a professor of creating writing at UC Riverside, comes out of academia. He has a BA in Religious Studies, an MTS degree from Harvard, and PhD in Sociology from UC Santa Barbara.[28] So his choices in *Believer* are exemplary of some of the common tropes of religious studies education. Aslan uses these methods to remedy a toxic kind of othering: "It's an opportunity to show religious traditions, practices, rites and rituals that may at first seem weird and foreign and exotic and unfamiliar—because you're unfamiliar with the metaphors underlying those ideas [...] At the end of an hour episode, they will all of a sudden become much more familiar and recognizable."[29] Over and over, Aslan has been clear about his motives in the series. The question that remains is *how* do these strange traditions become recognizable? In *Believer*, it is through a return to the "core" of all true religions. For Aslan that core is in the experiences of believers. This is a thoroughly universalizing tactic, one that Aslan openly admits to. Responding to a review of *Believer*, he notes that "[...] yes, the show is a 'canny sort of evangelism' for universal spirituality. That's my explicit goal: change how people think about religion."[30]

To do this, the show's format (the organization of each episode) remains constant even as the content changes. It begins with narration from Aslan on the topic of the show. This *hook* always hints at the dangerous, exotic, or surprising content that awaits the viewer, dangling the carrot of the bizarre in front of them. In the first episode on Hinduism, Aslan explains, "I came to Varanasi, India to do a show about Hinduism, about karma, reincarnation the caste system, and a little known Hindu sect called the Aghori [short pause]. That's when things got out of hand." Video of a naked man rolling around in the sand of a beach and appearing to throw urine at Aslan follows. As the man shouts threats at the crew, they run away, and a breathless Aslan says to the camera, "I'm pretty sure that was not the Aghori I was looking for." Each episode has a brief, and equally thrilling, teaser before the title sequence. And if the teaser is meant to titillate, the title sequence is meant to reassure.

The title sequence to the show legitimizes Aslan's role as expert, scholar, and tour guide. Dramatic music plays, and as clips from CNN news programming place Aslan onscreen with other famous talking heads, we hear a cacophony of narrators reinforcing Aslan's credentials. A woman's voice: "Reza Aslan is an author and scholar..." followed by Don Lemon: "Reza Aslan is a scholar of religions," another voice: "bestselling author Reza Aslan," and finally, Anderson Cooper addresses Aslan, "As a scholar, as a Muslim, as an American, let me ask you ..." As the question trails off, Aslan introduces himself: "I've been studying the world's religions for twenty years, and now I'm gonna live them." As he speaks, we see images of Aslan standing in a variety of sacred spaces (the Western Wall in Israel, the Ganges, the Dome of the Rock, a cemetery) and doing sacred things (reading the Torah, offering puja, participating in a voodoo ceremony, holding a Santa Muerte figure, wearing orange robes and standing at the helm of a boat on the Ganges). Every episode opens with this combination of a rousing teaser followed by Aslan's bona fides.

In the opening sequence Aslan is presented as a scholar of religion and a student of religion, as an expert and a seeker. His authenticity is partially constructed in the world of media and 24-hour news programming, which is a world that can be credited for some of his fame. It was his infamous exchange with Fox News' anchor Lauren Green in 2013 made him a viral figure.[31] It is also constructed in relation to his scholarly identity, his experience *studying* the world's religions for twenty years. However, both of these measures of his public and academic authority are then reconstructed in the realm of personal authenticity. Now, he tells us, he is going to *live* these traditions. Aslan is about to do the "real" work that he intimates his scholarship has merely prepared him for (but never achieved): he is going to experience the world's religions. For Aslan, *living* these traditions means taking a journey, and the journey becomes the basis of each episode.

As the show gets started, episodes follow a familiar narrative arc. They begin with the strange and move slowly into the more acceptable. Aslan travels to faraway (and sometimes not-so-faraway) lands. Along the way, he asks a lot of people what they personally feel and think. Periodically, the action breaks, and the focus shifts to Aslan's personal meditations on big questions. Each episode then ends with a montage of the characters we have met along the way, all of them professing "I believe …" statements that highlight the most acceptable parts of their belief systems (much like that online promotional campaign asked viewers to do). The format of the episodes delivers on Aslan's promised strange-to-familiar strategy. It also reinforces those categories, showing viewers what Aslan sees as good or bad kinds of belief and practice. And while he sometimes uses direct confrontation and value judgments to create these categories, I would argue that it is primarily through broader visual and rhetorical strategies of *comparison* and *confession* that Aslan reveals to viewers the good and bad of what they are seeing.

Content: Comparison and Confession

There are many ways that religion and authority on religion are constructed in the show, and the content of each episode highlights the tensions between good and bad religion at every turn. One key way this happens is through the juxtaposition of good and bad beliefs and practices. Comparison and contrast provide the viewers with a sort of taxonomy of good and bad religion. Thus the show does not simply make the strange familiar, it relies on some strange things staying strange. The first episode looks at Hinduism and caste, and contrasts reasonable Aghori groups that open schools for low-caste children not only with the Aghori cannibal gurus drinking urine on the beach (as extreme), but also with the traditional Hindu institutions represented by a Brahmin who describes caste by saying "the people who are living on this earth, they are not equal." Authentic Hinduism (the moderate Aghori groups as a form of good religion) is thus a humanist center that emerges between extremes of bad innovations and bad traditions. Through this kind of comparative framework, good and bad religion are constructed in each episode.

In another example, Aslan investigates a "doomsday cult" in Hawaii, led by a man named JeZus. In this episode Aslan again sets the scene by introducing the bizarre in the teaser; viewers see images of famous cults and hear a discussion of the failures of doomsday prophets. Aslan makes comparisons to cult leaders such as Jim Jones, David Koresh, and Marshall Applewhite, as well as mentioning failed prophet Harold Camping. He later compares JeZus's looks to Charles Manson. Examples of bad religion prepare the audience for interpretation of the group. Even if viewers come to sympathize with the aims of JeZus and his followers, it will be because they distinguish them from truly bad cults like Manson, Jonestown, and Heaven's Gate. There are many other key examples of "bad religion" throughout the series, and Aslan uses comparisons with "inauthentic" traditions to illustrate "good" religion.

In the Haredim episode, he begins with a discussion of the dangers of fundamentalism, and recounts his own family's story of fleeing Iran. Here, he sets up the good/bad dichotomy around dangerous religious fundamentalism that can destroy a secular state. In the Scientology episode, institutional corruption and control serve as the markers of bad religion. The show opens with a black screen that reads, "This show contains controversial material. After the episode was completed, the Church of Scientology contacted the producers to say the individuals featured in this show were expelled from the Church and can therefore no longer be considered TRUE Scientologists." After a short pause, the screen reads, "These believers have a different perspective." Aslan then goes on to tell us that, in addition to the outspoken critics of Scientology, "There are other voices you haven't heard from. Scientologists who've left the Church but who continue to practice the religion. True believers who are seizing for themselves the power to define one of America's newest faiths. I'm traveling the world to investigate the reformation of the Church of Scientology." Throughout the episode, Aslan compares the Independent Scientologists (who have been excommunicated from the church) with the true believers of the Protestant Reformation. He highlights that authentic religion happens when "individuals make it their own." Bad religion exists in corrupt traditions that ignore individual experiences, whether that tradition is Hinduism, Catholicism, or Scientology.

In addition to these comparative strategies, another tactic we see on the show is the "confessional" moment, in which Aslan has a heart-to-heart with the audience to share his feelings about what is happening. In episode one, Aslan walks along the banks of the Ganges; fires burn in the background. He speaks to viewers:

> Hinduism is a beautiful religion, I've always been fascinated by it. But I just can't wrap my head around this notion that there are people who simply because of their birth, or because they did things in a previous life, are then condemned to live life as an untouchable ... I just, I, I can't wrap my head around it.

His experience and interpretation (often framed as feeling) pull the narrative along, and they lead the viewer to the "good religion"—the light at the end of the tunnel—individual experiences and beliefs that we all share. The "good" is always in the individual interpretation of faith. And Aslan models this as he confides in the viewer about how to negotiate these feelings. At the end of each episode he sums up what he has found and how he feels at the end of the journey. In this episode, we watch Aslan participate in a Hindu ritual at the Temple of Baba Kinaram, founder of the moderate sect of Aghorism. We hear Aslan's voice narrating over dramatic, uplifting music:

> What does it mean to live without fear? It means recognizing that purity and pollution are just an illusion. It means knowing that nothing you do, nothing you eat, nothing you touch can cut you off from god. That if god lives inside you, as the Aghori believe, then nothing can defile you. The family you were born into, the color of your skin, the clothes that you wear, your education, your wealth, none of these matters. What matters is what you do, how you love, how you care for the least among you. So I will eat the ashes of the dead. I will drink the water from the Ganges. I will worship the god within me. I came to India to discover what it means to be Aghori. What I discovered is what it means to be human.

Aslan comes full circle. Through comparisons with a variety of other Hindu traditions that fall short, he finds an example of good religion that he can not only agree with, but also participate in. His own authentic experience in the temple at the end of the episode illustrates the universality of good religion. Aslan, a Muslim, sees himself in this tradition. A part of the authenticity of good religion comes from a universal applicability, which is revealed to viewers in personal, confessional moments with Aslan.

This confessional strategy is utilized in another way at the end of each episode. Viewers see not Aslan, but the characters of the show looking into the camera and explaining what they believe. Individual beliefs in the form of confessional statements reinforce the construction of good religion in each episode. Aslan does end, as he promises to, with something familiar, something viewers can see themselves in. The authentic individual experience is the pinnacle of good religion. The details, the content of those beliefs, change in each episode, but believers remain the centerpiece.

Critical Responses

CNN's *Believer* utilizes the notion of good and bad religion in its marketing, form, and content. It serves as an example of the ways in which liberal humanist notions of religion rely on this classificatory trope, even as they posit a universal religious impulse that pervades all cultures. It also clearly represents authentic religion as progressive and personal, utilizes orientalism, and occasionally reveals the limits of the very universalism it proposes. With this in mind, *Believer* exemplifies the ways in which Aaron Hughes' critiques of Islamic religious studies are more broadly applicable to both religious studies scholarship in general, and to representations of religion in the media more specifically.

Perhaps most appropriate is Hughes' critique surrounding the manufacture of liberal progressive religion that locates authenticity in in pluralism, justice, and egalitarianism. Often "in the service of correcting negative stereotypes," there is systematic engagement in the misrepresentation of the complexities of religion.[32] In *Believer*, authentic religion is characterized up and against not only negative stereotypes, but also bad religious forms (like deadly cults or non-secular religious regimes). This produces an over-simplified view of religion as fundamentally non-violent, personal, tolerant, and ultimately a good force in the world. This kind of religious studies, Hughes argues, is perhaps best called "crypto-theological," as it is "little more than a form of liberal ecumenicism in which all 'religions' are assumed to contribute to the betterment of human civilization."[33] Another of Hughes' critiques that applies to *Believer* is the way in which the show privileges the insider or convert view. Hughes' critique is levelled at Islamic religious studies scholars whose conversion becomes a type of authority.[34] In *Believer*, Aslan does not convert, but he participates; he legitimizes a particular kind of insider experience. Personal meaning and modern interpretations are what define authentic traditions in the series, and Aslan prescribes a role for the scholar that can transcend insider/outsider categories, drawing upon both for authority.

Outside of academic circles, the show has gotten a variety of reviews. Many of the show's critics focus on its liberal humanism and romantic individualism, but on the other end of the spectrum are critiques of *Believer* as a type of orientalism posing as anti-orientalism. This is reminiscent of Hughes discussion of apologetic, presentist, and theory-lite exoticism that draws upon orientalism even as it claims to reject it.[35] In this case, there is much to examine in the reviews of *Believer*'s first episode on Hinduism. Sigal Samuel sums up several of the criticisms from the American Hindu community in his *Atlantic* article. A pattern in their language emerges that highlights *Believer*'s exoticizing framework:

> The show is "shock religion porn," said Suhag Shukla, the leader of the Hindu American Foundation. It privileges "sensationalism over scholarship," said Ro Khanna, a Hindu Democratic congressman from California. It will "have a wider Hinduphobic societal impact," said Ajay Shah, convener of American Hindus Against Defamation. It "can create a perception about Indian Americans which could make them more vulnerable to further attacks," said Sanjay Puri, the chairman of the US India Political Action Committee.[36]

The critiques of the show's sensationalism also point to the limits of *Believer*'s universalism. Aslan's reliance on a good/bad dichotomy to make the strange familiar means that not all religions are portrayed equally. And many see this as actually working against the liberal humanist connectivity that Aslan espouses. In a *Huffington Post* blog, Vamsee Juluri accused CNN of perpetuating "a very racist, colonial era discourse of dehumanization and even demonization."[37] Beyond the Hindu community, other scholars have also levelled these critiques. Michael Altman compares Aslan's work to nineteenth century depictions of India, noting that neither is in the realm of scholarship.[38] The episode on the Aghori is not the only one that reveals the limits of the show's universalism. For instance, *Believer*'s broader humanist agenda promotes a privatized religion that challenges institutional religion, but it does not challenge the secular state. A critic in the *New Yorker* summed it up well, asking "Why do renegade Scientologists get the benefit of the doubt, while ultra-Orthodox Jews do not? Perhaps there is a limit to universalist tolerance, after all."[39] In all of these critiques of *Believer*, we see the problems that arise when the framework of good and bad religion is used to make the strange familiar.

Perhaps the most important example of the show's attempts to make the strange familiar through the use of this dichotomy comes in the depiction of a religion that is *not* the subject of an episode: Islam. Ultimately, Aslan himself is the real exotic other: intellectual, academic, Muslim, and seeker. He is the strange religion that Americans are truly being asked to make familiar; he is the believer that they should connect with in each episode. In a video series called "The Secret Life of Muslims," Aslan discussed the struggles of being Muslim in the US, particularly in relation to popular culture depictions. He notes his own role in this media construction, drawing upon his status as a commentator on many cable television news segments, "After about ten years of being cable news' favorite Muslim, I've come to the realization that I don't think it's doing any good." He goes on to say, "Bigotry is not a result of ignorance, it's a result of fear. And fear is impervious to data; fear is impervious to information. The only way that you're going to dissipate that fear is by getting people to know someone that they're afraid of."[40] In this interview, and in others, he notes that this is his motivation for turning to popular culture as a way to connect to the masses.[41] I would argue that *Believer* was ultimately Aslan's attempt to make Islam more palatable to the American viewer by letting them get to know a "good" Muslim.

The use of good and bad religion in media depictions is often a way of simplifying and generalizing complex realities for the general public. In the spiritual adventure documentary series *Believer*, this strategy is used to make strange religions familiar and to promote religious pluralism. It is addressing the very real problem of religious tolerance in the US. However, a close examination of the series reveals that this strategy does not make all of the exotic traditions palatable or even recognizable. Instead, the show maintains that some traditions really are quite strange, and leads viewers to see certain radicals, fanaticals, and cannibals, among others, as anything but authentic expressions of religion. The strange traditions that Aslan does manage to make familiar over the course of the series are all versions of a western individualism that mirror viewers' own understanding of authentic personal religious experience—an experience epitomized in the form of the *believer*. This is the issue at the heart of the good and bad religion dichotomy; it is not a neutral description of the world, it is a value judgment that reflects the intentions of those doing the classifying. In this case, the strategy ultimately fails in the service of Aslan's liberal humanist perennialism, as seen in the response from members of the American Hindu community.

The dichotomy also fails as scholarship. And this is the crux of the problem with this particular media depiction of religion. Aslan is clear about his perennialist intentions, but he never distinguishes them clearly from scholarship. Instead, he draws upon his role as a scholar to legitimate what he is doing. The show perpetuates the blurry distinction between religious studies and theology that already exists in American media landscape. The focus on good and bad religion hijacks the possibility of nuanced discussion around religion—of *how* and *why* some traditions are not accepted into American classifications of religion. Instead, *Believer* reinforces the very classification system of "toxic othering" that Aslan claims to be targeting with his perennialism. It does not break down the exotic other into familiar, human behavior. It maintains that some traditions are just too exotic to accept as religion.

Martha Smith Roberts is Assistant Professor of Religion at Denison University. Her primary research is a critical analysis of post-racial and post-ethnic theories of American religious pluralism. Roberts is also working on a co-authored manuscript analyzing the various spiritualities emerging within the hula hooping subculture. She is the Executive Secretary and Treasurer for the North American Association for the Study of Religion, and she also serves on the Board of Directors for the Institute for Diversity and Civic Life in Austin, Texas.

Notes

1. This chapter was originally presented as a paper in July of 2017. On the day of our panel, coincidentally, the series was cancelled by CNN. Aslan tweeted about US President Donald Trump, and the tweet was seen as out of line by CNN. While the ratings for the first season were good, the show will not have another season.
2. "CNN Original Series: "Believer" Promo," December 23, 2016, www.youtube.com/watch?v=h6xf6xttjPg.
3. Drew Kann, "We Are What We Believe: What CNN Readers Told Us About Faith," *CNN*, April 17, 2017, www.cnn.com/2017/04/05/us/believer-what-do-you-believe-stories-roundup/index.html (archived at www.webcitation.org/78tml7ap1).
4. Ibid.
5. Ibid.
6. One of the songs used in *Believer* is "Rain on Down" from Robert Homes and James Homes, 2015 *Down to the Swamp*.
7. "CNN Original Series: Believer with Reza Aslan," *CNN Promos*, January 1, 2017, http://edition.cnn.com/videos/tv/2017/01/06/believer-trailer.cnn-promos/video/playlists/believer-with-reza-aslan/.
8. "CNN Original Series: 'Believer' Promo," December 23, 2016, www.youtube.com/watch?v=h6xf6xttjPg.
9. Marianne Schnall, "Oprah Asks the Question, 'What Do You Believe?'," *Huffington Post*, October 14, 2015, www.huffpost.com/entry/oprah-asks-the-question-w_b_8288718 (archived at www.webcitation.org/78tn7Kq9G).
10. "Oprah Winfrey Presents 'Belief,'" *Oprah.com*, July 17, 2015, www.oprah.com/belief/oprah-winfrey-presents-belief.
11. Adelle M. Banks, "Oprah's 'Belief' Series Explores Faith From Many Perspectives," *Huffington Post*, October 15, 2015, www.huffingtonpost.com/entry/oprah-belief-series_us_561eb05fe4b028dd7ea6571d (archived at www.webcitation.org/78to5Yc17).
12. "Oprah Presents Landmark TV Event *Belief* Premiering Sunday, October 18 on OWN," *Oprah.com*, June 15, 2015, www.oprah.com/belief/oprah-winfrey-presents-landmark-television-event-belief.
13. Diana Butler Bass, "Oprah's New 'Belief' Series Shows How Dramatically the Nature of Faith Is Shifting," *Washington Post*, October 18, 2015, www.washingtonpost.com/news/acts-of-faith/wp/2015/10/18/oprahs-new-belief-series-shows-how-dramatically-the-nature-of-faith-is-shifting/ (archived at archive.today/cueRH).
14. "Sacred Journeys with Bruce Feiler," *Sacred Journeys with Bruce Feiler*, www.pbs.org/wgbh/sacredjourneys/content/home/ (archived at archive.today/cFx7O).
15. My work and discussion on the genre are limited to the English-language versions of it that have preceded *Believer*.
16. The studio website's description reads, "The series gives an objective view of the world's religious faiths and beliefs, including Catholicism, Protestantism, Hinduism,

Buddhism, Judaism, Islam, African religions, Taoism, Orthodox Christianity, New Age beliefs, and Ancestor Worship." For series description see "The Long Search" page at Ambrose Digital Streaming Video: www.ambrosevideo.com/screening-room/42-LS (archived at archive.today/UMK80).

17 Scholar Ninian Smart served as editorial consultant and author of the companion volume.
18 Ronald Eyre, *The Long Search: Reflections on the Long Search*, Episode 13, BBC Production, (1977, Ambrose Video Publishing). As Eyre attempts to present an objective answer and avoid value judgments, he utilizes the familiar perennial metaphor of mountain climbing to help explain the differences between religions. "Perhaps all religions say the same thing in the sense that all mountaineers climb mountains, but that doesn't mean that all the ascents are the same. Though it's perfectly true that all ascents are about going up."
19 Cited in Richard B. Pilgrim, "The Long Search Series," *Religious Studies Review* 6(1) (1980: 17.
20 Aaron W. Hughes, *Islam and the Tyranny of Authenticity: An Inquiry into Disciplinary Apologetics and Self-Deception*, London: Equinox, 2015, xiv.
21 CNN, Ted Turner's Cable News Network, launched as the first 24-hour news network in 1980.
22 Julia Felsenthal, "In Believer, Reza Aslan Gives Religion the Anthony Bourdain Treatment," *Vogue*, March 3, 2017, www.vogue.com/article/believer-cnn-reza-aslan-interview (archived at archive.today/5C2by). See also Jesse Singal, "Reza Aslan on His New CNN Show About Religious Rituals," *The Cut*, March 11, 2015, www.thecut.com/2015/03/reza-aslan-on-his-show-about-religious-rituals.html (archived at archive.today/8K1dD), and Elias Muhanna, "The Contradictions of Reza Aslan's 'Believer'," *The New Yorker*, April 9, 2017, www.newyorker.com/culture/culture-desk/the-contradictions-of-reza-aslans-believer (archived at archive.today/aQle1).
23 Singal, "Reza Aslan on His New CNN Show About Religious Rituals."
24 Felsenthal, "In Believer, Reza Aslan Gives Religion the Anthony Bourdain Treatment."
25 Singal, "Reza Aslan on His New CNN Show About Religious Rituals."
26 Ibid.
27 Mark Muesse, "Religious Studies and 'Heaven's Gate': Making the Strange Familiar and the Familiar Strange," in Russell T. McCutcheon (ed.) *The Insider/Outsider Problem and the Study of Religion*, London: Cassell, 1999, 390–394.
28 "About," http://rezaaslan.com/about (archived at archive.today/DLABz).
29 Stephen Battaglio, "In CNN's 'Believer,' Reza Aslan to Aim for a Window on World Religions," *Los Angeles Times*, March 21, 2015, www.latimes.com/entertainment/tv/la-et-st-reza-aslan-believer-cnn-20150321-story.html (archived at archive.today/x5CyD).
30 Reza Aslan, Facebook Post, April 10, 2017, 1:14pm. www.facebook.com/rezaaslanofficial/posts/1885929788320058 (archived at archive.today/szAqO).
31 See Adam Gopnik, "Fox News's Don't-Come-to-Jesus Moment," *The New Yorker*, August 2, 2013, www.newyorker.com/news/daily-comment/fox-newss-dont-come-to-jesus-moment (archived at archive.today/uEUsc); "Fox News Host Attacks Muslim Scholar Who Wrote About Jesus," *Clips 7*, July 27, 2013, www.youtube.com/watch?v=AQhMllQ-ODw (originally aired on *Fox News: Spirited Debate*, July 26, 2013).
32 Hughes, *Islam and the Tyranny of Authenticity*, xiv.
33 Ibid., 15.
34 Ibid., 59.
35 Ibid., 47.

36 Sigal Samuel, "Reza Aslan and the Risks of Making Religion Relatable," *The Atlantic*, March 12, 2017, www.theatlantic.com/international/archive/2017/03/reza-aslan-cnn-believer-make-religion-relatable/519147/ (archived at archive.today/kYehB).
37 Vamsee Juluri, "CNN's 'Believer' Is Reckless, Racist And Dangerously Anti-Immigrant," *Huffington Post*, March 5, 2017, www.huffpost.com/entry/cannibals-and-corpses-cnns-believer-is-reckless-racist_b_58bbc5fee4b02eac8876cfad (archived at archive.today/yPyuY).
38 Michael Altman, "Scholar or Retailer of Import Goods? Reza Aslan, His Guru, and His Critics," *The Immanent Frame*, March 27, 2017, https://tif.ssrc.org/2017/03/28/reza-aslan-his-guru-and-his-critics/ (archived at archive.today/hecYo).
39 Muhanna, "The Contradictions of Reza Aslan's 'Believer'."
40 "Secret Life of Muslims: Reza Aslan," *USA Today*, April 18, 2017, www.youtube.com/watch?v=9Z2G4iKpB0U.
41 "The Power of Storytelling: Reza Aslan's Path to Riverside and Beyond," *UCRHighlander*, May 18, 2015, www.youtube.com/watch?v=Pm29ayQmBiU.s

Chapter 9

The Journalist-Ethnographer, Religious Diversity, and the Euphemization of Social Relations

Carmen Becker

Watching the promo to CNN's production *Believer*, two traits which continue to imprint all six episodes immediately catch attention: The ethnographic mode in which Reza Aslan as a host casts himself and the navigation of a vocabulary of religious perennialism and liberal humanism embedded in the broader discourse of religious diversity. Martha Smith Roberts has fleshed out both elements in her anchoring essay. Appearance of both traits together in Aslan's *Believer* is not a coincidence, as I will argue in this contribution. The ethnographic mode used in media productions serves to authenticate and authorize specific claims. It is the claim to have unmediated access to a phenomenon that is at the heart of the ethnographic mode as employed by Aslan. The ethnographer is imagined as collecting meaningful raw data through physical presence and the sensory apparatus of the body. In the popular understanding, fieldwork is tantamount to experiencing and witnessing the world as it is, as "raw," "true," and unmediated.[1]

Some scholars have noted how the term "authenticity" has come to play a central role in contemporary societies (see Lindholm 2008; Fillitz and Saris 2012). For instance, foods and art have to be authentic in order to be appreciated, individuals are on the quest to realize their "authentic" self, and identities are considered to be authentic if the bearers of that identity can trace their biological heritage and act in an associated, culturally valued manner. Lindholm identifies two overlapping modes in which authenticity is constructed: (1) Genealogical or historical in terms of origin and (2) identity or correspondence in terms of content. In this sense, "[a]uthentic objects, persons, and collectives are original, real, and pure; they are what they purport to be, their roots are known and verified, their essence and appearance are one" (Lindholm 2008: 2). The same can be said for knowledge, truth, ideas and classifications or, in short, for any idea about the world produced in society. Journalists try to get to the core of an issue, aim to tell the story "as it really is" and catch the "authentic" culture of a collective. This idea of journalism is closely associated with the ethnographic mode I have outlined before.

In the case of *Believer*, the ethnographic mode leads the viewer to misrecognize the arbitrariness of Aslan's double classificatory work on what counts as, first of all, "religion" or "belief" and, secondly, as "good religion" or "good ways of believing" in the sense of acceptable and legitimate religion in the socio-political field.

His negotiation of religion while he travels different selected sites to encounter believers around the world fills this category with specific ideas and models of religious subjectivities which are offered as a blueprint for acceptable authentic religious experience.

My following argument is strongly informed by Pierre Bourdieu's notions of *field* and *symbolic power* through which he formulates a specific relational perspective on the production of power in different social arenas such as the media. As Loïc Wacquant highlights, Bourdieu's approach is highly agonistic in the sense that his perspective puts the focus on struggle (Wacquant 2013: 275–276). Social reproduction as both continuity and rupture emerges from the battlefields of social spaces. In this spirit, a field is

> a space of conflict and competition, the analogy here being with a battlefield, in which participants vie to establish monopoly over [...] scientific authority in the scientific field, sacerdotal authority in the religious field, and so forth—and the power to decree the hierarchy and "conversion rates" between all forms of authority in the field of power. (Bourdieu and Wacquant 1992: 17–18)

In conjunction with this perspective, the media field is one of the fields specialized in cultural production, similar to the fields of art, science, or religion, "wherein authoritative representations of the social world are produced and disseminated" (Wacquant 2013: 276). Positions taken in this field are first and foremost relational, not substantial, and embedded in conflicts over authority of identification, interpretation, and classification. The media field is thus nested in the public sphere, mediates classificatory work, and adjudicates debates over identities (see Bourdieu 1999). It is a site for "the struggle to impose the legitimate principle of vision and division" (Bourdieu 1989: 20–21) which produces the hegemonic categories of perception and classification. They in turn construct social reality and are the primary stakes of political struggle.

In order to gain authority in a specific field such as the media field, agents need to be endued with symbolic capital, which is the form that specific kinds of capital (e.g., cultural, economic, or social) take when recognized as legitimate (Bourdieu 1989: 17). In his recurring definition of symbolic capital, Bourdieu characterizes it as "any property (any form of capital whether physical, economic, cultural or social) when it is perceived by social agents endowed with categories of perception which cause them to know it and to recognize it, to give it value" (Bourdieu 1998: 47). The importance of the notion of authenticity in contemporary societies and the value attached to it indicates that the ability to perform in the ethnographic mode due to, for the most part, cultural capital, is evidence for the symbolic power of the specific agent: Based on cultural capital, the ethnographic mode produces authenticity which in turn is vested with symbolic power because social agents value it and recognize it as legitimate.

Symbolic capital grants power to those "who have obtained sufficient recognition to be in a position to impose recognition" (Bourdieu 1989: 23). This kind of power is the power of world-making, the power to consecrate and reveal things in terms of knowledge and by way of classification, identification, division, and distinction. To change the world then means to change socially essential classifications and divisions into groups and categories of things and beings. In order to be effective, symbolic capital works towards naturalizing and objectifying the particularity of the specific point of view that is taken by the bearer of that view from a particular point in the social field. Her vision becomes the universal vision; his point of view is turned into common sense and transcends, albeit temporarily, the competition for authority. In extension, symbolic power is most efficient when the genesis of classificatory systems from particular positions within the social field, and therefore from particular points of view of specific actors, is obscured and the power relations structuring the social field are euphemized in communication.

To return to Reza Aslan and *Believer*, in the course of this response I will first argue that the journalist who performs as an ethnographer—as Aslan does—claims to have privileged access to "authentic," that is unmediated, knowledge about the world. This claim is credited by specific forms of mostly cultural capital such as academic diplomas, language skills, or biographical narratives that are recognized as legitimate and authoritative in the media field. Through his employment of and his performance in the ethnographic mode, Aslan converts specific kinds of capital into symbolic capital based on which he strives towards objectifying his particular point of view on religion stemming from his specific position in the social field. The program naturalizes Aslan's particular negotiation of religion. It becomes common sense and a norm that forces itself on society. Concurrently, Aslan obfuscates the power relations that give rise to the specific discourse on religious diversity.

In a second step, I will briefly discuss a German TV production, *Der Moscheereport* (The Mosque Report), in which the journalist Constantin Schreiber also employs an ethnographic mode to produce a specific narrative pertaining to religious diversity but with a different strategic aim. It is not about perennialism and finding the true and good elements in each religious tradition. He focuses exclusively on Islam, which is part of the broader religious texture of German society, and aims to identify the elements that are crucial for "Islam" to be an "integral" part of German society. The underlying idea is that all other religions in this diverse, multi-religious society are already integrated and have become part of society. Islam is not (yet) that far and in need of change or adaptation.

The discussion of *Believer* and *Der Moscheereport* directs our attention to the more hidden ways through which symbolic capital achieves its purpose and produces (symbolic) power. It also brings the indeterminacy of (symbolic) power under scrutiny: The elements of the social world are elastic and can be interpreted in different ways which leads to a plurality of vision and to "the battlefields" of which Bourdieu and Wacquant talk, where the symbolic struggle over the legitimate perception of the social world is fought and never fully resolved (Bourdieu 1989: 20). Both, Aslan and Schreiber employ the ethnographic mode and try to produce hegemonic knowledge within the discourse of religious diversity. The ways in which they operationalize the ethnographic mode and the strategic positions taken within this discourse are, however, points of difference.

The Ethnographic Mode, Religious Diversity and the Master Narrative of Perennialism

Before turning to *Believer*, a brief discussion of the role of narration in the academic field of ethnography is necessary in order to understand how Aslan imports the ethnographic mode into the media field and what he achieves by doing so. The aim here is not to say that ethnography or fieldwork in the academic field is the same as in the media field. Rather, the debate within the academic field about the nature and effects of ethnography does us good service in order to understand strategies and dynamics taking place in the media field.

Ethnography is as much about writing or representation as it is about fieldwork. Ethnographers strive to produce convincing narrative accounts of specific cultural sites in their field notes and their ethnographies. The so-called Writing Culture Debate (see Clifford and Marcus 1986) and works of scholars like Hayden White have drawn our attention to the literary quality of cultural and social science texts and the work they do in representing reality. White (1980: 6) argues with Roland Barthes that the narrative form is inevitable for any account of how things happened or how one has experienced something, and that narratives are translatable "in a way that a lyric poem or a philosophical discourse is not." Ethnographers narrate in order to achieve the translation work from their research field to a broader audience which does not necessarily share the dispositions and socio-cultural habitus of those who are part of the research field. Van Maanen (1988) groups the different styles of ethnographic writing into three kinds of narrative: realist, confessional, and impressionist tales. Realist tales represent reality in a solid monological and monosemic master narrative, weaving different pieces of data provided by the subjects together. Confessional tales are highly personal accounts of the involvement of the ethnographer in the field revealing self-consciousness and emotional response to the research setting. Finally, impressionist tales are unique stories from the field that startle the audience and do not represent the ordinary course of events though they are meant to underline general features. Although all three kinds of narrative modes are used in contemporary ethnographies, anthropologists have noted a broad shift from "realist" to "confessional" and "impressionist" tales since the 1970s that has accompanied the growing emphasis in anthropological theory on notions such as practice, experience, performance, self, person, subject, and agent (see for instance Ortner 1984 and Tedlock 1991). Van Maanen's typology of narratives employed in ethnographies might help us to understand the narrative strategies in *Believer* and, concomitantly, in *Der Moscheereport*.

Turning to the media field and Aslan's *Believer*, we see a well-crafted mixture of all three kinds of narratives. Aslan uses impressionist and confessional narratives in the production in order to highlight experiences and emotions, to label them as religious, and to frame them as good or bad. In episode one on the Aghori Sadhus, Aslan confides to the audience how appalled and nauseated he feels at the prospect of entering the Ganges due to its obvious pollution. In another episode on the veneration of Santa Muerte in Mexico, he confesses that he feels connected to the figure of the saint. These confessional tales are mingled with impressionist scenes and narratives that can be expected to generate attention and views such as the Aghori drinking his own urine. However, these scenes do not work to unsettle the master narrative of religious diversity of humanity and perennialism. They are rather a building block of the "realist tale" that every religious tradition harbors authentic and good elements located in the realm of the personal: experiences, practices, and beliefs of individual believers. The "good" side is associated with so called reform or moderate groups which have been marginalized by the mainstream of the specific tradition such as the reform Scientologists who have been outcast by the Church of Scientology or the followers of Rabbi Nachman who strive for a continual state of happiness. It seems as if Aslan's distinction between good and bad religion opposes what is considered to be part of the orthodoxy of a specific tradition to what is considered to be heterodox. He also tends to shift in his semantic repertoire from the term religion to the terms belief and believer which highlights the shift away from institutionalized, men-made religion as embodied in the caste system, for instance, towards personal faith. Aslan has made this distinction in several interviews in which he also self-identifies as "a person of faith" (Fassler 2013).

Aslan's meta-narrative is vested with credibility by the cultural capital with the help of which he is able to occupy the interstice between the academic and the journalistic fields. His diplomas and titles in religious studies (BA) and theology, as well as fine arts (MA) and sociology (PhD) provide him with the institutionalized cultural capital necessary to be recognized in the public as an expert on religion. He is a faculty member of the Department of Creative Writing at UC Riverside which grounds him in the academic world. Furthermore, he highlights biographical narrative elements such as his own spiritual search and his family's migration from Iran to the US in 1979 in the course of the so-called Islamic Revolution. He embodies the "academic scholar of religion," the "person of faith," and the "victim of oppressive religion." In *Believer* he draws from this entire symbolic repertoire when he, for instance, introduces the audience to Orthodox Judaism, shares intimate spiritual moments, and discusses the repressive side of institutionalized religion.

Due to the sensibilities and dispositions that come with this cultural capital, Aslan is able to perform in the ethnographic mode and to produce the impression of unmediated and hence authentic experience and emotion. We can understand each episode as a short ethnography in the sense of field notes combining realist, impressionist, and confessional tales in order to weave the story of a multitude of religions and beliefs of which each has a true, universal, and "good" core. The latter, according to this storyline, is for the most part not to be found in the more orthodox strands of the belief traditions. By telling these stories, he delineates the realm of "true belief" from the realm of "bad religion" preferring the term belief whenever he narrates "good religion." The term belief indicates a conviction that is personally held and confidence in the truthfulness of something. These are notions that are intimately tied to the individual mind and body nexus. "Good" religion as authentic or "unmediated" belief is therefore to be found within the individual and not in institutions or congregations.

Aslan is not alone in telling a story about "good" and "bad" religion in the ethnographic mode. He competes with other actors in the media field as well as in the academic field. Another example of a production trying to uncover what is "really" going on and what people "really" believe, is the German series *Der Moscheereport*, aired around the same time as Aslan's *Believer*.

The Ethnographic Mode, Religious Diversity, and the Integration of Islam

In the spring of 2017, three episodes of *Der Moscheereport*, broadcast on German public television (Tagesschau24), received attention and critique in the public sphere.[2] In this production, acclaimed young journalist Constantin Schreiber, who is fluent in Arabic and has field experience in Muslim majority countries, visits mosques "trying to find out what is going on there." In the promo for the show, which was played as an intro at the beginning of every episode, he is seen entering a mosque while he states in a voiceover that "this is a threshold that only a few Germans cross, the threshold to one of the many mosques in our country. They are for most of us an alien world." He then asks a series of questions that are all geared towards the integration of Muslim communities and the role of mosques therein. This actually sets the stage of his approach to the mosque as an institution and a community: The people there, Muslim migrants, are not part of the imagined "us," the non-Muslim Germans.

The roughly 15-minute shows are divided in two main parts: In the first part, Schreiber and a camera team visit a mosque, provide some information on it, attend the Friday prayer, and show fragments of the sermon. Visitors of the mosques are only shown but not interviewed or talked to. At the end of the first part, the preacher or imam is interviewed in Arabic or German. In the second part, Schreiber is in a studio setting similar to a news room and interviews an academic expert on the mosque that has been portrayed before and its role in the process of integration. The focus of the show is on the *khutba*, the Friday sermon given in mosques and usually covering a specific topic that is of concern for the spiritual and social wellbeing of the community. While the production did not go further than three episodes covering three mosques with one *khutba* each, Schreiber discusses in his accompanying book *Inside Islam: Was in Deutschlands Moscheen gepredigt wird* (Inside Islam: What is being preached in Germany's mosques) his visits to Friday sermons in 13 different mosques. In interviews around the publication of the book, Schreiber voiced his concern over the role of mosques in the process of integration of Muslims in Germany and problematized the role of the imams. While stating that the book is not representative, he claims that the Friday sermons in general call for segregation from German society (see Franz 2017 or Sasse 2017). The results of his research were in Schreiber's own words "sobering": "In terms of content, I went home rather dissatisfied since most of the sermons did not have any reference to real life in this country" (Trotier 2017). A short promotional text accompanying the publication of the book paints the picture of a large amorphous section of the population that

> lives among us and still we hardly know anything about them. How many Muslims are there actually in Germany and how and where do they practice their faith? [...] Where can you find mosques and what do the imams preach during Friday sermon? How do they talk about Germany when no camera is present and people feel unobserved?[3]

A quick search through the public databases of the Federal Statistical Office and reading some of the ever-increasing amount of literature on Muslims in Germany produced in the academic field might already answer these questions. However, these questions are not posed in order to be answered. They are performed under the ethnographic mode: Schreiber is portrayed as someone stepping into yet unknown and uncharted territory. The promotional text furthermore claims that Schreiber conducts research in a reality that "is unintelligible for many and which affects our society as never before."

These brief glimpses into the story told by Schreiber embody the overall master narrative of the three episodes. They center on the examination of the "integrability" (Integrationsfähigkeit) of one specific tradition constructed as "Islam." The people subsumed under this tradition are marked as different as is the reality they live in. Schreiber's meta-narrative is therefore the fundamental foreignness of Islam—and in extension of Muslims in general—and the question of integration into a society constructed as secular. During the episodes and in interviews, Schreiber considers as authentic what happens behind the scenes, when no camera is present and the Muslim congregation deems itself "alone," that is with no non-Muslim among them. Due to this rhetorical move, everything that the imams say to Schreiber during the interviews remains potentially doubtful and suspect: After all, they might be saying something totally different in the intimacy of the mosque without the attentive eye of the camera. Schreiber claims to enter an "alien world" in order to find out what is "truly" going on there in terms of integration. However, this can result at best in a good impression, but how will "they" talk when "we" are not there? Doubt is there to remain.

The ethnographic mode Schreiber employs is purely observational. He purports to tell a realistic tale about a specific mosque from a neutral point of view. However, he replaces every practice that is linked to mosques with the Friday sermon. The Friday sermon is not the essential element of mosque life. He ignores a whole range of activities from Ramadan festivities, prayer for the dead, coaching for school, youth clubs, reading circles, advising, or just hanging out in the adjacent cafeterias or the main hall. He takes a specific, unique though regular element of mosque life, the Friday sermon, a specific practice that is not attended by the entire community, as *pars pro toto*, and zooms into it. He tells a realistic story by employing impressionist tales without contextualizing these impressions. Instead, what is happening there becomes the general, the true, the authentic. The Arabic title to the production "[shedding] light on the pulpit" (*dhuʾ ʿala al-minbar*)[4] is telling considering the logic which drives

Schreiber's ethnographic mode: finding the hidden, true meaning of Islam and bringing it to the attention of the German public by shedding light on the Friday sermon. Confessional elements are lacking since there is no interaction between the "journalist-ethnographer" venturing into "unknown," "alien" worlds and the "natives," the one exception being short interviews with the imams of the mosques. In the story told by Schreiber, he is not part of it, only its narrator. Perception is not mediated through him but constructed to be brought to the viewer pure and raw. Concomitantly, the first part of each episode is framed to comprise raw ethnographic data which in turn is analyzed in the second part of each episode together with an academic. The questions posed are evaluative and meant to provide the platform for the academic "expert" to adjudicate on the role of the mosque in terms of "integration." The second part defines the issues that are decisive for evaluating the "integrability" of Muslims. The focus therefore is on the role of women in mosques, on German language skills, or on citizenship.

It is for instance telling to consider what is actually meant when talking about language skills. It is not only the expectation that Muslims—and, first and foremost: "their" imams—master German sufficiently in order to participate. In one episode, Schreiber comments in a voiceover on the "broken German" (*brüchiges Deutsch*) of a person who is providing a brief summary of the sermon that had been given in Arabic just before. When listening closely to the summary, the person in question has an accent of somebody whose first language is not German. But he hardly makes any mistake. This is quite an achievement considering that he was providing the summary spontaneously while translating from his notes.

Similar to Aslan in *Believer*, Schreiber is visually and aurally the center of the production. His point of view is represented by the camera as it gazes into the mosque and hovers over the heads of attending people being immersed in what seems to be praying or reading the Quran on their smartphones. In the first episode for instance, he appears as the figure sitting on the cold floor among the community of a mosque located in an underground parking in Hamburg. While he seems to be close and to be sharing the space with "them," his body language communicates difference: He sits upright, does not look to the front where the *minbar* (pulpit) is located but watches in an exploratory and investigative manner every move of those around him. He scans the space and looks boldly into faces. During prayer and sermon, he positions himself at the side-line leaning against a wall while others are sitting, listening or performing the prayer. While Aslan takes his center position to lead the viewer to identify and participate with the "believers" on Aslan's terms, Schreiber in contrast positions the viewer as observer of a group of people, shunning interaction or contact but scrutinizing and inspecting the place and the people. In ethnographic terms, Aslan and Schreiber represent the two extremes of the ethnographic mode: "Going native" and constructing oneself as a neutral, detached, and objective access point to the world of the alien other.

Comparing their institutionalized cultural capital, Schreiber is firmly situated in the field of journalism while Aslan is primarily rooted in the academic field. Schreiber studied Law in Germany and spent some time in Egypt while an intern with a trading company where he perfected his Arabic. He says that he spent some time in Syria as a teenager but the context remains unclear. After his studies he trained as a journalist with Deutsche Welle, Germany's public international broadcaster, and received a grant to attend Oxford University. He held different positions with Deutsche Welle, such as correspondent based in Dubai from 2007 to 2008, and Arabic newspapers like Lebanon's *Daily Star*, for which he worked in 2006. From 2009 until 2011, he served as a social media aide to the German Federal Foreign Office and accompanied members of the government and the President of the European Commission on their travels to the Middle East. Since 2011, he has advanced his career in journalism working as host, producer, and correspondent based in Berlin. During the so called refugee crisis in Europe, he produced a TV show with the German news outlet N-TV called *Marhaba, Ankommen in Deutschland* (Marhaba [Arabic for "welcome"], arriving in Germany).[5] In this show he explains in 5-minute episodes "the Germans and life in Germany." He focuses on topics such as women in Germany or the German constitution. This production, for which he received a prestigious award for TV productions (Grimme Preis), was his breakthrough and firmly established him in the field of accredited journalism.

Conclusion: The Ethnographic Mode, Religious Diversity, and the Euphemization of Social Relations

Aslan and Schreiber produce a story that is nested in the broader discourse of religious diversity. The narrative is generated through an ethnographic mode and constructed as "authentic" in the sense of unmediated and raw. While telling their stories respectively, they define and mark central issues and use classifications that bind and thereby also divide. The ethnographic mode covers up this classificatory work achieved in both productions and sets the reality for religious diversity and religion in general. The different narrative strategies are not employed to lay bare the ambiguities, contradictions and power relations inherent to social life but to, to conclude with Bourdieu again, euphemize social relations according to their own classifications.

Narrative tales as the building blocks of the ethnographic mode are based on language in the broadest sense of the word. For Bourdieu, all language involves euphemization as a kind of "play off between form and information, dictated by the social conditions of production" (Grenfell 2011: 55). Euphemization denies or obscures economic or political truth. As a result, social relations and structures operating under the discourse on religious diversity are established and/or preserved according to the classifications of those exerting symbolic power. Euphemization can only remain effective as long as it achieves its misrecognition: as long as the contingent and partial systems of classification upholding specific social relations are perceived as natural and authentic.

Carmen Becker is a political scientist, Islamicist and scholar of religion working as a Lecturer and Researcher at the Religious Studies Unit of the Leibniz Universität Hannover, Germany.

Notes

1. Of course, this leaves out much of the academic debate on fieldwork and ethnography. In this contribution I am talking about the ethnographic mode as understood by the broader public.
2. All three episodes are available on the official channel of "tagesschau" on YouTube: https://youtu.be/Y_VU1BV6p_I.
3. From the author page of Constantin Schreiber on Amazon: www.amazon.de/Inside-Islam-Deutschlands-Moscheen-gepredigt/dp/3430202183 (archived at archive.today/77z46).
4. Interestingly, the Turkish, French, and English titles are literal translations of the German Der Moscheereport.
5. The five-minute videos are available on the website of N-TV: www.n-tv.de/marhaba/Man-muss-die-Menschen-direkt-ansprechen-article16028561.html (archived at archive.today/lxHqu).

References

Bourdieu, Pierre. 1989. "Social Space and Symbolic Power." *Sociological Theory* 7(1): 14–25. https://doi.org/10.2307/202060

Bourdieu, Pierre. 1998. *Practical Reason: On the Theory of Action*. Stanford, CA: Stanford University Press.

Bourdieu, Pierre. 1999. *On Television*. New York: New Press.

Bourdieu, Pierre and Loïc Wacquant. 1992. *An Invitation to Reflexive Sociology*. Chicago, IL: University of Chicago Press.

Clifford, James and George E. Marcus. 1986. *Writing Culture: The Poetics and Politics of Ethnography*. Berkeley, CA: University of California Press.

Fassler, Joe. 2013. "The Book that Changed Reza Aslan's Mind about Jesus." Interview with Reza Aslan. *The Atlantic*, August 6. Retrieved from www.theatlantic.com/entertainment/archive/2013/08/the-book-that-changed-reza-aslans-mind-about-jesus/278410/ (archived at archive.today/AjcQV).

Fillitz, Thomas and A. Jamie Saris. 2012. *Debating Authenticity: Concepts of Modernity in Anthropological Perspective*. New York: Berghahn Books.

Franz, Rüdiger. 2017. "Constantin Schreiber warnt vor muslimischen Parallelwelten." Interview with Constantin Schreiber. *Bonner General-Anzeiger*, May 22. Retrieved from www.general-anzeiger-bonn.de/news/politik/deutschland/Constantin-Schreiber-warnt-vor-muslimischen-Parallelwelten-article3561560.html (archived at archive.today/BlRRC)

Grenfell, Michael. 2011. *Bourdieu, Language and Linguistics*. London: Continuum.

Lindholm, Charles. 2008. *Culture and Authenticity*. Malden, MA: Blackwell.

Ortner, Sherry B. 1984. "Theory in Anthropology since the Sixties." *Comparative Studies in Society and History* 26(1): 126–166. https://doi.org/10.1017/S0010417500010811

Sasse, Sabine. 2017. "Hoppla, was wird denn hier für eine Meinung verbreitet!" Interview with Constantin Schreiber. *Der Tagesspiegel*, March 27. Retrieved from www.tagesspiegel.de/medien/der-moscheereport-mit-constantin-schreiber-hoppla-was-wird-denn-hier-fuer-eine-meinung-verbreitet/19570320.html (archived at archive.today/YP0c9).

Tedlock, Barbara 1991. "From Participant Observation to the Observation of Participation: The Emergence of Narrative Ethnography." *Journal of Anthropological Research* 47(1): 69–94. https://doi.org/10.1086/jar.47.1.3630581

Trotier, Kilian. 2017. "Gäbe es mehr wie ihn, wäre viel gewonnen." Interview with Constantin Schreiber. *Die Zeit* 15. Retrieved from www.zeit.de/2017/15/constantin-schreiber-inside-islam-interview (archived at archive.today/byibx).

Van Maanen, John. 1988. *Tales of the Field: On Writing Ethnography*. Chicago, IL: University of Chicago Press.

Wacquant, Loïc. 2013. "Symbolic Power and Group-Making: On Pierre Bourdieu's Reframing of Class." *Journal of Classical Sociology* 13(2): 274–291. https://doi.org/10.1177/1468795X12468737

White, Hayden. 1980. "The Value of Narrativity in the Representation of Reality." *Critical Inquiry* 7(1), 5–27. https://doi.org/10.1086/448086

Chapter 10

Scopophilia and the Manufacture of "Good" Religion

Leslie Dorrough Smith

I have the pleasure of teaching an interdisciplinary course called "Christianity and Film" with a colleague who is a documentary filmmaker. One of the most interesting aspects of this class, for me, is the manner in which she describes the importance of a predictable narrative arc to the financial success of a film. In other words, one important measure in whether we call something a "good" movie has to do with whether the plot resolves in a way that we find emotionally satisfying, or that gives us closure. Personally, I can relate rather well to this: I would far prefer to leave the theatre with a very particular sort of feeling (no matter if it's pleasant, or even one I didn't anticipate) rather than one laced with ambiguity.

What this means, more practically speaking, is that audiences are willing to pay money to see and hear a story that, in many ways, they've already seen and heard before. While that may seem a little silly (if not a bit boring) on the surface, social psychologists have argued that most people are rather clear in their preference for something familiar over something new, even when that new thing might be in their best interest or a more logical choice. Psychologist Jonathan Haidt (2012: 56) has argued, for instance, that most people don't make ethical decisions via a rational process; rather, most of us side with our pre-existing and often deep-seated biases or convictions—regardless of their logic—and then manufacture a suitable rationale after the fact to support that vantage point.

But of course, this is not how we often conceptualize our own thinking, which we usually believe to be tempered and rational. This is why I am intrigued by the fact that learning about an audience's desire for narrative predictability is frequently just as jarring to my (majority Christian) students as are controversial portrayals of Jesus in films like, say, *Jesus of Montreal* or *The Last Temptation of Christ*. Their discomfort at finding out that they, too, gravitate towards the safe and known does at least somewhat destroy the image of Hollywood that many of them hold dear, one of unique artistic expression that supposedly defies the status quo (predictability be damned!). Nevertheless, the larger injury is probably the realization that what felt like their own deeply personal response to their favorite film might actually have been a rather predictable, cookie-cutter, pre-planned emotional event orchestrated by people they don't know—and one that was explicitly designed to separate them from their wallets, at that.

So at the end of that class, when a student occasionally remarks that we've "ruined movies for them" (they always laugh nervously when they say this), I believe them, for it is uncomfortable and unsettling to find that an entire universe of economic motive and psychological manipulation is at work in the things that bring us enjoyment, not to mention our very perceptions of reality. Interestingly, students tell me the same thing about the way that they look at many of their day-to-day social interactions after having taken one of my courses on gender (where we also analyze aspects of our identities that are often taken for granted), and it is in this interesting overlap of media and gender that I would like to focus our attention in this essay.

As we consider how the media-consuming Western world understands religion today, it would seem that the picture is moving away from blatantly xenophobic portrayals. Most critical observers recognize that the very white, Christian bias of some Western media consumers is often reinforced in those conservative media outlets that still attempt to situate any number of non-Christian groups as weird, at best, but as downright dangerous, at worst. But equally as common, it seems, are the efforts of other media agencies to create an image of various religious groups that is, they argue, more even, more objective, and more diverse.

This is, in fact, much how Reza Aslan described the television show he created and hosted, called *Believer*, which originally aired on CNN in early 2017. Aslan pitched the program as something akin to the late Anthony Bourdain's popular show *Parts Unknown*, in which Bourdain, a chef, went globe-trotting in search of new and unusual international food experiences (Makarechi 2017). Although *Believer* was cancelled abruptly for reasons largely independent of its content (Aslan used a profanity when describing American President Donald Trump, and CNN responded with his firing and the show's cancellation), it is to this content that I wish to turn, for Aslan has been very vocal in portraying the now-defunct program as something that was immensely positive due in large part to its capacity to expose people to new ideas and thereby erase prejudice. He notes:

> We could give an audience an experience, unlike anything that they would normally have, to confront some of their own misconceptions and their prejudices, and to take them from a place of uncomfortableness to a place of understanding. It was one of the greatest joys of my life to see the overwhelmingly positive response that this show had on people, that it really did just blow people's minds. My career has been based on trying to break down the walls that separate us into different religions, or ethnicities, or races. In the back of my mind for years was always this germ of an idea to do a show in which I immerse myself in various religious traditions around the world as a way of opening up windows to other ways of thinking, other ways of believing, and to force people to recognize just how much they have in common with people that they think couldn't be more different than them. (Blyth 2017)

With the aforementioned references to security, safety, and predictability in mind, I am interested in challenging Aslan's argument that the show fundamentally markets newness and diversity by considering how *Believer* peddles in a specific form of objectification that feeds into certain safe and predictable stereotypes about religion. As I will discuss, this is accomplished through many of the visual and rhetorical dynamics of the show, dynamics that are designed to depict both Aslan and the show's other characters as domesticated, benign, and safe from the outset—rather than "different," as Aslan describes them.

To make this argument, I want to draw on Laura Mulvey's now famous 1975 media critique entitled *Visual Pleasure and Narrative Cinema*, in which Mulvey identifies Hollywood tricks of the trade that have, over time, created a seamless and naturalized image of a dependent and yet sexualized woman, one that is so familiar and appealing to audiences that they hardly question this character trope even as it remains highly constructed and, for all intents and purposes, unrealistic and misogynistic. I want to employ Mulvey's argumentation not because I believe that Aslan and the producers of *Believer* are sexually objectifying women in their program, but because Mulvey provides an interesting framework through which we can consider the process of how visual objectification operates. I use the term "objectification" not just to mean the symbolic transformation of people into objects (dehumanizing them in the process), but more to the point, the systems by which the relative power of various individuals is established. To Mulvey, this objectification transpires when women are turned into sexual objects; for *Believer*, this process occurs when its characters are transformed through liberal Western tropes about religion into "good religious people." I believe that thinking through Mulvey's argument can help us ask important questions about how *Believer* and other similar forms of media that tout their liberal educational value operate as agents of objectification and why they have such widespread appeal. So to better understand this dynamic, let's turn to Mulvey's argument.

Scopophilia and Audience Emotion

In *Visual Pleasure and Narrative Cinema*, Mulvey's aim is to explore how our pleasure in watching certain types of media is generated by a series of other pre-existing emotions that structure the world, thus unknowingly leading to that world's regeneration (Mulvey 1999: 833). Mulvey is interested, in other words, in thinking about why we like to look at certain images, and how looking at them repeatedly normalizes the states they depict. Focusing specifically on film, she argues (ibid.: 835) that the cinema is a type of voyeurism—where we, in a dark theatre, peek into the lives of others—that makes this emotional reproduction possible due in great part to *scopophilia*, which was Freud's term for the pleasure that we take in viewing certain images.

The ways in which we view film, she notes, are different from other sorts of performance (such as live theatre, for instance). The reason for this is that the very technologies of film (editing, shot angles, lighting, etc.) naturalize their otherwise manufactured state; we can only see, in other words, the image that the camera captured, and even then, can only see it in the way it was designed for our consumption (that is, in terms of editing, lighting, etc.) (Mulvey 1999: 843). But despite this rather intentional image construction, we are ready to adopt what we see on screen as some form of naturalized reality because such images tap into our larger cultural norms and desires (ibid.: 833). In the world of cinema, what is "real" is thus limited to what the camera shows.

Mulvey was the inventor of the concept "the male gaze," and that concept is critical in this work, for Mulvey's entire argument is that most movies are shot from the vantage point of a heterosexual male. In other words, if the camera is the movie goer's eyes, then most movies are designed to reinforce images that would be pleasurable to most heterosexual men functioning under patriarchy, which Mulvey understands in the traditional feminist sense as men whose masculinity is defined, in great part, by conquest, aggression, and the sexual desire of women. Thus when she argues that "the phallus" is always symbolically present in film, she means that the film is shot using subjects, angles, themes, acts, and emotions that reinforce a particular view of masculinity. As such, there is no actual moment when men are not at the center of every scene, even when no man is physically present in any one scene (Mulvey 1999: 837ff, 833–834).

With that background, there are two types of images that are scopophilic (Mulvey 1999: 837–839). The first are basic sexual images of women that are pleasurable to view because they create heterosexual male desire. Beyond simple bodily compartmentalization/objectification, where the camera is only focused on breasts, mouths, buttocks, etc., other classic examples of scopophilia include: (a) when the camera pans up the body of a woman, starting at her feet and moving to her face; (b) when the camera's center is right at the collarbone such that a woman's breasts are central even as we can still see her face; and (c) when women are posed in scenes in ways that they would not probably perform in real life so as to heighten some sexualized aspect of their appearance (bent over a desk, shown in profile so as to accentuate their breasts while their male counterparts delivers their lines facing the camera, etc.).

Beyond this more blatant sexual objectification, scopophilia can happen a second way, Mulvey observes. Here the visual pleasure occurs when the audience member emotionally subsumes the character of the protagonist, thereby becoming a surrogate protagonist, normalizing most everything that the protagonist does or represents (Mulvey 1999: 838). For Mulvey, the fact that most protagonists are not female is a critical example of scopophilic dynamics at work, for what is desirable viewing is, again, power; so while male viewers may vicariously experience a sensation of power (and thus pleasure) from watching a male protagonist, a woman is likely to experience something similar simply by virtue of the fact that the image of male power is safe and familiar. (Notably, Mulvey was also one of the first media analysts to demonstrate how sexism relegates women to secondary, accessory roles in narrative formation insomuch that their job is to further the usually male protagonist's character arc; ibid.: 833, 837–842.)

Scopophilia under Mulvey's analysis, then, refers to the various ways in which we take pleasure in viewing the acting-out of the power relations between characters in a film. While the role of sex as an instrument of power is a vital part of Mulvey's argument about film, I believe that we can generally de-sexualize her overall model and still come away with an important framework for understanding how power operates through different types of media offerings. If, as feminist scholars have long argued, the purpose of objectifying women is not just to turn them into objects, but in so doing, to domesticate or delimit their power, then it is interesting to consider what other media techniques assist audiences in performing the same mental domestication when they interact with new people or experiences. With that said, let me condense what I've just shared of Mulvey's work into five basic points that will be helpful in following my argument:

- First, objectification is a process by which one group asserts power over another by engaging in acts of compartmentalization and power differentiation; that is, certain characters are clearly secondary to others who are clearly primary. Primary characters (usually protagonists) tend to typify social norms of strength and dominance.

- Second, the camera is not neutral; what it shows in both content and form is representative of a particular hegemonic perspective.

- Third, the things we see induce pleasure because they induce desire, and we tend to desire power, or if we cannot have that, familiarity. Often, they are the same thing.

- Fourth, as such, the protagonist in most films not only represents cultural ideals of power, but is also the person to whom we relate, regardless of whether we actually embody those characteristics ourselves.

- Fifth, and finally, cultural "others" act as accessories that help along the protagonist's story.

Let me take a moment to point out what might be obvious, and that is that Mulvey's framework can be used to describe how many types of prejudice are socially instantiated and then replicated, including everything from sexism to racism to classism to ethnocentrism, particularly. But what is intriguing to me is how closely the structure of *Believer* and other similarly perennialist programs mirror Mulvey's model, for in breaking down each of Mulvey's key points, we will find that *Believer* relies heavily on the same symbolic themes (i.e., the establishment of a dominant character who embodies a taken-for-granted normativity; the secondary nature of other characters to the identity of the first; the pleasure in viewing that comes from the reinforcement of established power roles).

In this sense, *Believer* is specifically scopophilic precisely because watching it reinforces a variety of reassuring, familiar, and (from these) pleasurable power motifs that are used widely in more progressive public images of religion today. For many Western audiences, the threat of the religious "other" comes not just from fear of terrorism and other sorts of violent activity, but is more deeply embedded in perennialist assumptions that "authentic" religion is generally about love, acceptance, and liberal notions of social justice. But as with many perennialist claims, this positive attitude towards the institution of religion has a built-in mechanism that stops it from validating anything that might be considered extremist by Western standards, including any behavior that is socially uncouth to middle-class sensibilities. Even though a large proportion of religious people around the world display such "negative" behaviors as part and parcel of how they understand religion, what we see in *Believer* is one very selective, perennialized snapshot of religion that is intended, nevertheless, to stand in for "difference" more broadly.

Believer as a Scopophilic Experience

It might be helpful to think of *Believer*, and Aslan in particular, much in the way that the show markets him—as something like a tour guide taking us, the audience, on a particular adventure. But this portrayal might be somewhat misplaced, for my argument here is that the show is actually about Aslan, as I will further elaborate. The centrality of Aslan is actually fairly critical to his scopophilic portrayal, for he is identified as a scholar of religion at the beginning of every show, and refers to himself as such throughout. It is vital to keep in mind that, if objectification is a process by which one person is clearly in power over another, then Aslan's power dynamic in the show is already well-secured: he's the expert, the one in charge.

In addition to his role as expert, his power also stems from the fact that he is a translator of sorts. Aslan is the person who provides context and reason to the people and groups we meet; put differently, he is the filter through which the different is approachable, if not tamed. This may seem an unusual role for him to play, since he is a brown Muslim man. After all, for the (unspoken white Christian) audience, isn't he supposed to be the very "outsider" we're encountering along our journey?

This might be true except for the fact that Aslan is very privileged in so many clear ways in the show: not only is he clearly very cosmopolitan, traditionally handsome, and well-educated, but he comes across as extremely articulate, charismatic, and likeable. As the "voice of reason," he is also a person to whom we relate—he domesticates the foreign; he is the audience's "cool Muslim friend." In this sense, the audience not only relates to Aslan personally, but also takes on his—the protagonist's—perspective. This is one of those moments where Aslan's class and social capital not only overcome what might otherwise be his power liability (his race, religion, and ethnicity), but because he has secured these other traditional symbols of power, what began as liabilities are transformed into privileges of a sort: his status as friendly cultural "other" grants him symbolic insider weight to barter in the language of exoticism and spirituality, tapping into the longstanding Orientalist impulse.

This balance of things is vitally important, for if there is one sort of narrative pleasure that many Westerners seem to demand, it is the triumph of sentimental spirituality tempered by occasional appeals to reason. One could argue, in fact, that Aslan's role in the show is one of domestication. In many, if not most, episodes, he has a discussion with the camera as if the audience is his confidant, during which he first questions the logic of the members of the religious group in question, and, after usually finding their reason lacking, he next considers their motives. From a content perspective, the questions he asks participants are clearly intended to push the religious person to justify themselves according to the standards of Western Protestant rationality ("Do you really believe in this guy?" he asks a follower of a man named "JeZus," who lives in a self-built hut in a rural Hawai'ian jungle and who engages in gibberish ranting and wild gesticulating as a means of introducing Aslan to his religion).[1]

Yet Aslan stops short of pressing the rationality issue too forcefully, generally following the perennialist script by concluding that so long as his subjects are experiencing some sort of spiritual awakening that doesn't hurt anyone else, then they've tapped into "real" religion—that is, until they make him uncomfortable. In one noteworthy episode where this occurs, an Aghouri Hindu man who Aslan at first reveres as a guru (Aslan has, in fact, sought him out for spiritual guidance) is later clearly deemed something of a fraud when the man throws excrement at Aslan as he attempts an interaction.[2] This has gone too far; Aslan physically runs away from the man, as the audience might be inclined to do, as well. But as a foil to that emotional shock, the episode ends with a conversation with another Hindu man—this one from a different anti-caste group committed to social equality—who, in addition to wearing Western clothing and engaging in traditional acts of charity (helping orphans, running schools for the poor, etc.), counterbalances what we have previously seen by reaffirming the very popular Western—if comparatively less popular Indian—notion that God wants love and equality for everyone.[3]

Indeed, each episode closes with a summative narrative that attempts to situate the group's idiosyncrasies within a context of their perennialist merit. This is often accompanied visually by instances of physical objectification, wherein many disembodied close-ups (often in slow-motion and still shot) of eyes, hands, and smiling faces are set to new-age style music. In addition to these shots, there is also the matter of Aslan's partial (if not, at times, total, blurred-out, full frontal) nudity, and here it might be fair game to re-enlist the sexual elements of Mulvey's model. Throughout several episodes, Aslan's body is on display when he is accomplishing some sort of "spiritual task" or other feat of strength (of which there are at least one or two per episode). Anytime other men around him are not wearing their shirts, he joins in readily. In one episode he literally walks around nude after a ritual challenge.[4]

Apart from these sexualized elements that litter the show, the very presentation of Aslan's subjects induce pleasure, insomuch as they involve two of pleasure's elements – novelty and control: (1) the audience is watching new, exotic things from the safety of their homes; (2) they have Aslan as the masculinized scholar whose physical and mental prowess keeps the show psychologically safe, since he "pulls the plug" if things get too much (in addition to the aforementioned Aghouri guru, in another episode he cannot spend the night in a cave as an initiation ritual because he is too uncomfortable);[5] and (3) almost every episode ends with the smiling faces of the group members in question, so that the unease of knowing that "people like that" are out in the world can be satisfactorily resolved by their good intentions.

From the Protagonist's Eyes

With all of this said, I think it's naïve to think that *Believer* is about anyone but Aslan, as Mulvey might agree is true of the centrality of the protagonist to most scopophilic media. I don't mean that as a personal indictment per se, nor do I say this necessarily as a larger critique of perennialism (although with more space and in another venue, that critique does have merit). Rather, my comment is a response to the fact that Aslan describes *Believer* as a show depicting the process by which the audience watches *him* become "immersed" in a particular religion so as to explain it back to them, thereby channeling all new experiences through his own familiar, safe persona. This explains not just Aslan's behaviors during the episodes, wherein he engages in the very sorts of controversial acts that make the groups upon which he focuses interesting, such as eating human brains, drinking blood, slaughtering animals, etc. It also accounts for the fact that, in virtually every episode, he describes his interactions with the group as something like his own insider conversion (along the way making claims such as "I feel Jewish today") that he can promptly shake off once the new episode airs.[6]

Several Hindu groups (among others) have taken offense at his portrayal of their religion on the grounds that he sensationalizes and oversimplifies their beliefs and practices to the degree that he may, ironically, turn audiences against them (Safi 2017). But while these debates over the "true" depiction of a religion focus on authenticity claims that usually involve status disputes between groups rather than objective states that can be definitively measured, my critical interest in this critique of Aslan lies with what he omits in his presentation. By focusing on a series of ritual acts and assorted belief claims, Aslan manages to divorce religion almost entirely from the historical-cultural contexts that create it in the first place. For example, no serious scholar of Hinduism can discuss contemporary caste dynamics (as does Aslan) without—at the very least—in-depth consideration of the political and historical dynamics that have characterized nineteenth- and twentieth-century India, for this is, in great part, where those very dynamics come from. And yet severing these acts from their history not only makes for easier-watching TV, but also reinforces the popular perennialist notion (that so wooed my own students in their movie watching) that our feelings and experiences are just that—our own—and thus are only tangentially connected to the outside world.

As such, what we are watching is Aslan's own character arc, assisted by the "others" around him, rather than a show about the others to which Aslan is only a sideline accessory. It is interesting—but certainly fitting—that the cutaway shots of Aslan used for commercial breaks feature him looking over his shoulder with a concerned look on his face, as if something threatening is near. As virtually all filmmakers will tell you, people have no interest in watching a character if s/he encounters no formidable challenges that create narrative tension—and thus audience interest. While there are several moments when the groups Aslan studies are presented as threats (whether to their own cultures, Aslan, or reason itself), most of the time he resolves this tension in a way that is emotionally satisfying. That is, true to the Hollywood narrative, we ride the wave of conflicts alongside Aslan, where he must navigate new and different people with strange ways, until we come to a resting place where things are different, but safe, again precisely because he is different, but safe, again.

Mulvey's argument about scopophilia, then, demonstrates both how and why we like to watch certain images, and reinforces the idea that we are quick to reconcile something new or different in rather predictable, personally fulfilling ways. I am reminded of writer David Mamet's related argument, which is that no matter how many atrocities one shows on the screen, and the complexity of the moral dilemmas portrayed therein, audiences will almost always walk away from the theatre feeling like moral heroes. In other words, Mamet argues, audiences believe that they would themselves have been on the side of the protagonist if the filmic situation were real, a phenomenon that Mamet (1996: 141) once called "emotional pornography."

I have long been intrigued by the fact that many of us—Aslan included—teach about religion via sensationalism, or by approaching it from the far sides of a continuum. In other words, just as we all know that there is no religious group that would have made it onto *Believer* without somehow appearing to first violate Western religious and cultural norms, we also know that their selection depended just as much on them conforming to some sort of "normalcy" to make them suitably presentable by the end of the episode. We often approach the study of religion by those things we think are most interesting, from snake-handlers, to UFO believers, to "cult" members, etc., without considering *why* our interests tend to gravitate to such social groups. Certainly, there is merit in J. Z. Smith's now famous argument that the scholar's task in identifying basic social processes will necessarily involve engagement with both the strange and the familiar in order to sharpen our perceptual skills of the politics that created those categories, more broadly (Smith 1982: xiii). But what I think *Believer* may help us see is that our pleasure in creating categories of difference often comes in our ability to domesticate the people we believe they describe, and in so doing, to exercise a very satisfying sense of control as it regards the feeling that we have understood religion's "authentic" nature via that act of domestication.

Leslie Dorrough Smith is Associate Professor of Religious Studies and Director of the Women's and Gender Studies program at Avila University (Kansas City, MO, USA). She is author of *Righteous Rhetoric: Sex, Speech, and the Politics of Concerned Women for America* (Oxford, 2014), and *Compromising Positions: Sex Scandals, Politics, and American Christianity* (Oxford, 2020).

Notes

1 *Believer*, Season 1, Episode 2. The episodes of *Believer* that were once available while Aslan was still employed by CNN have been removed from social media. Short clips of his *Believer* interviews remain on YouTube, and parts of this episode can be accessed at www.youtube.com/watch?v=oexpMQklaLo&list=PLUaTQYFkj9_47R8O LBZm5hUTvUfeMTdF&index=18 (accessed January 7, 2018).

2   *Believer*, Season 1, Episode 2. A short clip of this particular episode can be accessed at www.youtube.com/watch?v=i_6ltfDWF0Q, February 27, 2017 (accessed January 7, 2018).
3   *Believer*, Season 1, Episode 2.
4   *Believer*, Season 1, Episode 3. A short clip of this particular episode can be accessed at www.youtube.com/watch?v=W8A02LCbtyw, March 10, 2017 (accessed January 7, 2018).
5   *Believer*, Season 1, Episode 2.
6   *Believer*, Season 1, Episode 6. The promotional material for this particular episode can be accessed at www.youtube.com/watch?v=xxtPOx6jais, April 9, 2017 (accessed January 7, 2018).

References

Blyth, Antonia. 2017. "Believer's Reza Aslan on CNN's Firing Over Anti-Trump Tweet: 'I Don't Regret the Sentiment'." *Deadline*, June 17. Retrieved from http://deadline.com/2017/06/reza-aslan-believer-cnn-firing-interview-1202115267/ (archived at archive.today/ttDLi).
Haidt, Jonathan. 2012. *The Righteous Mind: Why Good People Are Divided By Politics and Religion*. New York: Vintage Books.
Makarechi, Kia. 2017. "Reza Aslan on *Believer*, and the Stakes of America's Identity Crisis." *Vanity Fair*, February 21. Retrieved from www.vanityfair.com/hollywood/2017/02/reza-aslan-believer-american-identity (archived at archive.today/d4O4U).
Mamet, David. 1996. *Make Believe Town: Essays and Remembrances*. Boston, MA: Back Bay Books.
Mulvey, Laura. 1999. "Visual Pleasure and Narrative Cinema." In Leo Braudy and Marshall Cohen (eds.), *Film Theory and Criticism: Introductory Readings*, 833–844. New York: Oxford University Press.
Safi, Michael. 2017. "Reza Aslan Outrages Hindus By Eating Human Brains in CNN Documentary." *The Guardian*, March 10. Retrieved from www.theguardian.com/world/2017/mar/10/reza-aslan-criticised-for-documentary-on-cannibalistic-hindus (archived at archive.today/BJ0ks).
Smith, Jonathan Z. 1982. *Imagining Religion: From Babylon to Jonestown*. Chicago, IL: University of Chicago Press.

Chapter 11

Naturalizing the Transnational Capitalist Class: Reza Aslan's Believer and the Ideological Reproduction of an Emerging Social Formation

Craig Prentiss

In the spring of 2017, Reza Aslan's CNN series, *Believer*, sparked a furious wave of essays, blog posts, and Facebook discussions among scholars of religion. The critiques were wide-ranging, and most angles of criticism have been covered by the other papers in this section. I confess that as the commentary was being generated, I had not yet seen the show. When I finally watched my first episode, the six-part series had almost concluded. As such, I struggled to evaluate it with fresh eyes as mine had already been clouded with the foreknowledge that *Believer* was guilty of presenting the communities and individuals it treated with excessive sensationalism, of muddying classificatory waters, of ignoring important political contexts in favor of simplistic narratives, and of resurrecting theoretical approaches to religion that some would like to imagine (despite substantial evidence to the contrary), are behind us.

At the same time, I came to the series with the hope that I would find something redeemable about the program. I had this hope because I had spent a day with Reza Aslan a few years ago when he spoke at my university and found him to be a charming, sharp, and friendly person who could engage people in conversation with the ease of a long-lost friend. And sure enough, those personal characteristics translated well to the screen and were central to fashioning *Believer* into a series that, while meriting most of its criticism, made for some very good television. Production value was high, the camerawork was beautiful, Aslan proved himself an adept interviewer, and the program did provide an entryway into communities and practices that most viewers were likely unfamiliar with. Whether it made for good scholarship, however, is another question entirely.

As I watched the series, my interest was consumed primarily with the binaries Aslan continued to produce, his not-so-deeply hidden theoretical framing of "religion," and what I took to be the ideological work being done by *Believer*. In this essay, I would like to situate a set of claims and themes Aslan routinely invoked in each episode of the series within the framework of an emergent social formation marked by the rise of a transnational capitalist class. I am especially interested in Aslan's discourse regarding the individual in relation to collective structure and the ideological load this discourse carries in the series. My argument is that

Believer participates in the naturalization of a distinctive social formation that has emerged with the advent of a transnational capitalist class. Furthermore, the distinctive material conditions and practices of this social formation shape what Aslan counts as "good" or "bad" religion. Indeed, I contend that the boundaries for what gets to count as "good" or "bad" religion at any given historical moment reflects those conditions and practices characterizing reigning social formations. The ideological and discursive fruit of transnational capitalism, like all emergent social formations, remains in conflict with the ideological and discursive residue of alternative social formations past and present. Therefore, we are always left with multiple, competing conceptions of "good" and "bad" religion. Reza Aslan's *Believer*, as an ideological artifact in this struggle, does what ideological artifacts always do: it participates in constituting subjects fitted for the social formation from which it emerges. And it does this by naturalizing the ideology necessary to sustain and reproduce the material and social order from which it arises.

Let's begin by looking at the outlines of social formation theory and the assumptions that guide it. When Louis Althusser sought to expand upon Marx's notion of Superstructure in his famous 1970 essay, "Ideology and Ideological State Apparatuses: Notes towards an Investigation," hoping to more explicitly identify the mechanisms through which ideology was produced, he worked under the assumption that the material conditions at the base of a social formation were bound within the confines and activity of the state or equivalent governing structure. Like Marx, Althusser viewed the state as a repressive apparatus dependent upon the threat of violence and existing to preserve the particular means of producing and distributing resources, while maintaining the socio-economic hierarchies these means produced. Complementing the violent apparatus of the state, Althusser, explained, were an array of nonviolent apparatuses that forwarded these objectives. He referred to these as "Ideological State Apparatuses" (ISAs) and identified eight ISAs: educational, familial, legal, political, trade-union, communications, cultural, and of course, religious. Reflecting a common usage of the term in France at the time, Althusser's (1971: 143) understanding of "religion" referred to "the system of different churches." Presumably in light of the Roman Catholic Church's important status in France, despite its systematic disentanglement from the State in the centuries after the Revolution, Althusser explained that only in recent history had educational systems surpassed religion as the most important ideological apparatus engaged in doing the work of naturalizing the social order.

While religion was identified as an ISA, by the late twentieth century we see signs that Althusser's framework of state-bound systems—frameworks central to virtually all economists until recently—required some amending. One might even reach back to economist Peter Drucker's 1969 classic, *The Age of Discontinuity*, to see the roots of this transformation. Drucker coined the term "knowledge economy" to describe the increasing importance of "knowledge workers" (a term he introduced a decade earlier in *Landmarks of Tomorrow*) to the functioning of the American economic system, foreshadowing a transformation throughout the

West. Notably, these knowledge workers were distinguished by their not being bound to the same material resources and connections to the land previous laborers had been, rendering them less confined to the dictates of a landed state. Businesses built upon knowledge labor were also slowly freed from these limitations (Drucker 1969, esp. ch. 12). The revolution in communication technology along with the digitalization of financial transactions accelerated the importance of knowledge workers exponentially, while at the same time enabling a previously unimaginable level of coordination between traditional manufacturers and distributors worldwide. By the 1980s, Dutch political economist Kees van der Pijl had begun documenting the transformation Drucker had identified with a detailed historical analysis of capital's internationalization and the resulting reformulation of dynamics between the fractional interests of the capitalist class (Van der Pijl 1984). This transformation would give rise to the discourse of "globalization" we have been immersed in for at least two decades (notwithstanding the rise of Trump, Brexit, and Le Front National).

A turning point in the documentation of the decline of state-bound capitalism came with Leslie Sklair's 2001 study, *The Transnational Capitalist Class*. Sklair was instrumental for not only identifying the material conditions through which this transnational class has emerged, but also for illustrating the ways in which economic globalization has been and continues to be shaped by this new class. For Sklair, the term "transnational" is distinct from "international" by its reference to "forces, processes, and institutions that cross borders but do not derive their power and authority from the state" (Sklair 2001: 2). He argues that this emerging transnational class is made up of four fractions: "corporate executives, globalizing bureaucrats and politicians, globalizing professionals, and consumerist elites" (ibid.: 4; Sklair 2002: 144). Sklair's work, which was based in part on extensive interviews with corporate CEO's, is especially significant for its interrogation of the interactions between those accumulating global capital and those who promote their interests in other sectors. Others have built on Sklair's work, including William I. Robinson (2004: 38) who contends that "the globalization of production and the extensive and intensive enlargement of capitalism in recent decades constitute the material basis for the process of transnational class formation." He has gone so far as to argue for the rise of a transnational capitalist state—an argument that Sklair, for one, rejects. Most recently, sociologist William K. Carroll paid tribute to Sklair's work with a 2012 study, *The Making of a Transnational Capitalist Class*. Carroll analyzes the intricate web of social connections between transnational corporate elites and their innumerable overlapping affiliations.

Of course, multi-national corporations are not new. We could trace them to the British and Dutch East India Companies in the earliest days of European colonial expansion. But these scholars contend that a new transnational order outside the bounds of the state has been forming in recent decades, stressing substantive changes to industrial organization in the age of global companies. For instance, by the late 1990s, Al Zeien, CEO of Gillette Corporation, differentiated multinationals from these global companies:

A multinational has operations in different countries [while] a global company views the world as a single country. We know Argentina and France are different but we treat them the same. We sell them the same products, we use the same production methods, and we have the same corporate policies. We even use the same advertising, in a different language of course. (Robinson 2004: 33)

If these scholars are correct and we are witnessing a substantive reformulation of at least a key element of the economic order, social formation theory would dictate that these reformulations would be reflected in the ideological production of a range of apparatuses—even if those apparatuses, in this case, are not properly identified as "state" apparatuses. This brings me back to Aslan's *Believer*. The series participates in the naturalization of the ideological scaffolding necessary to sustain and reproduce the transnational capitalist class. It does so, as a television program, while straddling the apparatuses of religion, communications (which, for Althusser, included television), and culture. While we could identify a multitude of potential pieces that make up this ideological scaffolding in the series, I would like to focus on three which are nurtured through each episode of *Believer*: (1) a deregulated order, (2) the primacy of the individual as the driving force of economic growth, and (3) the transportability of capital beyond boundaries which is the transnational capitalist class's most distinctive feature. I contend that these ideological features of the burgeoning economic order condition Aslan's reading of what constitutes "good" or "bad" religion and are naturalized in this series.

Let's start with deregulation. The heroes of each installment of *Believer* are those who refuse to succumb to the regulatory schemes of the dominant institutional orders from which they emerge. The Aghori in India reject the binary structures of purity and pollution that regulate so much of Indian social structure. They do so in the name of a monism that gives rise to not only the subversion of the complex system of *jati* or caste—a subversion which Aslan celebrates—but also to the subversion of deeply conditioned notions of hygiene and bodily taboos—a subversion which Aslan, a self-described "germaphobe," was unable to fully embrace. JeZus with a "Z" and his followers have opted for isolation on a Hawaiian Island in preparation for an environmental apocalypse while rejecting both the social and theological norms regulating the dominant strands of Christian apocalyptic sentiment. Likewise, Voudou stands as the ultimate deregulatory force in Aslan's narrative through its role in overthrowing the supreme regulatory practice of bodily enslavement. In this vein, Voudou assumes the vanguard of Haitian resistance to colonialist Christianities—both Roman Catholic and Evangelical Protestant—that seek to regulate Haitian life through control of schools, hospitals, and economic enterprises. Aslan portrays Voudou as co-existing with Christianities on the island in a state of cold-peace—one threatened by aggressive Evangelicals linking the former to Satan.

Aslan also features renegade Scientologists resisting the regulation of the Church of Scientology's notoriously controlling hands. The apostates he interviews each recount troubling tales of the personal and professional costs they have incurred at the hands of Scientology's Los Angeles based hierarchy. Devotees of Santa Muerte have created, in Aslan's words, "a brand new religion" outside the regulatory clutches of Roman Catholicism which rejects veneration of the skeletal saint as devotion to a satanic cult (despite the plurality of her devotees continuing to self-identify as Roman Catholic). And finally, Aslan portrays the Na-Nachim as an apolitical force in Israel, committed to rejecting the larger Haredi movement's attempts to impose regulatory codes legislatively across Israel in favor of a personal, mystical spirituality built upon the joyful encounter with God. (Though it is worth noting Aslan ignores the marginal but certainly *political* party, Kulanu Chaverim-Na Nach, meaning "we are all friends-Na Nach," that has been promoting the interests of the Na-Nachim in the Israeli Knesset since 2012).[1] In Aslan's examples, the de-regulators are the "good guys." Each stands as an exemplum of "good" religion, paralleling the transnational capitalist class's insistence on minimal state regulation to maximize growth. The dominant institutional structures against which each featured group struggles can be understood as a stand-in for the regulatory state.

Next, the view that the entrepreneurial individual is the driving force behind economic growth has been the most consistent truism of capitalist discourse since Adam Smith. The ideology of individual primacy serves to both protect the inalienable right of private property as well as safeguard the accumulated wealth of capitalists from the hands of labor, the State, and the less fortunate by concealing the social networks upon which wealth creation depends. In the US, for instance, the appellation "job creators" has been consistently applied in recent years to the wealthiest Americans as a tool for authorizing disproportionately large tax cuts that, presumably, facilitate their role as creators of jobs. The language succeeds in crafting an image of the wealthiest individuals as having attained wealth in isolation, free from systems of labor, state enforced contract law, patent and copyright law, favorable tax codes, federally negotiated trade deals, a publicly financed telecommunications network, brick-and-mortar infrastructure, and a dizzying web of economic exchange throughout the social order that created the markets for their products. At the same time, "job creators" paints the same class as noble benefactors whose munificence merits the benefit of a regressive tax structure. The fetishizing of the individual is an ideological tool that renders those at the bottom of the capitalist hierarchy as victims of their own poor choices—being equally free to have chosen the path of a titan of industry instead of the path of a welfare recipient dependent on the largesse of the taxpayers. Obscuring the social networks in which individual subjects are both constituted and operate has been endemic to all variations of the capitalist order, not only the emergent transnational class. Individualism is paramount to capitalist ideology.

Believer is a six-episode celebration of individual choice and the absolute freedom we imagine we have to make those choices. After all, Aslan embodies this individual freedom himself as the American Muslim man who, on six separate occasions over six weeks, will make the choice to "experience" these exotic traditions through immersion. As the episode among the Aghori in India closes, he asks:

What does it mean to live without fear? It means recognizing that purity and pollution are just an illusion. It means knowing that nothing *you* do, nothing *you* eat, nothing *you* touch, can cut *you* off from God. That if God lives inside *you*, as the Aghori believe, then nothing can defile *you*. The family *you* were born into, the color of *your* skin, the clothes that *you* wear, *your* education, *your* wealth ... none of these matter. What matters is what *you* do. How *you* love. How *you* care for the least among you. So *I* will eat the ashes of the dead, *I* will drink the water from the Ganges. *I* will worship the god within me. *I* came to India to discover what it means to be Aghori. What *I* discovered is what it means to be human. (Episode 1, emphasis added)

This is a seductive and beautifully phrased sentiment. With a cavalcade of "you," "you," "yous" and "I," "I," "Is," Aslan assures us of our freedom. It is not a freedom before God, but the freedom actualized by the God dwelling within each of us.

At the conclusion of episode 2, Aslan says of the commune built around JeZus with a "Z": "They may seem like a bunch of lost souls [...]. But they've created a community. A place where they belong. And that's a good reminder about *what religion truly is*" (emphasis added). At this point, we might be tempted to imagine that Aslan has pivoted from the individual as holding primacy in "good" religion, but we quickly discover that his community parallels Rousseau's "Social Contract," built on individual consent to bow to the will of the majority for the preservation of good order, rather than a community as a social structure whose collective practices and norms constitute the individual. He continues,

Because it's one thing to look for an authentic religious experience, something that's real, or grounded, or historically accurate, but I think that misses the point. Because, in the end, religion is what people make of it [...]. Religion isn't about scripture, or temples, or priests, or rules or regulations. *It's about the individual and the quest for meaning.* (Episode 2, emphasis added)

While he told us earlier that community is what "religion truly is," he soon abandons this for the assertion that it is the individual quest for meaning that characterizes religion. We may choose collective living, but we do so as a means of staying true to our individual quest.

Aslan's renegade Scientologists are "true believers who are seizing for themselves the power to define one of America's newest faiths" (Episode 4). He entitles episode four "The Scientology Reformation" and draws constant parallels between the unregulated Scientologists and sixteenth-century Protestant reformers who, Aslan explains, were marked by their desire to "interpret the Church for themselves." Of course, none of the sixteenth-century reformers would have celebrated the individuality Aslan celebrates here, nor claimed the right to interpret for themselves. Instead, possessed of an exegetical optimism, they imagined themselves submitting to the self-evident, unmediated, plain meaning of scripture—a plain meaning Roman Catholics had deviated from. But the chasm separating conceptualizations of individuality in the sixteenth century from the twenty-first is not Aslan's concern here:

> We are witnessing a Scientology reformation [...]. A religion can only expand and grow if *individuals* feel free to make it their own [...] and that's what's happening here [...]. And it doesn't matter whether they're right or wrong. What matters is that all religions go through this process. (Episode 4, emphasis added).

Individual experience dominates other episodes. For instance, Aslan highlights the "strange [...] personal connection" he begins to feel for his recently purchased statue of Santa Muerte. And among the Na-Nachim in Israel, individual happiness is paramount. As one of his informants explains, "Each one has to find his way to how to connect to HaShem." This final episode culminates with a trip to the woods for, as Aslan explains, "some alone time with God." He explains that Rabbi Nachman of Breslov, the group's progenitor, made it his custom to go to the woods or the water to be alone with God. "Hitbodedut," a Hebrew word for self-seclusion, his informant explains, animates the Na-Nachim practices. "It means to be alone. Making a personal relationship with God. Talk to HaShem in your own words. Tell him 'thank you' for all the good things that you feel that he gave you. Ask him for things you want to get."

Aslan's hope for the redemption of Haredi Judaism rests in the Na-Nachim emphasis on individual freedom to seek happiness in God. It is worth noting that in capitalism, individualism also functions to divide the collective action of organized labor. A primary appeal of globalization in the West has been the promise of finding cheaper labor in territories unsullied by unions and state-enforced worker's rights. Maximizing surplus value in this order depends upon divide-and-conquer strategies pitting one segment of the labor force (both globally and within the nation state) against another to drive down labor costs. Aslan's natural order of things gives primacy to the individual's pursuit of personal satisfaction. A spirituality disconnected from institutional structure is the consistently celebrated. If the individual practitioner is analogous to the individual laborer in *Believer*, the message is that you do not have to settle for the imperfect and sometimes corrupted structures that seek to coopt your body and your spirit in the service of a unified front. The heroes of *Believer* are consistently those who say "no" to unity, or whose unity comes only on their personal terms.

Finally, while the prior features of the ideological fruit stemming from a transnational capitalism can be said to be endemic to all forms of capitalism, the salient feature of this emerging social formation is the transportability of capital beyond national borders. Aslan's *Believer* is a testament to the meaninglessness of those borders. Each episode takes place in a different part of the world and focuses on what Aslan himself has described as a conversion. "I convert," he told Melanie McFarland during an interview with *Salon* magazine. "I become one of them. I join their cult or their religion [...]. [Y]ou're going to learn about these faiths by watching me live these faiths." So Aslan, an Iranian-American Muslim academic, performs six acts of immersion in which the audience is asked to view every boundary one might protest as standing in the way of suddenly becoming a Na-Nach or an Aghori for a day, as meaningless. Moreover, these acts of immersion are performed in the service of fostering cross-cultural understanding. What many will "see in the first few moments" of each episode, Aslan explained, "might seem really foreign and exotic and frightening and weird, and then by the end of the hour [...] they'll probably think to themselves [...] 'Well, not that weird actually. Not as foreign as I thought, and actually I kind of agree. I share similar beliefs'" (McFarland 2017).

As a liberal Westerner, and an academic who values the task of "making the strange seem familiar and the familiar seem strange," Aslan's professed hope resonates with me. But this resonance stems from my being an interpellated subject of a late capitalist social formation as well. At the same time, I am also conditioned by the rites and practices of my field of study, which have included years of reading scholars interrogate positionality with respect to ethnography and scholarship in general. These rites and practices have conditioned me and other religious studies scholars in such a way that hearing Aslan's claim to "become one of them" is almost bound to elicit a wince. It is a wince born of a learned conviction that in any act of translation, explanation, or theorizing, borders like those Aslan seeks to dismantle do, in fact, matter. Where we sit shapes both what we claim to see and how we claim to see it.

Yet in the world of *Believer*, boundaries are inconsequential, and Aslan's perennialist impulses help to erase those boundaries. Yet Aslan's perennialism appears to differ from the Ottonian articulation of *Das Heilige*, or the Eliadan encounter with hierophanies, whose universalist pretentions imagined the individual aligning with and submitting to the overwhelming power of "the sacred." Instead, Aslan's perennialism is a universal quest for individual happiness that need not answer to the dictates of a transcendent force, particularly if that force is articulated within the confines of an imperfect institutional structure. His brand of cosmopolitan spiritual adventurer encourages viewers to feel as much at home at a dinner party sipping wine with friends in Los Angeles or Haifa as when being washed clean by the waterfall at Saut d'Eau in Haiti, or being audited by a reformed Scientologist in Reno, Nevada. One could imagine a series set entirely in Los Angeles that explores the practices and ideas of an array of "believers" every bit as diverse as those Aslan traversed the globe to find. But why be bound to the narrow confines of your hometown? Much in the same way one might ask, why be bound by the narrow confines of one's home nation state? Or your own country's banking system?

The classification of groups or movements in *Believer* as "good" or "bad" is, in the end, contingent upon whether those groups or movements resonate with the ideological pillars necessary for reproducing the conditions of transnational capitalism. Those more easily aligned with the ideological imperative of a deregulated order and a celebration of the individual, at least in Aslan's telling, exemplify the good. Moreover, those ecumenically-minded enough to dispense with boundaries long enough for him to engage in the performance of immersion—privileging broadly binding concepts like equality, self-actualization, happiness, and love over more limiting conceptions of doctrinal acceptance and submission to sanctioned authorities—land on the side of the good as well. The "bad guys" in this story can be traced to residual social formations whose days have passed. *Believer* castigates the caste-consciousness of an India steeped in hierarchical social structures dating back to the *Vedas*, the organic and hierarchically bound ideology of a Roman Catholicism forged in the arena of Western feudalism, the authoritarian tendencies of an Evangelical Protestantism springing from the birth of national consciousness and mercantilist loyalties, and even the controlling and protectionist impulses of a Church of Scientology that guards its technologies and secrets with the ferocity of a rising management class burgeoning under the shadow of the Cold War in mid-20th-century United States. At any given moment, prevailing social formations stand in conflict with the echoes of residual social formations and the confident cries of emerging ones, like transnational capitalism. As Reza Aslan's *Believer* invites us to pursue our individual, deregulated spiritual path in a world without borders, it acts as a salvo in the naturalization of an ideological cocktail. The long-term success of transnational capitalism demands that we drink of that cocktail.

Craig Prentiss is a professor of Religious Studies at Rockhurst University in Kansas City, Missouri. He is the author of *Staging Faith: Religion and African American Theater from the Harlem Renaissance to World War II* (NYU Press 2014) and *Debating God's Economy: Social Justice in America on the Eve of Vatican II* (Penn State University Press 2008).

Note

1   For more on Kulanu Chaverim–Na Nach, see www.zissil.com/topics/Kulanu-Chaverim---Na-Nach (archived at archive.today/0q5zs); on the origins of Kulanu Chaverim, see Kordova (2012).

References

Althusser, Louis. 1971. "Ideology and Ideological State Apparatuses: Notes Toward an Investigation." In *Lenin and Philosophy and Other Essays*, 127–186. New York: Monthly Review Press.
Believer with Reza Aslan. 2017. Episodes 1–6. CNN. March 5–April 9.
Carroll, William K. 2012. *The Making of a Transnational Capitalist Class*. London: Zed Books.
Drucker, Peter. 1959. *Landmarks of Tomorrow: A Report on the New "Post-Modern" World*. New York: Harper & Row.
Drucker, Peter. 1969. *The Age of Discontinuity*. London: William Heinemann. https://doi.org/10.1016/B978-0-434-90395-5.50005-5
Kordova, Shoshana. 2012. "Word of the Day Na Nach." *Haaretz*, December 10. Retrieved from www.haaretz.com/.premium-word-of-the-day-na-nach-1.5270473 (accessed July 18, 2017) (archived at archive.today/H1hkF).
McFarland, Melanie. 2017. "Failed Conversion: Believer with Reza Aslan Wants to Touch Faith but Embraces Sensationalism Instead." *Salon*, March 2. Retrieved from www.salon.com/2017/03/02/failed-conversion-believer-with-reza-aslan-wants-to-touch-faith-but-embraces-sensationalism-instead/ (archived at archive.today/9JVLp).
Robinson, William I. 2004. *A Theory of Global Capitalism: Production, Class, and State in a Transnational World*. Baltimore, MD: Johns Hopkins University Press.

Sklair, Leslie. 2001. *The Transnational Capitalist Class*. New York: Wiley-Blackwell.
Sklair, Leslie. 2002. "Democracy and the Transnational Capitalist Class." *The Annals of the American Academy of Political and Social Science* 581: 144–157. https://doi.org/10.1177/000271620258100113
Van der Pijl, Kees. 1984. *The Making of an Atlantic Ruling Class*. London: Verso.

Chapter 12

Authentic Religion—or, How to Be a Good Citizen

Steffen Führding

Martha Smith Roberts's chapter describes and analyses CNN's television series *Believer*, hosted by Reza Aslan. In the following essay I would like to switch the focus from the North American context to the German context—from *Believer* to *Was glaubst du denn?* (*What Do You Believe In?*), a German documentary about three young people speaking about their religious experiences.

Since 2008, the Arbeitsgemeinschaft der öffentlich-rechtlichen Rundfunkanstalten der Bundesrepublik Deutschland (ARD, Consortium of Public Broadcasters in Germany) has offered so called "theme weeks" once a year, aiming to initiate discussions about important social issues (see https://themenwoche.ard.de). Each week has been dedicated to a specific topic, such as "mobility," "homeland," "death," or the "future of work." In 2017, they chose the topic "What do you believe in?". For an entire week they broadcasted a series of diverse programs on television and radio connected to this specific topic—documentaries, reports, movies, series, etc.,—some of which were produced especially for this occasion (ARD 2017).

Even though an analysis of the whole theme week would be worthwhile, I have confined myself to one single contribution for the time being, *Was glaubst du denn?* by Jan Teuwsen (2017). In this roughly half-hour film, three young people speak about their religion: Laila is introduced as Muslim, Boris as Jewish, and Patric as Catholic. The three tell the audience about their beliefs, how they practice their religion, which problems they are confronted with by virtue of this identity, and what their religion means for their lives. The film was produced in 2017 for *Planet Schule* (Planet School), which is a multimedia educational platform produced by Südwestrundfunk (SWR, Southwest Broadcasting) and Westdeutscher Rundfunk (WDR, West German Broadcasting), channels that both belong to the ARD. The website www.planet-schule.de offers online models, animated media, and additional in-depth information regarding the broadcast as well as teaching advice and worksheets for the creative design of lessons or e-learning-modules for self- and interactive learning. Moreover, the material refers to different school curricula used in Germany to make its application to the classroom relatively seamless (Planet Schule 2016).

While *Believer* comes off as a high gloss product, *Was glaubst du denn?* appears a bit more conventional. The quick camera cuts and high drama of *Believer* are missing; instead, the three protagonists tell an invisible and silent interviewer about their lives in common interview settings (such as their homes), and are also accompanied to various daily life activities such as religious ceremonies, shopping, or going to a climbing park. This form of representation helps to legitimize and authorize a specific populist image of these types of religion as "real," and thus as authentic and good, while subtly allowing the audience to delegitimize other forms of religion that do not directly manufacture "good citizens" who secure the stability of the community.

The documentary describes the lives of the three very closely and empathetically. Even some of their friends and companions get a chance to speak. This move displaces the "expert presenter" motif of Aslan in *Believer* or Constantin Schreiber in *Moschee Report* (Mosque Report; see Becker, Chapter 9, this volume) who "explains" to the audience what they have been watching and thereby determines the plotline.[1] Instead, this "expert" role is turned over to three apparently common young people (and, occasionally, their friends), who speak about their religion from their point of view and their experiences living in a religiously diverse environment. This is the common thread connecting the three (otherwise independent) stories.

While Aslan's series gives priority to exotic and strange phenomena in order to locate them in the "realm of a perennialist worldview, where all good religion, no matter how exotic, shares common forms" (Roberts, Chapter 8, this volume), the German documentary chooses a different approach—there is no exotic setting, no hysterical tone. Some of the aspects of religion presented in the documentary will, no doubt, seem unfamiliar or strange to the audience,[2] even though the protagonists are presented as rather common people. Their convictions and practices are recorded and explained in a considerate and calm tone, inviting the audience to sympathize with them even when their views fall outside of the mainstream, or incite controversy, such as when Boris explains why circumcision—which has been discussed controversially and critically in the German public within the last few years (see Perlentaucher 2012)—has such an important and positive meaning for him and therefore for Judaism itself.

Other elements of controversy include Patric's decision to become a priest and Laila's choice to wear the headscarf, both practices that are often treated with prejudice and/or incomprehension in German society. Especially where these topics are concerned, the individual decision of the protagonists are emphasized. For instance, Laila tells the viewer that she has never been forced to do anything by her family regarding her religiosity. Instead, her family has set an example of religious life which influenced her positively, thus influencing her decision. At school she first wore the headscarf at the beginning of 11th grade and was very excited and anxious at the time. Close friends and her parents encouraged her to take the plunge and in the end "I just did it. I did, what my heart told me to do" (Teuwsen 2017: 1:19–1:20; my translation, emphasis added). Laila considers the headscarf a symbol for her devotion to her belief. In her opinion, she has become a strong and self-confident person by living out this belief in public. Boris's decision is also described as an individual act. "I was twelve, when I discovered the whole Judaism for myself. And sometimes I thought okay, 13 is the age of *bar mitzvah* and I am going to celebrate *bar mitzvah* [...] told my mother, I want to do it. I deem it important" (ibid.: 7:37–7:57; my translation, emphasis added). As with Laila, this religious act it is not only an individual and personal decision, but it also implies that religion enables these individuals to experience a wholeness or more highly developed sense of self that non-religious people do not experience. So Boris "likes it that it (his religion, SF) always reminds you of who you are" (ibid.: 7:15–7:16; my translation). Patric mentions similar considerations. Religion is described not only as a personal matter, but also as something that plays a central role in giving him a complete sense of identity.

The point of engaging many of these controversial topics, it seems, is to normalize specific religious behaviors for a wary public by portraying these individuals as innocuous citizens who are merely engaging in an act of personal choice and belief. The message that is conveyed is that the viewer does not have to fear attempts at conversion or harm in any way. He or she is just invited to get an inside look into the world of ideas and experiences of the believer. This is exemplified by Boris's statement at the end of the film: "I live my belief for myself. I don't want to convince others, that's nonsense"(Teuwsen 2017: 27:40; my translation). As mentioned earlier, the topics discussed are often targeted at current prejudices within German culture in order to enable the audience to understand the religious person's motives. The same applies for less controversial subjects, like prayer in Islam. It is presumed that most viewers would not understand why someone takes on the burden to pray five times a day voluntarily, and yet Laila is portrayed as someone who appreciates this "burden." Instead of understanding prayer as an annoying and restrictive duty, Laila tells that the audience that the prayer ritual helps to structure her day usefully and that it offers breaks from an otherwise stressful daily routine (ibid.: 12:50–12:57).

These subjects are further normalized when the camera follows them into various other, "non-religious" realms of life. Thus you can see Boris recording a rap song with his friend in a park, Laila shopping with a friend, or Patric climbing with a friend in a climbing park; all of them quite "normal" activities. The fact that they are often featured with friends helps to portray them as well-integrated parts of modern society—not as isolated outsiders. These images reinforce the impression that what we are dealing with is three quite normal young people, people like you and me. This opposes a common German understanding of "being religious" as something otherworldly, backward, or even fundamentalist.

In these ways, religion is portrayed as an act of faith and private matter. It has nothing to do with coercion or force, but is an act freely chosen. Self-doubts and self-reflection are an integral part of this religion. Moreover, religion is depicted as something that is not just a part of an individual's identity, but that is important to identity development. It gives shelter, orientation, and community, keeping the person grounded. In short, the picture of religion that is constructed here is that of "good" and "authentic" religion. It is up to par with the ideology of religious pluralism and interreligious dialogue (see McCutcheon 2001: ch. 10; McCutcheon 2005: ch. 2), and thus fits the needs of the liberal nation state (I will elaborate on this below). "Other" forms of religion are hardly mentioned in this documentary and this, it seems, is intentional, for it is clear that, in the program's subtext, all religions that do not accept these principles of individuality, choice, and reflection are problematic or bad. Thus, it is striking that the images we are presented with in the news (which has focused on Islam by examining ISIS for example) or in formats such as *Mosque Report* (which deals with common prejudices and anxieties regarding Islam) are missing here.

The conceptualization of religion in *Was glaubst du denn?* follows classical notions of liberal political beliefs. The propagated image of religion is harmless to the state's claim to power. By locating religion in the private (and internal) realm, it ultimately becomes a matter of personal preference. Each must live as she or he sees fit, as long as this does not encroach on the public order and the state monopoly on legitimate violence.

This understanding of religion and the associated notion of religion in the state public sphere—which, to many of us seems so natural and which is manifest in most Western constitutions, for example—is the result of a relatively new discourse. The origin of this discourse can be dated temporally and geographically: namely the Early Modern Age and (Western) Europe (see e.g. Arnal 2000; Fitzgerald 2003; McCutcheon 1999, 2003). Above all, the consequences of the Reformation and the "Wars on Religion" (e.g. Thirty Years War) made the representatives of (liberal) political philosophy (e.g. Thomas Hobbes, John Locke, Jean-Jacques Rousseau) think about how the state can succeed against the backdrop of competing absolute truth claims. They attempted to create parameters that would allow for the coexistence of different confessions—that is, parameters that would create religious tolerance.

As a result, the state was denied the right to interfere with the religious beliefs of its citizens on condition that these did not threaten public order or public welfare. This was possible because religion was declared an exclusively private matter, of no significance to public affairs of any kind. That notion is common among liberals, namely the generation of two individual domains that are thought to be isolated from one another: a political public sphere and an apolitical private one. Religion is allocated to the apolitical sphere, where it appears less threatening (cf. Martin 2010: 33–57). Thus, different sectors are assigned to one or the other sphere. The sectors that are more about taking action directly (economics, politics, etc.), are attributed to the public sphere.

The (rhetorical) construction of the two spheres created the basis for the successful formation of the modern national and constitutional state. What were originally central and unbridgeable truth claims, which encompassed the whole area of human life and society, were depoliticized and moved into the "private" realm. As discussed elsewhere (Führding 2013), contemporary representatives of liberalism generally assume the same logic. For them it is necessary to locate religion within the private realm in order to guarantee the state and its stability even though religion can still be understood as an important factor in creating social cohesion. The state is indeed not entitled to interfere in the production of social norms and values but must ensure conditions in which the citizens are allowed to decide independently about the ideological norms and values which are binding and necessary for social cohesion. In accordance with this thinking, religion and its relationship to the state are configured in a way that they are not explicitly seen as a danger to the commonwealth. Rather, religion is rendered basically as "individual religious experience," which belongs to the private sphere and thus seems decoupled from the question of power.

This leads us back to *Was glaubst du denn?*, which represents many of these same ideas. The documentary is not intended to be scientific, nor does it adopt a religious studies perspective. This is at least somewhat different from *Believer*, where Aslan's authority as a scholar of religion—even if poorly executed—is designed to contrast the outsider with the insider by inserting an "expert" opinion into the narrative. *Was glaubst du denn?* uses only the insider report which is not broken down by outside expert opinion. As known from different debates concerning the insider/outsider problem within the study of religion (Knott 2009; McCutcheon 1999), the insider approach tries to understand religion from the believer's perspective. "It involves looking at religious texts and religious rituals in order to find out significance of these for practitioners and subsequently describes their contents and performances to others," as Aaron Hughes (2013: 27) states.

With this in mind, the protagonists of the documentary are portrayed as the real experts on their religion. As insiders, they are depicted as authentically reporting on their religious experiences and their meaning for their lives. Their individualized, neo-liberal, peaceful religions are now authorized to be authentic, while other forms of religion are at least indirectly denigrated. Such forms of religion that are contrary to the concerns of a liberal-democratic constitutional state, those that disturb the public order and provoke the state monopoly on legitimate violence, are, according to this interpretation, not authentic religions at all. One can illustrate that very well if one draws on the extreme examples of Boko Haram and ISIS used by Hughes in his introduction of *Islam and the Tyranny of Authenticity*. These groups are generally not understood as authentic and thereby as a good form of Islam. Instead they are seen as terrorist groups that hijack religion—in this case "the" Islam—for their criminal and political aims (Hughes 2015: xi–xii).

In addition, the problem of such an exposition, which is basically inherent to *Was glaubst du denn?*, is that it assumes a specific perspective on religion that is both authorized and naturalized. Even if the documentary does not pretend to describe religion in a scholarly way, it is problematic that any kind of contextualization and critical questioning of the picture is missing. This problem would not be resolved merely by including mention of more extreme religious forms, for as Russell McCutcheon has shown, neutrality is not achieved by comparing authentic religion and inauthentic religion, for those very concepts "authentic" and "inauthentic" are strategic in so much that they are "social sites where specific sorts of political work is being done through the artful deployment of distinctive sets of classifications" (McCutcheon 2005: 13). This is an especially important omission within the school context—for which this documentary is also intended—since one central aim of school education, required by law, is that schools teach students to think critically and independently about bias and political interests (see e.g. Darm 2017; Darm and Lange 2018).

This does not, of course, only happen in this field; a look to methodological issues in the development of educational curricula shows similar issues, as Wanda Alberts stresses in her chapter in this volume:

> Learning about religion from a critical, unbiased point of view is rarely part of school curricula. On the contrary, school systems in general tend to promote the instrumentalization of religion rather than its critical study. The frameworks in which religion is studied in school shows its peculiar status. It is part of most school curricula, but hardly ever by the same standards as other subjects. (Alberts, Chapter 19, this volume)

And further:

> The rationale behind [... religious education is, SF] to educate the pupils to become good Christians or good Muslims and thereby good citizens. The whole debate about Islamic Religious Education shows that very clearly, including the role of Islam as the "significant other" that always has to face the hermeneutics of suspicion. Only when the fear of the phantom of Islamic terrorism grew stronger, the need for Islamic RE [Religious Education, SF] was acknowledged, with the clear aim of teaching "good" Islam in order to prevent radicalization. (Alberts, Chapter 19, this volume)

The engagement with religion at school and in other various fields aims at imparting ethical values in order to bring up good, ethical people and, as a result, good citizens.

The critical study of religion is meant to show such mechanisms and to challenge, instead of reproducing and thereby authorizing, them. The force of these mechanisms—like the good/bad rhetoric—is much more significant than mere words, for they entail concrete consequences in terms of power. They facilitate very specific forms of social "reality" by designating and controlling ways of organizing and acting in the community. If one directs the focus in this direction, the discipline of the study of religion can become a critical social science. As such, it can contribute important insights into power relations and legitimacy practices, thereby making an important contribution to social debates. The work of the conference participants and of the conference itself, the results of which are documented in this volume, set an impressive example of such a kind of research within our discipline. This is an encouragement for the future of the study of religion.

Steffen Führding, PhD, teaches at the Department for the Study of Religion at Leibniz University Hannover. He has published on the history of the study of religion and theoretical debates within the discipline, including the monograph *Jenseits von Religion* (transcript, 2015).

Notes

1 It is characteristic that Jan Teuwsen, who is the author and director of photography and therefore responsible for the documentary, occurs in name only in one place, the

end title. He also does not appear in the supplementary materials nor in the film itself, giving ultimate priority to the three teens.

2 There is a hierarchy of strangeness, so to speak. While Islam and Judaism are usually portrayed as strange and unknown in general (particularly, in Islam, with reference to the oppression of women), this is different in the case of Catholicism. In principle it is not about Catholicism; what is portrayed as "strange" is that Patric would want to become a priest.

References

ARD. 2017. "Themenwoche Woran glaubst Du?" Retrieved from www.ard.de/home/themenwoche/ARD_Themenwoche_2017_Woran_glaubst_Du_/3981220/index.html (archived at www.webcitation.org/78knK6MYQ).

Arnal, William. 2000. "Definition." In Willi Braun (ed.), *Guide to the Study of Religion*, 21–34. London: Continuum.

Darm, Ricarda. 2017. *Demokratiebildung als kritisch-reflexive Selbstbildung: Die Kritische Diskursanalyse als Prinzip der Didaktik der politischen Bildung*. Hannover: Unveröffentlichte Masterarbeit an der Leibniz Universität Hannover.

Darm, Ricarda, and Dirk Lange. 2018. "Mündigkeitsselbstbildung als Referenzpunkt der Demokratiebildung." In Steve Kenner and Dirk Lange (eds.), *Citizenship Education: Konzepte, Anregungen und Ideen zur Demokratiebildung*, 49–59. Frankfurt/M.: Wochenschau Verlag.

Fitzgerald, Timothy. 2003. *The Ideology of Religious Studies*. New York: Oxford University Press.

Führding, Steffen. 2013. "Religion, Privacy and the Rise of the Modern State." *Method and Theory in the Study of Religion* 25(1): 118–131. https://doi.org/10.1163/15700682-12341251

Hughes, Aaron W. 2013. *The Study of Judaism: Authenticity, Identity, Scholarship*. Albany, NY: SUNY Press.

Hughes, Aaron W. 2015. *Islam and the Tyranny of Authenticity: An Inquiry into Disciplinary Apologetics and Self-Deception*. Sheffield: Equinox.

Knott, Kim. 2009. "Insider/Outsider Perspectives." In John R. Hinnells (eds.), *The Routledge Companion to the Study of Religion*, 2nd edn, 259–273. London: Routledge.

Martin, Craig. 2010. *Masking Hegemony: A Genealogy of Liberalism, Religion and the Private Sphere*. London: Routledge.

McCutcheon, Russell T., ed. 1999. *The Insider/Outsider Problem in the Study of Religion: A Reader*. London: Continuum.

McCutcheon, Russell T. 2001. *Critics Not Caretakers. Redescribing the Public Study of Religion*. Albany, NY: SUNY Press.

McCutcheon, Russell T. 2003. *The Discipline of Religion: Structure, Meaning, Rhetoric*. New York: Routledge. https://doi.org/10.4324/9780203451793

McCutcheon, Russell T. 2005. *Religion and the Domestication of Dissent: Or, How to Live in a Less Than Perfect Nation*. London: Routledge.

Perlentaucher. 2012. "ESSAY Ein Linkdossier zur Beschneidungsdebatte." Retrieved from www.perlentaucher.de/essay/beschneidungsdebatte.html (archived at www.webcitation.org/78kodNFOz).

Planet Schule. 2016. "Was glaubst du denn? Unterricht." Retrieved from www.planet-schule.de/wissenspool/ich-und-die-anderen/inhalt/unterricht/was-glaubst-du-denn.html# (archived at www.webcitation.org/78kovLki5). https://doi.org/10.13109/9783666702228.toc

Teuwsen, Jan. 2017. *Was glaubst du denn?*. TV documentary. 24:44 min. Südwestrundfunk. Retrieved from www.planet-schule.de/sf/php/sendungen.php?sendung=10559

Part IV

University

Introduction to Part V

Leslie Dorrough Smith, AVILA UNIVERSITY
Steffen Führding, LEIBNIZ UNIVERSITY
Adrian Hermann, UNIVERSITY OF BONN

The university campus is an important public space for the negotiation of different understandings of religion in modern society. A large variety of disciplines claim to be studying the various traditions of the "world religions," an endeavor that religious studies is still participating in, while also critically reflecting on this legacy. But debates about religion on the campus reach far beyond such traditional scholarly work as the category of "religion" becomes embroiled in broader political struggles and is wielded strategically by a variety of social actors.

The contributions in Part IV deal with representations of "good" and "bad" religion at the university and in particular with the application of the "religion" label to current student protests. The anchoring essay comes from *Adrian Hermann* and *Stefan Priester* (Chapter 13), who discuss the "new campus religion" of "political correctness" as identified by mass-media commentators like William Deresiewicz and others. They ask how such current debates can be analyzed in light of our interest in the public rhetoric of "good" and "bad" religion, and focus on two things: first, the role played by the polemical use of "religion" and adjacent terminologies in the descriptions of current protests; second, how an insider/outsider logic familiar to the study of religion seems to be at play in these controversies. Moving beyond this case study, they ask what the study of religion can learn in regard to the often discussed insider/outsider problem by drawing on feminist standpoint theory to better understand the epistemic effects of marginalization and oppression.

The other three chapters in this section reflect on religion on the university campus by taking Hermann and Priester's considerations as a starting point and comparing this case with other instances of "good" and "bad" religion.

Stephanie Gripentrog's response (Chapter 14) focuses on the relationship of scholarly normativity and political pressure. Drawing on the work of Russell T. McCutcheon and Thomas Gieryn, she argues that scholars are always engaged as public intellectuals and involved in negotiating the boundaries of what can count as real scholarship. In a "post-truth world," she argues, the study of religion is challenged to recognize the constructedness of the stories it tells, but at the same time has to demonstrate the value of a perspective that constantly questions normative claims in scholarship and the broader society.

In Chapter 15 *Christopher R. Cotter* explores the "rhetoric of good and bad religion" in regard to recent scholarship on "non-religion." Engaging with Aaron Hughes's description of the ways in which this rhetoric is active in "Islamic Religious Studies," he demonstrates that scholars writing on "non-religion" equally make use of these tropes. He also argues that such rhetoric allows "religious" and "non-religious" moderates to build alliances against anything that is seen to challenge the legitimacy of the liberal, secular state. In conclusion, Cotter highlights that the Christian assumptions perpetuated by non-religion studies and its tacit promotion of neoliberal values have to be critically reflected upon.

David Kaldewey (Chapter 16) provides elements of a sociology of knowledge perspective on the contemporary student protests examined in Hermann and Priester's essay. He argues that a new ideal of the university as a "safe space" becomes apparent in the protest discourse. In pointing to some research desiderata, Kaldewey addresses the theoretical foundations of the protesters and suggests that what is needed is a historical encyclopedia dealing with the new vocabularies and the traveling of the concepts employed by students.

Taken together, the four chapters of Part IV make visible that questions of "bad" and "good" religion at the university go far beyond the "world religions paradigm" and that the rhetoric explored in this volume has become a central element of current society-wide debates about the present and future of the university as an institution.

Chapter 13

'Bad Religion' on the University Campus: "Political Correctness" and the Future of the Insider/Outsider Problem in the Study of Religion

Adrian Hermann and Stefan Priester

You might have missed it, but apparently a new form of 'bad religion' has appeared on the scene in the last couple of years: the "new campus religion" of "political correctness," as critic William Deresiewicz described it in a blog post on *The American Scholar* in March 2017.[1] We want to reflect on this case of the rhetoric of 'bad religion' that differs in some important regards from other instances discussed in this volume. We will ask, on the one hand, what we can learn from these debates in regard to our interest in the public rhetoric of 'good' and 'bad' religion, and, on the other hand, what critical perspectives the study of religion can develop from the scholarly and public discussion regarding the events and phenomena we will detail below. As a case study, we will present some aspects of the mass media reaction to recent student protest movements at primarily US colleges and universities in order to focus on two things: first, the way in which the term "religion" and adjacent terminologies ("inquisition," "heterodoxy," "blasphemy," "ritual") have been used in a polemical way to describe such events; second, how an insider/outsider logic familiar to the study of religion seems to be at play in these controversies; following this, we will move beyond the exemplum of the student protests and ask what the study of religion can learn in regard to the insider/outsider problem by drawing on feminist standpoint theory to better understand the epistemic effects of marginalization and oppression.

A New 'Bad Religion' Has Arrived on the University Campus

A new 'bad religion' is troubling the university—or rather, to be precise, it is troubling certain mass media columnists, bloggers, and twitter commentators writing about this "new campus religion" (Deresiewicz 2017). One could argue, however, that this 'new religion' is not really a completely recent development. Almost a decade ago, in his book on the history of the concept, scholar Geoffrey Hughes (2010: 24) claimed that "political correctness […] politically can be seen as a new form of orthodoxy" and described it as having "its roots in ethics and religion." He refers to an entry in the 1991 *Random House Webster's College Dictionary* which defined the term as "marked by or adhering to a typically progressive orthodoxy on issues involving especially race, gender, sexual affinity, or ecology." Between 2010 and today one can find a variety of posts by conservative commentators and bloggers describing the "ancient evil religion of political correctness" or stating that "Political Correctness Has Replaced Christianity As the Religion of the West" (Huntwork 2014; CanSpeccy 2015). All this leads us to observe that a not altogether new, but increasingly prominent form of rhetoric about 'religion' has been established in the North American (and in some ways also the European) public sphere. And, interestingly, it clearly is a case of 'bad religion.'

Most readers will be at least somewhat familiar with an increasing list of recent controversies and student protests at universities and colleges, particularly in the US—but also in the UK and in Germany, where the dynamics are different and such clashes not (yet) equally widespread. Just to list a few:

- In February 2017, a planned appearance of right-wing provocateur Milo Yiannopoulos at University of California Berkeley led to violent clashes between protesters and university police (Fuller 2017).

- In March 2017, at Middlebury College (Vermont), a private liberal arts college, students (encouraged by some faculty) protested and disrupted an event where Charles Murray, controversial author of *The Bell Curve*, was supposed to speak about his new book (Seely 2017).

- In May 2017, a controversy developed when biology professor Bret Weinstein criticized plans for a "Day of Absence" at Evergreen State College in Washington State, in which a tradition of minority students and faculty members absenting themselves was reversed and white students and faculty were asked to not come to campus for one day (Hartocollis 2017).

- In the UK, in November 2015, Australian professor and feminist author Germaine Greer gave a talk at Cardiff University in the midst of protests against that lecture on the basis that Greer held transphobic views, while in Germany, in May 2019, the protests of a small student group against a conference on the "Islamic Veil" as a "Symbol of Dignity or Oppression?" at the University of Frankfurt led to a media debate about "academic freedom" (Johnston 2015; Kehler and Davydov 2019).

Recent years have seen many other big and small instances of such public, media-fueled controversies. Since these events all have very different histories and issues addressed by student protestors and activists are by no means identical, one could question whether it is actually legitimate to treat them here as a consistent list of exempla for what follows. Nevertheless, we want to see what we can learn in regard to the public rhetoric of 'bad religion' by analyzing them in this way, especially since there is a consistent pattern in media reactions to these controversies that sees them as part of a cohesive 'movement' and a common expression of a 'threat to free speech' on the university campus. One of the interesting aspects of this reaction is that media commentators using this 'rhetoric of bad religion' are located all across the board, from Christian and conservative critics, to liberal and progressive writers.

Andrew Sullivan, for example, in a post on the *New York Magazine* website, asks: "Is Intersectionality a Religion?" (Sullivan 2017) and William Deresiewicz (as already quoted above) describes "political correctness" as the "new campus religion" (Deresiewicz 2017). A *New York Times* op-ed calls for "[t]hese Campus Inquisitions" to stop (Bruni 2017), while a conservative online magazine describes "identity politics" as a "progressive religion" in which "members of oppressed identity groups are elevated to a kind of sainthood" (Metzgar 2019). In Europe, for example, a German online magazine has picked up Sullivan's characterization and identified "a kind of religious ritual" in the new student protests (Mühlbauer 2017). Many other recent examples could be listed.[2] On what criteria do these commentators base their assessments?

Sullivan takes the March 2017 protests against a talk that controversial political scientist and author Charles Murray was supposed to give at Middlebury College in Vermont as his starting point and writes:

> "Intersectionality" is the latest academic craze sweeping the American academy. [...] It is operating, in Orwell's words, as a "smelly little orthodoxy," and it manifests itself, it seems to me, almost as a religion. It posits a classic orthodoxy through which all of human experience is explained [...]. Its version of original sin is the power of some identity groups over others. To overcome this sin, you need first to confess, i.e., "check your privilege," and subsequently live your life and order your thoughts in a way that keeps this sin at bay. [...] The saints are the most oppressed who nonetheless resist. [...] The only thing this religion lacks, of course, is salvation. It operates as a religion in one other critical dimension: If you happen to see the world in a different way [...] you are not just wrong, you are immoral. [...] And you are not just complicit, your heresy is a direct threat to others, and therefore needs to be extinguished. (Sullivan 2017)[3]

Sullivan considers "intersectionality" as "almost a religion" and describes the ways in which he sees its 'religious nature' at work in the campus protests with a large variety of concepts borrowed from the history of Christianity, such as 'original sin,' 'confession,' 'saints,' 'salvation,' or 'heresy.' He goes on to characterize what happened at the students' protest against Murray's planned talk in similar terms:

> And what I saw on the video struck me most as a form of religious ritual—a secular exorcism, if you will—that reaches a frenzied, disturbing catharsis. When Murray starts to speak, the students stand and ritually turn their backs on him in silence. The heretic must not be looked at, let alone engaged. Then they recite a common liturgy in unison from sheets of paper." [...] "Hey hey, ho ho! Charles Murray has got to go." Then: "Racist, Sexist, Anti-gay. Charles Murray, Go away!" [...] Murray has long supported marriage equality. [...] But none of that matters. Intersectionality, remember? If you're deemed a sinner on one count, you are a sinner on them all. (Sullivan 2017)

In a similar vein, Deresiewicz, in the above-cited article, argues that "[s]elective private colleges have become religious schools." In this case, the 'religion' in question is not Christianity or any other of the 'world religions,' but "an extreme version of the belief system of the liberal elite." Attending such a school, according to Deresiewicz, equals being "socialized, and not infrequently, indoctrinated into that religion" (Deresiewicz 2017). What is he referring to?

> What does it mean to say that these institutions are religious schools? First, that they possess a dogma, unwritten but understood by all: a set of "correct" opinions and beliefs, or at best, a narrow range within which disagreement is permitted. [...] Secularism is taken for granted. Environmentalism is a sacred cause. Issues of identity—principally the holy trinity of race, gender, and sexuality—occupy the center of concern. The presiding presence is Michel Foucault [...]. The fundamental questions [...] are understood to have been settled. The assumption, on elite college campuses, is that we are already in full possession of the moral truth. This is a religious attitude. [...] Which brings us to another thing that comes with dogma: heresy. Heresy means those beliefs that undermine the orthodox consensus, so it must be eradicated: by education, by reeducation—if necessary, by censorship. (Deresiewicz 2017)

Just like Sullivan, Deresiewicz makes extensive use of terms from Christian theology and history to elaborate on his characterization of the "new campus religion." He sees an "orthodoxy" at work that has established a left-wing consensus and—as any good 'religious dogma'—does not allow any questioning of these beliefs.

The German online magazine *Telepolis* has also picked up on these descriptions, with author Peter Mühlbauer arguing that the point of the new campus protest movements is "an unreflective form of self-assurance in something like a religious ritual [...] that serves to confirm one's own purity which would be sullied by different opinions." He also claims that the "intellectual equipment for this new religion stems from the teaching methods of certain [academic] disciplines" (Mühlbauer 2017).[4] Here, not only are the descriptions cited above being reproduced, but we also see that the blame for the emergence of this problematic 'new religion' is put on particular disciplines at the university (mostly identified by the author as 'postmodern' cultural studies and gender studies).

A comprehensive take on the issue appeared in the self-described "broadly liberal and humanist" online magazine *Areo* (see https://areomagazine.com/submissions) in December 2018 (written by James A. Lindsay and Mike Nayna), proving that such descriptions are still being furthered (Lindsay and Nayna 2018). The article provides an "inordinately long" almost "short book on the topic" under the heading "Postmodern Religion and the Faith of Social Justice." On the basis of a Durkheimian understanding of religions as "moral communities" the authors argue that "Social Justice"—based on "identity politics and political correctness (along with the more recent buzzworded concepts of equity, diversity, and inclusion)"—can be shown to possess "many religion-like qualities." Rather than arguing that it *is* a religion, however, the article goes on to claim that "it is certainly religion-like enough to treat in a way that's similar to how we should treat religions—that is, we should approach them with an attitude generally associated with secularism." Unlike Sullivan, therefore, Lindsay and Nayna suggest that the solution to this new religion's spread seems to be not a reinstatement of the central societal role of traditional religion but rather a strengthening of "secularism" as the "committed prevention of institutionalizing religious doctrines and practice in liberal governments."[5] This perspective is connected with a particular view of the current political situation as a struggle "between universal liberalism and identity politics" that Lindsay describes in another co-written essay (Pluckrose and Lindsay 2018). "Identity politics" is seen here as a movement seeking the "political empowerment" of particular identity groups understood as "monolithic, marginalized entit[ies]." Instead of promoting "the worth of the individual regardless of status of race, gender, sex, sexuality, or other markers of identity," proponents of "identity politics" are described as convinced that "for true equality to exist, the knowledge of women and racial and sexual minorities, which are understood to be different and products of lived experience, should be foregrounded." This view, the authors argue, is based on the idea that there is an "authoritative form of identity-based knowledge that cannot be disagreed with by anyone outside that group" (ibid.). Lindsay and Nayna (2018) describe this "faith that group-based identity is real, meaningful, and a site of oppression" as a central aspect of the "postmodern religion" they discuss. We will take up this topic of 'insider knowledge' in the following sections.

Pronouncements of the 'religious character' of the contemporary student protests do also provoke pushback to these descriptions, like atheist writer Lauren Nelson's response on the blog *Friendly Atheist*. She writes:

> [I]ntersectional beliefs are no more a "religion" than feminism, or anti-racism, or a political party, or any other cultural ideology. There is no deity being praised. There are no churches. There are no sacraments. These ideologies don't stem from books written thousands of years ago with centuries of suspect revisions and politicized interpretations. It stems from actual modern lived experiences. [...] This isn't about virtue. It's about basic dignity. (Nelson 2017)

This claim that there is nothing 'religious' about intersectionality is then taken up by another blogger, who argues why religion can be understood in a broader sense:

> To summarize, Nelson tries to refute Andrew Sullivan's argument about intersectionality being a new, secular religion. [...] Nelson tries to do this by highlighting the differences [between intersectionality and religion]. Let's review each one and see what's wrong with it.
> There is no deity being praised. *Irrelevant, as not all religions praise deities.*
> There are no churches. *Irrelevant, as not all religions have houses of worship.*
> [...] These ideologies don't stem from books and instead stem from actual modern lived experiences. *Contradicted by evidence.* [...] (Shadow To Light 2017)

We can only offer a limited glimpse at these debates here, and thus acknowledge that they might not be fully representative of the way that the general public reacts to the recent controversies on college and university campuses, now described by some popular commentators as another 'free speech crisis' (see e.g. Slater 2016; Haidt and Lukianoff 2018). Nevertheless, in the context of this volume, this is an interesting discursive phenomenon, since what is discussed as a 'bad religion' is not a particular interpretation of one of the 'world religions' or any other 'religious movement.' Instead, the term 'religion' is used in a polemical sense to describe the student protest movement as rigid, irrational, and closed to debate.

A Critical Religious Studies Perspective on the "New Campus Religion"

Why should the study of religion engage with the emerging discourse of the "new campus religion" that we have presented here? There are at least two aspects of this. On the one hand, studying the contemporary usage of the category 'religion' in the public sphere is itself an important topic for the study of religion; this includes contextualizing and historicizing such usage as described above. On the other hand, could the study of religion as an academic discipline—attracted to this topic by the overt use of the marker "religion"—make a contribution not only to the study of this rhetoric of 'bad religion,' but also provide some further reflection on debates about "political correctness," "intersectionality," "free speech," and "identity politics" that increasingly seem to be taking place (or at least the mass media discourse makes us think so) not only in the US but also in Europe?

We will address the first aspect here and come back to the second in the next two sections of this essay. What contributions to analyzing this rhetoric of 'bad religion' could the study of religion make? We want to shortly discuss at least two approaches: (a) first, we can embed this particular rhetoric of 'bad religion' into a genealogy of religion as a derogatory term (and thereby highlight its implicit 'Protestant bias'); (b) second, we can try to show how 'religion' as a label for these campus protests facilitates the creation of new alliances between ideologically divided camps such as liberals, conservatives, and those on the Christian right.

One way in which this analysis could proceed is to relate this case of a rhetoric of 'bad religion' to a genealogy of particular negative connotations—'religion' as a derogatory term—in order to show the location of this discourse both in the history of critiques of religion and in interreligious polemics. The 'bad' elements of religion listed by the commentators, which include confessional pressure, the ritualistic nature of the protests, and the dogmatic orthodoxy of intersectionality, reflect particular Protestant critiques of the backwardness and mindlessness of Catholicism.[6] Even a public Catholic like Andrew Sullivan in this sense reveals somewhat of a 'Protestant' bias in his polemics against intersectionality. Such a religious critique of this new 'false' religion therefore can find common ground here with general critiques of all religion as ideological irrationalism (see below).

Additional questions could be asked: What historical understandings of 'religion' do these descriptions of the "new campus religion" draw on and how is that connected to the purchase and plausibility they seem to have in the (US) public sphere? In what way do existing elements of the rhetoric of 'bad religion,' as described by other chapters in this volume, also make an appearance in this discourse? What roles do certain understandings of science and the scientific worldview as 'rational' play (as opposed to the presumed 'irrationality' of religion)? How does a distinction between 'the religious' and 'the secular' figure here if the "Faith of Social Justice" is analyzed as a "secular moral ideology," as in the *Areo* magazine piece quoted above (Lindsay and Nayna 2018)? How could this case therefore help us to come to a more concise understanding of the role that such rhetoric plays in contemporary public discourse?

While we cannot go further here in attempting to answer the questions raised above for the sake of brevity, we nevertheless want to address one more issue: Who is the audience for this type of rhetoric? One possible answer could be that these descriptions are so successful precisely because they allow two usually opposed camps to meet in their opposition to this "new campus religion." The rhetoric of 'bad religion' allows self-identified 'conservative' and/or 'religious' people who see these movements of "Social Justice" as a 'false religion' (as opposed to 'true religion,' often Christianity) to find common ground with self-identified 'non-religious,' often 'liberal' people or 'atheists' who see all religion as 'bad' (and current "Social Justice" movements as just one more instance of irrationality).[7] In this way, this discourse of 'bad religion' creates new alliances between a certain class of 'liberal leftists' and the '(Christian) right' that is opposed to certain progressive movements and the perceived dominance of 'postmodern (or gender studies) ideology' on campus.[8] Similar transformations might be at work in the category of 'free speech' more generally, which is quickly becoming a red herring for particular right-wing political positions (see Battaglia 2014; Sultana 2018). This opposition to the perceived ideological nature of "political correctness" can apparently also provide common ground for otherwise very different intellectual positions, as seen recently in a public debate between Slavoj Žižek und Jordan Peterson (Marche 2019).

What unites our preliminary analyses of the 'bad religion' rhetoric regarding the "new campus religion" is that our second-order critical perspective does not engage with the descriptions of "political correctness" as "religion" by taking a side in this debate and arguing for or against this point of view. Rather, we attempt to contribute to a second-order evaluation of this emerging discourse by contextualizing and historicizing it. The critical study of religion that this volume espouses does not itself participate in the rhetoric of 'good' and 'bad' religion, declaring 'religion' in general (or any particular religious expression for that matter) as a phenomenon that is either good or bad. Rather, as we argue here, the fact that people describe religion alternatively as an essentially positive or negative phenomenon is itself our object of study, and what we find is that the concept of religion in contemporary society is an 'essentially contested category.' Not only is 'religion' being debated as being either helpful or harmful to individuals and society at large, but the application of the labels 'religion' and 'religious' to a particular phenomenon is often being debated hotly in itself.

The Insider/Outsider Problem in the Study of Religion and the Current Campus Protests

As a critical enterprise, the academic study of religion is particularly well-suited to contribute to an analysis of debates of this kind, not because it has amassed so much knowledge about 'religion' as a phenomenon in the world, but because there has long existed an intense reflection on the fact that societal disputes about a concept like 'religion' already precede any scholarly analysis. Wherever scholars of religion look in contemporary world society, everywhere they will find situations where 'religion' is being contested. Drawing on this history, Anne Koch (2006: 255) has described the discipline as a potential "Theorienschmiede" (*forge of theories*) of theoretical and methodological reflection for all cultural studies disciplines, as "its history is pervaded by a permanent self-criticism and the withdrawal of more or less concealed religious models" from its own analytical perspective. The academic study of religion can therefore, on the one hand, critically analyze and contextualize the use of 'religion' in public discourse (as briefly demonstrated in the section above). On the other hand, the discipline might be able to contribute to an analysis of current societal conflicts about "political correctness" that is occasioned by descriptions of some aspects of these controversies as "religious" without at the same time accepting the premises underlying this example of the rhetoric of 'bad religion.'

One of the things at stake in the campus protests is the question of how to engage with truth claims put forward by actors that identify as being part of particular (often marginalized) groups. In their elaborate critique of such protests as having "religion-like qualities," the authors of the *Areo* magazine article already quoted above argue that "standpoint epistemology" as "the philosophical powerhouse behind intersectionality" implies the demand to value the identities and experiences of "moral tribalists" over the scientific objectivity envisioned by the "rational skepticism of the Enlightenment" (Lindsay and Nayna 2018). As a solution to this problem of "identity politics," they claim that in "secular societies" such forms of "pocket epistemologies" should be rejected or relegated to the private sphere, just like any other religious position. The point here—in an explicit parallelization of student protesters and religious actors—is that insiders' claims should not inform public policy in "liberal societies." Rather, such societies "have already developed and made one of their cornerstones" the idea that "secularism," understood as "forming a bulwark between church and state" is the adequate "answer to dealing with groups that forward special knowledge as though it is knowledge" (Lindsay and Nayna 2018). We can therefore understand this as one of the central issues at stake in the critique of the campus protests and the broader movements of "Social Justice"—namely, the question of how to deal with the truth claims of *insiders* both in a scientific context and in society as a whole. It is here where one could argue that scholars of religion, because of the discipline's history and the ways it has reflected on its object of study, have expert knowledge and might be able to contribute.

There have always been those who have argued that an important starting point for the academic study of religion is the commitment to 'respect' all religious positions, often at the same time leading to an exclusion of questions of (religious) truth from the things that scholars of religion engage with. At the same time, because truth-claims have often been seen as a central aspect of its object of study, a large variety of perspectives on how to address this relationship between the academic study of religion and questions of (religious) truth have been developed.

For the US context, Alan J. Levinovitz (2016: 16) has recently argued for the "value of intolerance" in the religious studies classroom as a space where debate about religious truth claims has to be possible. He dismisses (ibid.: 10) what he calls "bumper-sticker postmodernism" (a position he describes as "It's true for him so it's true; there's no way to prove beliefs right or wrong; facts are just social constructs—and so on.") and equally rejects a second option he sees as prevalent in religious studies: silence. Those who refuse relativism, he says, often choose to remain silent about anything that could be seen as critical of or offensive toward religious claims. Part of this problem is, of course, the 'world religions discourse' and the idea that in the end all religions are somehow compatible or 'the same' so that it is not necessary to debate about their truth claims. Instead, Levinovitz argues, in the context of a university classroom there is a need for spaces "where religiously intolerant confrontations can take place, confrontations that force [...] existential challenges" to the religious convictions of the students, as this for him is "the essential purpose and unique objective of higher education" (ibid.: 27). The classroom should therefore be a place where we discuss beliefs rather than relativizing them or being silent about them.

Crucially important to Levinovitz's argument is his understanding of the special nature of the classroom. The *university* as a broader space has to be distinguished from the *classroom* as the space in which these "intolerant" debates take place. While the university is a broad institution that also has to include a variety of "safe spaces," the classroom is a place where one should expect to be challenged even in regard to deeply held beliefs. He argues:

> Students and teachers expect different norms to govern offices, dorm rooms, and classrooms. These can be thought of as forming an arc: at one end are spaces in which people expect not to be engaged in dialogues about their religious beliefs—the bathroom, say, or one's personal residence. At the other end are spaces explicitly dedicated to the pursuit of truth. (Levinovitz 2016: 32)

It is clear that—on the basis of his teaching experience in a particular US context, where most students probably come to the classroom with some form of explicit religious conviction—Levinovitz sees it as the task of religious studies instruction to debate the relative value of particular religious truth claims. This is probably not the position that most scholars in this volume would take. At the same time, they would probably argue that their alternative positions are not exhausted by the two positions Levinovitz criticizes: postmodern relativism and silence about truth claims. Additionally, one could say that his concept of questioning and debating truth claims in the religious studies classroom mirrors the relationship which theology as an academic discipline entertains with Christianity. The version of religious studies advocated by Levinovitz could be called a kind of 'generalized theology' since it constructs the scholarly engagement with religious beliefs of any kind after the model of Christian theology: a critical and rational exchange about propositional beliefs.

The questions raised by Levinovitz regarding if and how (religious) truth claims should be debated in the religious studies classroom point to an issue that the study of religion, like all humanities scholarship, has been grappling with from the beginning. It can be generalized as a particular version of the insider/outsider problem. Following Russell T. McCutcheon (1999), four classic positions in regard to this issue can be distinguished: empathic, explanatory, agnostic, and reflexive.[9] While an empathic stance aims at 'taking seriously' the meanings of people's actions and beliefs in an attempt at understanding, an explanatory perspective instead is interested in exploring the generalized regularities that govern human behavior with little regard to the insiders' convictions (ibid.: 5). As a mediating position, an agnostic perspective attempts to avoid either quickly validating insiders' claims or dismissing them outright. It consists of a 'bracketing out' of all truth claims through 'methodological agnosticism,' leading to a focus on description, cataloguing, and comparison, rather than explanation (ibid.: 7–8). A fourth option, the reflexive stance, sees the scholar's experiences itself as the bridge between insider and outsider, on the one hand allowing for a projection of "the researcher's experiences on the other," and on the other claiming that "all observations are inextricably entwined with the self-referential statements of the observer" (ibid.: 9). To these four, McCutcheon (ibid.: 369) adds his own position of "critical inquiry" that tries to avoid taking a side between description and explanation and argues for the necessity of both—historically detailed contextualization *and* second-order theory-building—if the academic study of religion wants to avoid turning into advocacy instead of critical inquiry.

Even though reflections on this problem have arisen at different points in the history of a number of humanities disciplines,[10] there is an argument to be made why it was and is particularly pressing for the study of religion. Many scholars wonder what good a study of religion could be if questions of religious truth claims are being treated as beyond the scope of the discipline. In this sense, a pressing need to engage with the object of study on the level of first-order observation has accompanied the history of the discipline in different versions, as seen in the need to 'take religion seriously,' as well as in the conviction that scholarship must be communicated in a way that the religious people studied can agree to the scholarly descriptions, etc. All of this points us once again to the question of whether insider experiences and insider perspectives on the object of study have to play a certain role in research.

It is here where this rather academic debate from the study of religion connects to larger contemporary societal issues. A general aspect of the current debates about what has been termed "political correctness" and "identity politics" seems to be the question of the value of insider perspectives and experiences not only in determining the rules of our collective life (for example in regard to discrimination, marginalization, and racism; see Baer 2017), but also in regard to the *study* of specific cultures and groups (what makes the issue also particularly important in regard to the university). What role should the experiences of marginalized people play in their study and in the study of marginalization in general? And is it helpful—or possibly even necessary—to have experienced marginalization and discrimination oneself in order to study it?

This question of the necessity of insider experience has featured in the study of religion from the beginning: is it necessary to be religious oneself in order to really understand religion? Is someone who is religiously "unmusical," as Max Weber put it, able to 'really understand' religion? In other words: is insider experience a necessary condition for the study of a particular subject matter? Most humanities disciplines, especially those that are comparative, have probably, at one point or another, found themselves engaged with this question.

Such discussions about the insider/outsider problem have once again become heightened in our contemporary moment. One the one hand, there is renewed emphasis on the question of whether scholars, who (traditionally) acted as *outsiders* to the religions and cultures they were studying, are able to fully grasp the objects of their study. On the other hand, because of the increasing diversity of scholarly discourse itself, there is a growing number of scholars from formerly underrepresented groups who are *insiders* in a particular culture and at the same time act as scholarly outsiders studying their own culture. How does this changed situation affect debates about the insider/outsider problem?

Maybe it is here where a reflection on the history of the study of religion might be helpful. While for many disciplines like anthropology or sociology the vocal presence of an increasing number of scholars who themselves claim a particular insider expertise is a new situation (as there were not many established scholars e.g. from non-Western cultures or from socially marginalized groups before), the parallel existence of a large number of vocal insiders-as-scholars has always been the status quo for the study of religion. *Theology*, as an academic insider-project has a much longer history as a scholarly discourse than religious studies. In this sense, there have always been privileged insiders—theologians—present in the broader field of disciplines studying religion. And as far as academic (Christian) theology is concerned, these insiders were not only insiders in the sense of religious experts but also insiders in another sense: scholarly insiders, as (Christian) theology has had—and in many places still has—a strong and privileged position within the university.

While other disciplines are now confronted with an increasing number of 'insiders' who are at the same time credentialed scholars, this has therefore always been the case for the study of religion. Maybe we can learn something from the history of engaging with this problem of insider scholarship in the study of religion and develop a more general model to address this situation, even if we cannot do much more than raise such questions in this essay.

At the same time, the recent campus activists differ in at least one important respect from Christian insiders in most theology departments, since the majority of them speaks from *non-privileged positions*. While both theologians as well as non-privileged campus activists can be described as insiders in regard to their respective experience, these experiences are presumably quite different in practice. This leads us to the question: how does the insider/outsider problem intersect with questions of privileged/non-privileged speaking positions?

As discussed above, the study of religion has a pronounced tradition of self-critical analysis towards its object of study. We argued that the issues raised by Levinovitz in regard to the religious studies classroom can be generalized as a version of the insider/outsider problem, towards which McCutcheon, as described above, has distinguished four approaches, plus his own position of "critical inquiry." We now might be able to see that all of these five attempts at resolving the insider/outsider problem fail to systematically take into account the question of whether the insiders are privileged or non-privileged in a particular social situation. Our argument here, then, is that one aspect of the campus protests that might be interesting for the study of religion is that they push us to systematically complement the insider/outsider distinction and the problems connected to it with a distinction between privileged and non-privileged positions. Both Levinovitz and McCutcheon do not give this second distinction enough space. McCutcheon (1999: 369) hints at its importance by describing it as the job of scholars of religion to "investigate [...] marginalized social formations in an effort to learn not only how to describe accurately their behavior and belief systems but also how to use this information as the basis for investigating the utter complexity of all human behavior," but he does not develop this into a systematic argument. Similarly, Bruce Lincoln (1999: 396–397), addresses the question of privilege in this 8th thesis on method, when he argues that we should not take the statements of privileged insiders as representative for a particular group or culture. In his 13th thesis, however, he then states (ibid.: 398) that "[w]hen one permits those whom one studies to define the terms in which they will be understood[,]" a critical scholarly perspective is suspended and replaced by other non-scholarly attitudes like advocacy or cheerleading. We might learn from the contemporary campus protests and the increasing presence of scholars from non-privileged contexts that upholding the distinction between those doing the studying and those being studied might not be as simple.

We have also highlighted the distinction between the classroom and the university at large (developed by Levinovitz) that points us to consider different ways the insider/outsider problem should be addressed depending on what social space we are talking about. This makes the complexity of the problem even more apparent and connects it to broader questions of university's role in society. If we follow the mass media commentators on the campus protests, the issue at stake is often described as a danger to "freedom of speech" at the university. One could argue however, that in order to develop a more complex view on the issue, we first have to distinguish between the principle of "free speech" as governing the public sphere at large from the idea of "academic freedom" as the normative basis of the modern university. As Robert Mark Simpson and Amia Srinivasan (2018) propose, it is the latter that should govern interactions in the university classroom and probably also on the university campus. Rather than being oriented towards the value of "free speech" as guaranteeing everyone the right of public expression of their ideas, "academic freedom" is meant precisely to support "academic disciplines in amplifying the speech of experts and marginalizing the speech of non-experts" (ibid.: 196). On this basis, academic freedom, can be understood as compatible with the "exclusion of speakers and viewpoints"—as well as with the privileging of others, e.g. particular insiders—"for content based [...] reasons" (ibid.: 205). It is in this way, that an engagement with the 'bad religion' rhetoric applied to the campus protests could be an occasion for the study of religion to extend its consideration of the insider/outsider problem in regard to a differentiation between different spaces on campus as well as between a variety of social spaces in modern society.

Concerning the question of the role of insider experiences and perspectives in the academic field, we therefore have *three* distinctions to work with: insider/outsider, privileged/non-privileged, and classroom/university (or university/society). What we end up with, then, are the contours of a more complex model of what has been discussed as the insider/outsider problem, intersecting this existing distinction with two additional ones: a distinction between privileged/non-privileged and a distinction between a variety of social spaces in which the recognition of insider and outsider perspectives might be variably important. If the contemporary campus protests have something to do with the ways in which the experiences and positions of non-privileged insiders should be considered in scholarship and on campus, then the study of religion should take this as an occasion to recognize that its current ways of engaging the insider/outsider problem have been insufficiently complex.

Some Future Challenges for the Study of Religion in Regard to the Insider/Outsider Problem

Analyzing the 'bad religion' rhetoric in regard to the "new campus religion" and related current debates about "political correctness" and "identity politics" has led us to a re-engagement with the insider/outsider problem as a central question for the study of religion. Our preliminary proposal is to complement this distinction with two additional intersecting aspects: privileged/non-privileged and the broader question of different social spaces that Levinovitz's classroom/university distinction has pointed us to. What happens if we look at this in a more global perspective?

Two issues take precedence here: how does the insider/outsider problem have to be rethought in regard to a future postcolonial comparative study of religion beyond the West? And what could feminist standpoint theory that tries to show how positions of marginalization or oppression can serve as a basis for specific epistemological privileges contribute to the complexification of the insider/outsider problem with the other two distinctions mentioned above?

In an overview article, Kim Knott (2009) highlights two recent contributions to the insider/outsider debate. On the one hand, she notes how Peter Collins (2002) takes a postmodern stance, arguing that a more dynamic way of conceptualizing the self and society allows the insider/outsider binary to become irrelevant, making it visible as "an unhelpful consequence of a modernist view of self and society" (Knott 2009: 269). On the other hand, she describes Arvind-Pal Mandair's (2001) proposal of a more radical argument that the insider/outsider debate is representative of the dominance of a Western, secularist, and objectivist understanding of scholarship that should be abandoned in favor of a study of religion that is "at once a form of self-discovery, no less spiritual than political, no less therapeutic than classificatory" (ibid.: 68–69).

Even if one does not agree with this formulation or with Mandair's project as such, it seems that as part of a critical post-secular analysis that denaturalizes a secularist perspective without renaturalizing a supposedly more primal religious one (see Parmaksız 2018), questions regarding the role of second-order observation have to be raised. What can the future of scholarly second-order observation be in light of the complexity of the insider/outsider problem, especially if a discipline depends on it as much as the study of religion? We might follow Jürgen Mohn (2012: §16), for example, in arguing that a difference between the critical scholarly discourse and the religious discourse, however much it may be constructed or co-constituted by the scholars doing the study, is foundational for the study of religion as an academic discipline. Likewise, Knott (2009: 270) recognizes that a project like Mandair's—"no longer [...] compartmentalis[ing] the world of faith and the world of scholarship"—runs the danger of making the scholarly study of religion indistinguishable from religious activity and forms of writing: "For some scholars this would be a step too far, one which undermines the distinction between those doing religion and those observing it, between theology and the study of religions, indeed the very *raison d'être* of the latter as a field of study with its own terms of reference" (ibid.).

Even if we ourselves sympathize with the views of Mohn and Knott in seeing the maintenance of the distinction between a first-order religious discourse and a second-order scholarly observation as a necessary requisite for the future of the discipline, this distinction should not be understood as an essentialist difference between two forms of discourse. Instead, it is the result of the construction of a certain scholarly perspective that makes the particular intellectual project of our discipline possible. This is the challenge, then: to retain this distinction but to recognize the problems connected to it and to reformulate it in a non-foundationalist, nonessentialist way. And this implies a reflection on the epistemic consequences that should be drawn in light of the criticism as exemplified by Mandair.

On a more global level, the study of religion, being confronted with the complexification of the insider/outsider problem along the lines developed above, can therefore ask itself what the future of the discipline would look like if it takes the political content of the student protests discussed in this essay into account. This could mean that we start to more systematically pay attention to questions of privilege in addressing the insider/outsider problem in the study of religion.

In doing so, we could draw on insights developed in the context of feminist standpoint theory: that "those who are subject to structures of domination that systematically marginalize and oppress them may, in fact, be epistemically privileged in some crucial respect. They may know different things, or know some things better" (Wylie 2003: 26).

It seems important, however, both for the contemporary moment in which such issues are discussed in terms of "identity politics" and in particular as a contribution to thinking about the insider/outsider problem in the study of religion, to *not* immediately (and non-reflexively) associate demands for a broader recognition of (formerly) marginalized perspectives with two positions: an "*essentialist* definition of the social categories or collectivities in terms of which epistemically relevant standpoints are characterized," and the idea of an "*automatic epistemic privilege*" in the sense "that those who occupy particular standpoints [...] automatically know more, or know better, by virtue of their social, political location" (Wylie 2003: 28).

Instead, as Wylie (2003: 30) tries to show, "[n]onfoundationalist, nonessentialist arguments [...] for attributing epistemic advantage to some social locations and standpoints" can be given, even if, in her opinion, such arguments will not allow us to posit "ahistorical, translocational foundations." A critical study of religion, not least because of its history, can in any case not be interested in such foundations. This is what we share with Lincoln (1999). But in a certain respect it might be necessary to move beyond his opposition between insider/outsider, since the epistemological problems posed by the study of marginalized groups cannot be solved by solely forbidding "those whom one studies to define the terms in which they will be understood" (ibid.: 398). While this claim is justified insofar as that first order experiences should not be allowed to dictate the second order notions used in the study of religion, the decision not to replace second order observations with first order experiences does not sufficiently address the question of how to pay adequate attention to both socially and intellectually marginalized subjects and their experiences. In order to do so, we suggest to complement the insider/outsider distinction with considerations of privilege and the difference between particular social spaces that we have discussed above, and to therefore—in some cases—take into account insider perspectives and experiences as part of our critical scholarship.

This differential treatment of some insider perspectives depending on privilege and context does not have to defy the distinction between insider practices and the academic observation of these practices. While a more comprehensive recognition of the importance of listening to marginalized groups is the result of the subjective expressions of (formerly) unheard or silenced voices, the *form* which the preferential treatment of these perspectives takes still has to remain a decision of the scholar. This decision has to be based on the logics of second order observation established by religious studies as a discipline. The consequences that the preferential treatment of experiences put forward by (formerly) non-privileged groups will have therefore still depends on the theories, methods, and empirical knowledge that constitute religious studies as an academic discipline. Thus, recognizing the importance of non-privileged subjectivities does not mean to replace second order scholarly notions with first order lived experiences. Instead, it points to an intensification of an ongoing process of translation that takes power into account.

However, as the conceptual frame of the study of religion has been most strongly influenced by Christian theology and by Western secularism, a special focus on the insider experiences of those marginalized by these dominant discourses offers great potential for enriching the discipline's concepts and categories. Adopting a perspective that pays special attention to these historically excluded points of view may ultimately lead to a revision of concepts and theories. These changes, while still being decidedly realized in a scholarly second order mode of observation, would not be possible without taking into account the first order experiences of the (formerly) marginalized.

This process of integrating (formerly) excluded first order experiences into the process of constructing the notions that constitute our objects of study may be able to correct some of the Eurocentric biases of our discipline. Nevertheless, even such a revised version of religious studies would still remain a decidedly Western project given that the distinction between first and second order observations of religious phenomena still defines the epistemic horizon of the discipline. Religious studies cannot accept any rejection of its theories, methodologies, or empirical knowledge that is based on anything but arguments formulated within the cognitive boundaries of its disciplinary context. Consequently, truth claims that are solely based on insider or religious grounds do not take on relevance within the context of religious studies as an academic discipline.

The question of how to integrate non-privileged positions equally arises in the context of teaching. The function of the classroom is to put the students into the position to adopt a religious studies perspective. In order to do so the students need to learn how to differentiate between first and second order observations of religious practices—not to convey the superiority of religious studies, but to help the students develop the ability to adopt a point of view that is grounded in a logic of second order observation and that thus can make use of the theories, methods, and empirical knowledge produced by religious studies as an academic discipline.

A central lesson to be learned in a religious studies classroom continues to be that religious and scholarly truth claims operate in different modes of observation. Thus, subjective 'religious' sensibilities cannot dictate what is or is not taught. But the distinction between privileged and non-privileged positions should at least lead us to question how teaching the value of this distinction between first and second order observation can proceed in ways that at the same time are sensible to the specific subjectivities of those that come from marginalized backgrounds. Epistemic privilege in the sense of Wylie does not mean that a knowledge claim can be justified by simply pointing to the subject which utters the proposition in question. Instead, her argument stresses that positions of oppression or marginalization offer unique epistemic privileges which can be used to gain exclusive knowledge. To be able to act as an expert regarding the lived experience of (formerly) marginalized groups requires both: some kind of knowledge that can only be gained by being an insider of the marginalized group and the critical capacity to distinguish between a first order observation in the context of one's insider culture and a second order observation from a scholarly point of view.

The religious studies classroom has to deal with this confrontation between someone's beliefs and their own critical reflection on these views when attempting to look at a phenomenon to which one is an insider from the second order perspective of a scholarly observer. Concerning the distinction between the classroom and the university campus this means that while the former has to be a space of open inquiry into all knowledge claims including the first order religious experiences of the members of marginalized groups, the later has to be a safe space which enables the participation of (formerly) marginalized groups or subjectivities.

Thus, in regard to the study of religion as an academic endeavor, current controversies about the relevance of the subjective experience of non-privileged persons in the classroom and on campus are not about freedom of speech, but about the freedom of everyone, including marginalized groups, to participate in and contribute to the knowledge established by religious studies as a discipline. Such a treatment of the insider/outsider problem that is sensible to the difference between privileged and non-privileged positions constitutes one of the most important steps for the future of any comparative cultural studies discipline, in which 'insiders,' formerly marginal to the Western scholarly enterprise, are becoming equally established as scholars in their own right.

Adrian Hermann is Full Professor of Religion and Society and Director of the Department of Religion Studies at Forum Internationale Wissenschaft, University of Bonn. His work focuses on the global history of the concept of "religion," the use of non-fictional media in contemporary religious movements, and the religious history of the globalized world. He is the author of *Unterscheidungen der Religion* (Göttingen: Vandenhoeck und Ruprecht, 2015) and is currently working on a monograph on Philippine independent Catholicism around 1900.

Stefan Priester is a post-doctoral researcher at Forum Internationale Wissenschaft, Universität Bonn, Germany. He received a D.Phil. in sociology from the University of Hamburg, Germany in 2018. His work focuses on world society theory, the early history of film as art, and questions of digital sociological theory and methodology.

Notes

1. We use single quotation marks as scare quotes and double quotation marks to indicate direct quotes from sources.
2. See e.g. the video series on "The Grievance Studies Affair" (www.youtube.com/playlist?list=PLLHyNSlsz449SOhzpo7ClMEKe9WkXt5GO) by Mike Nayna, contributing author to *Areo* magazine (see below).
3. It is clear that Sullivan is not primarily interested in engaging with the complex history of the concept of "intersectionality" and its successful spread beyond academic circles. On this see Hancock (2016).

4 What "disciplines" Mühlbauer has in mind to is not made explicit, but a link to a caricature referencing "Microagressive White Privileged Anglo-European Imperialistic Western Culture" lets us imagine some form of 'postmodern' and 'postcolonial' cultural studies as the culprit.
5 We cannot further analyze here the role that ideas of "secularism" and "secularity" play in these debates in which a number of commentators are linked to the broader field of "New Atheism" and what Bari Weiss in the New York Times has called the "Intellectual Dark Web." See Weiss (2018). It would be an interesting project for critical scholars of religion to trace the usage of these concepts in the statements and articles discussed here.
6 As Birgit Meyer (2017: 305-306) argues, "[c]urrent commonsense discourses about religion [...] often mobilize stereotypical views of Catholic and Protestant religiosities that are grounded in long-standing tensions between these two strands of Christianity." See also Carroll (2007).
7 Sullivan's opinion piece, to only give one example, is referred to approvingly both by the secular humanists of the *Areo* essay on "Postmodern Religion" quoted above and conservative Christian university administrator Everett Piper in his 2017 book *Not a Day Care: The Devastating Consequences of Abandoning Truth*. Another example of such conservative Christian use of the trope is Metzgar (2019).
8 Another Areo essay describes both "postmoderns on the left and the premoderns on the right" as "enemies of modernity," which at the same time opens the door to an agreement with right-wing critiques of "Postmodern relativism." See Lindsay and Pluckrose (2017).
9 Knott (2009) offers a different typology, distinguishing the positions of "complete observer," "observer as participant," "participant as observer," and "complete participant" along a continuum from outsider to insider.
10 See e.g. for religious studies McCutcheon (1999), for anthropology Headland et al. (1990), and for sociology Merton (1972).

References

Baer, Ulrich. 2017. "What 'Snowflakes' Get Right about Free Speech." *New York Times*, April 24. Retrieved from www.nytimes.com/2017/04/24/opinion/what-liberal-snowflakes-get-right-about-free-speech.html (archived at archive.today/mnSe0).

Battaglia, Adria. 2014. "Opportunities of Our Own Making: The Struggle for 'Academic Freedom'." *AAUP Journal of Academic Freedom* 5. Retrieved from www.aaup.org/sites/default/files/Battaglia.pdf (archived at archive.today/PQNs0).

Bruni, Frank. 2017. "These Campus Inquisitions Must Stop." *The New York Times*, June 3. Retrieved from www.nytimes.com/2017/06/03/opinion/sunday/bruni-campus-inquisitions-evergreen-state.html (archived at archive.today/7xAji).

CanSpeccy. 2015. "Political Correctness Has Replaced Christianity as the Religion of the West." July 22. Retrieved from http://canspeccy.blogspot.de/2015/07/political-correctness-replaces.html (archived at archive.today/GLxHi).

Carroll, Michael P. 2007. *American Catholics in the Protestant Imagination: Rethinking the Academic Study of Religion*. Baltimore, MD: The John Hopkins Univ. Press.

Collins, Peter J. 2002. "Connecting Anthropology and Quakerism." In Elisabeth Arweck and Martin Stringer (eds.), *Theorising Faith: The Insider/Outsider Problem in the Study of Ritual*, 77-95. Birmingham: Birmingham University Press.

Deresiewicz, William. 2017. "On Political Correctness: Power, Class, and the New Campus Religion." *The American Scholar*, March 6. Retrieved from https://theamerican scholar.org/on-political-correctness (archived at: archive.today/UhP6d).

Fuller, Thomas. 2017. "A Free Speech Battle at the Birthplace of a Movement at Berkeley." *The New York Times*, February 2. Retrieved from www.nytimes.com/2017/02/02/us/university-california-berkeley-free-speech-milo-yiannopoulos.html (archived at archive.today/HhHTh).

Haidt, Jonathan and Greg Lukianoff. 2018. *The Coddling of the American Mind: How Good Intentions and Bad Ideas Are Setting Up a Generation for Failure*. New York: Penguin Press.

Hancock, Ange-Marie. 2016. *Intersectionality: An Intellectual History*. Oxford: Oxford University Press. https://doi.org/10.1093/acprof:oso/9780199370368.001.0001

Hartocollis, Anemona. 2017. "A Campus Argument Goes Viral. Now the College Is Under Siege." *New York Times*, June 16. Retrieved from www.nytimes.com/2017/06/16/us/evergreen-state-protests.html (archived at archive.today/wTTJt).

Headland, Thomas N., Kenneth L. Pike, and Marvin Harris (eds.). 1990. *Emics and Etics: The Insider/Outsider Debate*. Newbury Park, CA: Sage.

Hughes, Geoffrey. 2010. *Political Correctness: A History of Semantics and Culture*. Malden, MA: Wiley-Blackwell.

Huntwork, David. 2014. "The Ancient Evil Religion of Political Correctness." *RenewAmerica*, May 12. Retrieved from www.renewamerica.com/columns/huntwork/140512 (archived at archive.today/PpyRc)

Johnston, Ian. 2015. "Germaine Greer: Author Gives Cardiff University Speech Despite Protests Against Her Comments on Transgender People." *The Independent*, November 18. Retrieved from www.independent.co.uk/news/people/germaine-greer-author-gives-cardiff-university-speech-despite-protests-against-her-comments-on-a6739746.html (archived at archive.today/8f8mi)

Kehler, Marie Lisa, and Alexander Davydov. 2019. "Protest begleitet Kopftuch-Konferenz." May 8. Retrieved from www.faz.net/aktuell/rhein-main/widerstand-um-kopftuch-debatte-an-der-frankfurter-uni-16176483.html (archived at archive.today/JWDLG).

Knott, Kim. 2009. "Insider/Outsider Perspectives." In John R. Hinnells (ed.), *The Routledge Companion to the Study of Religion*, 2nd edition, 259–273. London: Routledge.

Koch, Anne. 2006. "The Study of Religion as Theorienschmiede for Cultural Studies: A Test of Cognitive Science and Religious-Economic Modes of Acces. *Method and Theory in the Study of Religion* 18(3): 254–272. https://doi.org/10.1163/157006806778553543

Levinovitz, Alan Jay. 2016. *The Limits of Religious Tolerance*. Amherst, MA: The Amherst College Press. https://doi.org/10.3998/mpub.10033802

Lincoln, Bruce. 1999. "Theses on Method." In Russell T. McCutcheon (ed.), *The Insider/Outsider Problem in the Study of Religion: A Reader*, 395–398. London: Continuum.

Lindsay, James A., and Mike Nayna. 2018. "Postmodern Religion and the Faith of Social Justice." *Areo*, December 18. Retrieved from https://areomagazine.com/2018/12/18/postmodern-religion-and-the-faith-of-social-justice (archived at archive.today/fUQB2).

Lindsay, James A., and Helen Pluckrose. 2017. "A Manifesto Against the Enemies of Modernity." *Areo*, August 22. Retrieved from https://areomagazine.com/2017/08/22/a-manifesto-against-the-enemies-of-modernity/ (archived at archive.today/KTUnR).

Mandair, Arvind-Pal Singh, 2001, "Thinking Differently About Religion and History: Issues for Sikh Studies." In Christopher Shackle, Gurharpal Singh and Arvind-Pal Mandair (eds.), *Sikh Religion, Culture and Ethnicity*, 47–71. Richmond: Curzon.

Marche, Stephen. 2019. "The 'Debate of the Century:' What Happened When Jordan Peterson Debated Slavoj Žižek." *The Guardian*, April 20. Retrieved from www.theguardian.com/world/2019/apr/20/jordan-peterson-slavoj-zizek-happiness-capitalism-marxism (archived at archive.today/MY9q5).

McCutcheon, Russell T. (ed.). 1999. *The Insider/Outsider Problem in the Study of Religion: A Reader*. London: Continuum.

Merton, Robert K. 1972. "Insiders and Outsiders: A Chapter in the Sociology of Knowledge." *American Journal of Sociology* 78(1): 9–47. https://doi.org/10.1086/225294

Metzgar, Jayme. 2019. "Hate Hoaxes Are What Happen When Your Religion Is Identity Politics." *The Federalist*, February 20. Retrieved from https://thefederalist.com/2019/02/20/hate-hoaxes-happen-religion-identity-politics/ (archived at archive.today/E9UQw).

Meyer, Birgit. 2017. "Catholicism and the Study of Religion." In Kristin Norget, Valentina Napolitano, and Maya Mayblin (eds.), *The Anthropology of Catholicism: A Reader*, 305–315. Oakland, CA: University of California Press.

Mohn, Jürgen. 2012. "Wahrnehmung der Religion: Aspekte der komparativen Religionswissenschaft in religionsaisthetischer Perspektive." *Erwägen–Wissen–Ethik* 23(2): 241–254.

Mühlbauer, Peter. 2017. "Deutscher Hochschulverband kritisiert 'Erosion der Debatten- und Streitkultur an Universitäten'." *Telepolis*, April 19. Retrieved from www.heise.de/tp/features/Deutscher-Hochschulverband-kritisiert-Erosion-der-Debatten-und-Streitkultur-an-Universitaeten-3687599.html (archived at archive.today/cDvBz).

Nelson, Lauren. 2017. "No, Andrew Sullivan, Intersectionality is Not a Religion." *Friendly Atheist*, March 14. Retrieved from https://friendlyatheist.patheos.com/2017/03/14/no-andrew-sullivan-intersectionality-is-not-a-religion/ (archived at archive.today/ZVu7f).

Parmaksız, Umut. 2018. "Making Sense of the Postsecular." *European Journal of Social Theory* 21(1): 98–116. https://doi.org/10.1177/1368431016682743

Piper, Everett. 2017. *Not a Day Care: The Devastating Consequences of Abandoning Truth*. Washington, DC: Regnery Faith.

Pluckrose, Helen, and James A. Lindsay. 2018. "Identity Politics Does Not Continue the Work of the Civil Rights Movements." *Areo*, September 25. Retrieved from https://areomagazine.com/2018/09/25/identity-politics-does-not-continue-the-work-of-the-civil-rights-movements/ (archived at archive.today/UfIMd).

Seely, Katharine Q. 2017. "Protesters Disrupt Speech by 'Bell Curve' Author at Vermont College." *New York Times*, March 3. Retrieved from www.nytimes.com/2017/03/03/us/middlebury-college-charles-murray-bell-curve-protest.html (archived at archive.today/eHXBM).

Shadow To Light. 2017. "Social Justice Atheist Tries to Explain Why Intersectionality is not a Cult." March 20. Retrieved from https://shadowtolight.wordpress.com/2017/03/20/social-justice-atheist-tries-to-explain-why-intersectionality-is-not-a-cult/ (archived at archive.today/AJnzS).

Simpson, Robert Mark and Amia Srinivasan. 2018. "No Platforming." In Jennifer Lackey (ed.), *Academic Freedom*, 187–209. Oxford: Oxford University Press. https://doi.org/10.1093/oso/9780198791508.003.0011

Slater, Tom (ed.). 2016. *Unsafe Space: The Crisis of Free Speech on Campus*. London: Palgrave Macmillan.

Sullivan, Andrew. 2017. "Is Intersectionality a Religion?" *NYMag*, March 10. Retrieved from http://nymag.com/daily/intelligencer/2017/03/is-intersectionality-a-religion.html (archived at archive.today/tE4cb).

Sullivan, Andrew. 2018. "America's New Religions." *NYMag*, December 7. Retrieved from http://nymag.com/intelligencer/2018/12/andrew-sullivan-americas-new-religions.html (archived at: archive.today/NZe5d).

Sultana, Farhana. 2018. "The False Equivalence of Academic Freedom and Free Speech: Defending Academic Integrity in the Age of White Supremacy, Colonial Nostalgia, and Anti-Intellectualism." *ACME: An International Journal for Critical Geographies* 17(2): 228–257.

Weiss, Bari. 2018. "Meet the Renegades of the Intellectual Dark Web." *New York Times*, May 8. Retrieved from www.nytimes.com/2018/05/08/opinion/intellectual-dark-web.html (archived at archive.today/pDIY9).

Wylie, Alison. 2003. "Why Standpoint Matters." In Robert Figueroa and Sandra Harding (eds.), *Science and Other Cultures: Issues in Philosophies of Science and Technology*, 26–48. New York: Routledge.

Chapter 14

Studying Religion in a Post-Truth World

Stephanie Gripentrog

What forms does the distinction between 'good' and 'bad' religion take on at the university? Looking at the examples discussed by Adrian Hermann and Stefan Priester, it is not so much about the normative discourse on the objects of study. It's more about how normative scholarship *itself* can become again with regard to its own standards and rules under circumstances of unexpected strong political pressure. Hermann and Priester point to the media coverage of a current 'fundamentalism' of political correctness at American universities, sometimes described as a very dogmatic religion in itself. Is normativity entering scholarly discourse again?

If we take a look back at the history of the academic study of religion in the nineteenth and early twentieth century, this has been an embattled field ever since. On the one hand, it had to clearly set itself apart from religious or normative discourse to become an accepted scientific discipline and constitute its distinct disciplinary identity.[1] For representatives of that approach, the 'good' religion was the religion that stayed out of science. On the other hand, representatives of phenomenology of religion for example followed an explicit religious agenda when saying that religious truth claims had to be taken seriously (cf. e.g. Heiler 1961: 17). However, we have now come to the point where the approach mentioned first has become constitutive and a more or less unquestionable precondition for the academic study of religion.

But recently, paradigms changed significantly again: Especially from research in fields such as postcolonial studies we know how difficult it is to deal with the aspect of perspective, and that all our knowledge cannot be but culturally, historically, linguistically, and maybe also religiously bound and stands in the context of power-relations that we can never really get rid of (cf. Ashcroft, Griffith, and Riffin 2006). Furthermore, the advent of post-structuralist theories brought back questions of power and politics to the heart of our discipline. This leads to two outcomes: First of all, nothing can be claimed as necessary, natural, empirical, or just 'real' anymore—things appear as socially constructed instead. Secondly, this causes new pressure to position oneself and to make decisions and positions (also scholarly ones) plausible again, but this time without corresponding to necessity or 'the truth.'

The consequences of this have been described very clearly by Russell T. McCutcheon: Scholars are *always* "public intellectuals," and: those who cannot accept this fact, should not publish. Following this argument, the question is not whether or not the academic study of religion is positioned in the public (and therefore also in the religious) field—it *always* is—, but *how* it wants to be positioned there. McCutcheon's answer to that question was that researchers in the academic study of religion have to be critics, not caretakers of religion (cf. McCutcheon 2001). Apart from that, scientific discourse is coined by further 'non-scientific' interests—or as Thomas Gieryn (1999) puts it, reflecting on science as *boundary work*: Science is not motivated only by genuinely scientific objectives, but by the pursuit of authority over material and symbolic resources and the concern to establish or defend scientific autonomy. To put it briefly: there is no such thing as a stable substance defining science. Science is negotiated and ever-changing, and so are its objects of study.

Maybe this is a good point to add some further observations on current political developments in the US and to relate them to the points mentioned above:

With the election of the word 'post-truth' as word of the year 2016 the *Oxford English Dictionary* defined the adjective as "relating to or denoting circumstances in which objective facts are less influential in shaping public opinion than appeals to emotion and personal belief" (Oxford Languages 2016). Furthermore, it was especially the election of Donald Trump to the American presidency that intensified the discussion on post-truth with regard to political questions. But how was science affected by that? The main point is, that it became less important as a basis of knowledge for policy-making. While Obama usually had his science advisor at the decision-making table, a year after taking office Trump had not even appointed a new director of the White House Office of Science and Technology Policy (Lane and Riordan 2018). So the remarkable thing is that some—for example American philosopher Daniel Dennett[2]—have started to blame post-structuralist thinking to be exactly one of the facilitators of that kind of post-truth politics that is so hostile towards science.

Thus, to resume: (1) there is a recognizable politicization and—as some observers claim—maybe even 'religionization' of some scholarly discourse at US universities as described above, (2) there is a marginalization of science in current US politics, and (3) there is a criticism of post-structuralist approaches, saying they enabled exactly that kind of post-truth politics. So the question is: What can be said about post-structuralist scholarship and its relation to questions of normativity in these times of political tension?

There are many possible reactions to that question, but the two most diametrical are: As we can't produce 'objective' or 'neutral' knowledge anyway—we could fully accept the challenge of becoming political/normative and the fact that boundaries between science and other fields are unstable. This also entails admitting the 'social construction of reality' (and therefore of science as well) and through that, losing the possibility of claiming 'facts' or 'the truth.' On the other hand, we could attempt to return to 'facts', so that we have something to say against those (representatives of post-truth politics) who just create their world based on their own interests and feelings. But *can* there be such a return to facts at all? Are there any 'right' or 'wrong' stories about the so-called reality or truth, and about religion as well? Or: Do 'right stories' simply *have* to exist, so that science and science-based politics can be meaningful again?

The answer I would like to suggest here lies somewhere in between. I do think that we cannot go back to 'pure' reality. But this does not necessarily mean the entry of arbitrariness into science, as criticism of post-structuralist approaches claims. Because: there is a difference between creating the world according to one's own interests and feelings, completely ignoring 'the world out there,' and a description of the conditions and means by which such a social construction of 'the world out there' is done by *others*. The latter is what cultural studies such as the academic study of religion should do—and this only can and has to be done by employing accurate methods, being far from arbitrary. The result of such research is a social construction, for sure. But it is a construction done along certain scientifically accepted rules that are shared or at least discussed and accepted by the current scientific community and that always have to be made plausible in that context.

Insights into the spread and success of lies show that a made-up story can't be questioned successfully by just saying it is wrong. You have to set your own, new story against it. The fake story still works better than no story. And a counter-story only works if it is completely different from the fake one (cf. Nyhan and Reifler 2015). Therefore, perhaps the most important question is: What kind of stories do we as scientists want to tell in times of post-truth politics? My answer to that question is: The specific contribution of the academic study of religion to society is that it tells stories that consequently question claims of normativity instead of raising new ones. This doesn't lead to the arbitrariness of post-truth politics, but to the creation of an enabling space where the plurality of possibilities becomes visible again. Which possibility *choose* then, is a decision that doesn't lie within the realm of scientific discourse.

Stephanie Gripentrog is a tenured post-doctoral researcher in the study of religion at the Christian-Albrechts-Universität zu Kiel, Germany. She received a D.Phil. in the study of religion from the University of Basel, Switzerland in 2013. Her work focuses on psychology of religion, the history of the concept of religion, discourses on abnormality and religion, and the Arab Spring. She is currently working on a habilitation thesis dealing with the question of the meaning of 'scripts' for the relation of religion and revolution in comparative perspective.

Notes

1 Cf. e.g. the proceedings of the first international congress in Paris: *Actes du premier congrès international d'histoire des religions* (2 vols, Paris: Ernest Leroux 1901–1902).
2 In an interview, Dennett stated: "I think what the postmodernists did was truly evil. They are responsible for the intellectual fad that made it respectable to be cynical about truth and facts." See Cadwalladr (2017).

References

Ashcroft, Bill, Gareth Griffiths and Helen Tiffin (eds.). 2006. *The Post-Colonial Studies Reader*, 2nd edn. London: Routledge.

Cadwalladr, Carole. 2017. "Daniel Dennett: 'I begrudge every hour I have to spend worrying about politics'." February 12. Retrieved from www.theguardian.com/science/2017/feb/12/daniel-dennett-politics-bacteria-bach-back-dawkins-trump-interview (archived at www.webcitation.org/6z10il8Qd).

Gieryn, Thomas F. 1999. *Cultural Boundaries of Science: Credibility on the Line*. Chicago, IL: University of Chicago Press.

Heiler, Friedrich. 1961. *Erscheinungsformen und Wesen der Religion*. Stuttgart: Kohlhammer.

Lane, Neal F., and Michael Riordan. 2018. "Trump's Disdain for Science." *The New York Times*, January 4. Retrieved from www.nytimes.com/2018/01/04/opinion/trump-disdain-science.html (archived at archive.today/tEJob).

McCutcheon, Russell T. 2001. *Critics Not Caretakers: Redescribing the Public Study of Religion*. Albany, NY: SUNY Press.

Nyhan, Brendan and Jason Reifler. 2015. "Displacing Misinformation about Events: An Experimental Test of Causal Corrections." *Journal of Experimental Political Science* 2(1): 81–93. https://doi.org/10.1017/XPS.2014.22

Oxford Languages. 2016. "Word of the Year 2016." Retrieved from https://en.oxforddictionaries.com/word-of-the-year/word-of-the-year-2016 (archived at www.webcitation.org/6z10ITh2z).

Chapter 15

The Good, the Bad, and the Non-Religion: The Good/Bad Rhetoric in Non-Religion Studies

Christopher R. Cotter

> It's a dangerous slip, a conscientious shift
> In the spirit of resistance you gotta hold your grip
> Lest the state of your resolve makes you quickly devolve to a fundamentalist
> You're an archetype that they can pin to the wall
> When you cling to your convictions like a farm animal in its stall
> Never thinking of the bigger world outside, as they take you for a ride ...
> —Bad Religion, "The Resist Stance" (2010)

Greg Graffin's lyrics above appear in "The Resist Stance," the third track of *The Dissent of Man* (2010)—the fifteenth studio album from legendary Californian punk rockers Bad Religion (1980–present)—and epitomize the band's relentless critique of religion, closed-mindedness, irrationality, unchecked capitalism, traditionalism, war, and the political elite. Having been a die-hard fan of the band for twenty years, I couldn't resist utilizing them in my opening gambit for this essay on the public rhetoric of 'good religion' and 'bad religion.' Although the band's output for the most part contributes to a dominant anti-religious discourse—that *all religion is 'bad religion'*—it also, as can be seen in the lyrics above, doesn't let the 'non-religious' off the hook. The greater sin in this case is to "devolve to a fundamentalist," to "cling to your convictions" and never think "of the bigger world outside"—a sin even more egregious when committed by an atheist. If *Bad Religion*, through their anti-establishment rhetoric of autonomy and critical thinking, see themselves as instantiating a form of 'good non-religion,' then this hypothetical atheist epitomizes the 'bad.' In this essay, I take this volume's focus on the rhetoric of good and bad religion and see what happens when we rhetorically add a 'non-.'

The first decades of the twenty-first century have seen a rise of a "rhetoric of authenticity" in public discourse about religion, whereby "good religion" which is "egalitarian, progressive, pluralistic, democratic, and so on" is constructed as "the real or authentic version" and set against its dichotomous opposite, "bad religion" (Hughes 2015: xiv-xv). This essay places academic scholarship on this rhetoric into conversation with recent work on 'non-religion.' I first introduce the rhetoric before briefly demonstrating that it also manifests in public discourse on good and bad 'non-religion.' I then dive into Aaron Hughes's critique of the rhetoric within Religious Studies—particularly in what he calls 'Islamic

Religious Studies'—before demonstrating that this critique can also be applied to 'Non-Religion Studies' (for want of a better term). I conclude that this matters because of a host of Christian assumptions that are perpetuated by non-religion studies, and because of the tacit participation of non-religion studies in the machinations of the neoliberal state.

The Public Rhetoric of Good/Bad Religion

The dubious rhetoric of there being good versions of religion and bad versions of it—particularly popularized in the political sphere by former UK Prime Minister Tony Blair—constructs "good religion" as something that "conforms to, and does not challenge, liberal secular principles" (Fitzgerald 2015: 306). A classic recent example of this rhetoric would be its use by the successor to Tony Blair's neoliberal ideology, former UK PM David Cameron in September 2014, following the killing of David Haines at the hands of ISIS:

> The fact that an aid worker was taken, held and brutally murdered at the hands of ISIL [ISIS] sums up what this organization stands for. They are killing and slaughtering thousands of people: Muslims, Christians, minorities across Iraq and Syria. They boast of their brutality; they claim to do this in the name of Islam. That is nonsense. Islam is a religion of peace. They are not Muslims, they are monsters ... (eNCA 2014)

We also see this rhetoric in, for example, the writings of 'New Atheists' such as Sam Harris (e.g. 2007) and philosophers such as Rawls and Habermas (see March, in Brown et al. 2015). This discourse separating good/authentic forms of religion from bad/inauthentic forms is not restricted to opponents of Islam—think of the recent controversy surrounding a Northern Ireland bakery's refusal to make a cake with a slogan supporting same-sex marriage (BBC News Online 2018), historical histrionics surrounding 'cults' or 'new religious movements' (Beckford 1985), or the debates about 'political correctness' at focus in the anchoring essay for this section.

The rhetoric that ISIS represent not only 'bad Islam' but no Islam at all might be understandable socially and politically, but this is hardly a neutral or agenda-free notion. As we should all know "religion is intrinsically neither good nor bad but is instrumental in cultivating (or, enforcing) specific types of behaviours and practices, regardless of the moral value of such behaviours and practices" (Eyl 2017: 42).

In the dominant discourse, however, 'bad religion' is the enemy of tolerance. This ties into official and media constructions of tolerance as a 'British value' (HM Government 2015b; cf. HM Government 2012, 2015a, 2012), posited in opposition to "a fantasized Islamic world of pure intolerance," and perpetuating a civilizational, integrationist discourse (Brown, in Brown et al. 2015, 161; see also Knott, Poole, and Taira 2013: 99).

As Titus Hjelm has argued, the designation of particular religions, practices deemed religious, or religion in general as problematic "gives us important clues about the struggles to define regional, national, local, and individual identity"

(2014: 214). Every time an "other" is constructed, so too is a self, and so "every European version of Islam, wherever found, is also a construction of Europe" (ibid.: 214). As Hermann and Priester argue in their chapter, it is this rhetoric of good and bad religion, who gets to define it, what position they are speaking from, and why, that is the object of analysis of the critical study of religion and related categories. Indeed, this "is an especially pertinent question in a time where religion is increasingly co-opted by governments for welfare and diversity management purposes" (Hjelm 2014: 214).

In my own empirical work, and that of others, we see this dominant discourse conflating 'good' with 'moderate' and 'tolerant' entangled in tactical declarations of indifference among the UK populace (Cotter 2017). Declarations of faith are positioned as 'unusual'—or 'bad'—among a UK populace who "pride themselves on their self-proclaimed 'moderation'" (Bagg and Voas 2010: 94; cf. Beckford 1999: 34; Davie 2015: 179). Mortimer and Prideaux describe this dynamic as originating in a "secular sacred boundary around the concept of inclusivity" (2018: 72) rooted in a "desire to project publicly an inclusive attitude towards those with different beliefs" (ibid.: 77). This noble but, as I will argue below, cynical discourse of moderation is part of a tactical discourse deployed in the face of the pervasive, powerful and strategic discourse of moderation (i.e. strategic indifference)[1] that demonizes those who take "religion too seriously" (Bruce 1995: 3), encourages Britons to keep quiet "on the subject unless formally prompted" (Knott, Poole, and Taira 2013: 120), and discourages "the open expression of religion in many public arenas" (Woodhead 2012a: 25).

The Public Rhetoric of Good/Bad Non-Religion

Unsurprisingly, this discursive entanglement extolling 'moderation' concerning questions of religion in interpersonal interaction, and demonizing 'militancy' or 'extremism' also implicates seemingly 'non-religious' subject positions. It is a common theme in contemporary theological critiques to castigate the 'New Atheism' of Richard Dawkins and others for its non-philosophical nature. According to Alvin Plantinga, "many of [Dawkins'] arguments would receive a failing grade in a sophomore philosophy class" (2007: 1–2), and certain critics even lament that this atheism is not up to the standards set by "Feuerbach or Marx, Schopenhauer or Nietzsche" (Aslan 2010: xiii–xiv; cf. Fergusson 2009: 3). A recent article in *The Guardian* dubs New Atheism "a topical subgenre of the right-wing backlash against the supposedly suffocating atmosphere of 'political correctness'" (Poole 2019; see also Hermann and Priester, Chapter 13 this volume) and castigates it as "faith as noxious as any other" due to "its messianic conviction that it alone serves the cause of truth." And a colleague of mine has even playfully used Aaron James's *Assholes: A Theory* (2013), to discuss how the 'New Atheists' language tends to be overly critical and yet simultaneously exude an aura of being "immune to counter criticism because their position is incapable of being incorrect" (Quillen 2015). According to James's definition, it seems that New Atheism is asshole non-religion.

This discourse is also common in the identity politics of atheists. One frequently encounters phrases such as 'I'm definitely not a fundamentalist …' or 'I'm an atheist, but not a Dawkins atheist …' and critiques such as the following, from within the online atheist community, which go into more detail:

> There's something that I've been seeing, and it's really disappointing me, man. And I know if it's getting to me, it's getting to other people as well. And that thing that I'm seeing is atheists being way too damn hostile, man. And I know they're doing it to me, they're going to do it to me anyway, they're gonna troll me … atheists are nitpicky. They watch a whole ten-minute video and point out one thing they didn't like, instead of telling you anything they did like and being supportive. We already know this; we already know that the community is like that. If you didn't know, well, now you know … (GodWorksOut 2015)

One finds similar reservations in the UK media, where "some versions of atheism and secularism are conceptualized as unwanted and a potential threat to society" (Knott, Poole, and Taira 2013: 116). This is, as Knott, Poole, and Taira argue, a relatively recent development, as back in the early 1980s "atheism and secularism […] were not seen as a threat or enemy of the Churches" (ibid.: 169). This is a point worth remembering as this essay continues. Moreover, the strategic discourse of moderation and the performance of indifference discussed above similarly implicate 'non-religious' subject positions. For example, in my empirical work in Edinburgh's Southside (Cotter 2020), some interviewees attested to feeling limited in their ability to manifest their religion-related identities in 'secular' public space, and pointed to 'bad' visible expressions of non-religion in the form of atheist bus adverts and irreverent material culture (see Lee 2017; Tomlins and Bullivant 2016). Thus, we see the same public rhetoric of 'good' and 'bad' religious and non-religious positions. The discourses have the same structure, although they are populated with different religion-related discursive objects (Potter and Hepburn 2008: 275; cf. Cotter 2020).

The Rhetoric of Good/Bad Religion in Religious Studies

Turning to the academic study of religion, for expediency's sake I will rely on Aaron Hughes's assessment in *Islam and the Tyranny of Authenticity: An Inquiry into Disciplinary Apologetics and Self-Deception* (2015), but this resonates with the work of many in the critical study of religion, including the other chapters in this volume.

Hughes examines the work of scholars such as Sherman Jackson, Amina Wadud, Ingrid Mattson, Kecia Ali, and Jonathan Brown, to argue that

> The Islam of Boko Haram and ISIS [and so on …] conflicted with what these Western scholars believed to be the authentic version of the religion—one that was, for example, liberal, inclusive, pluralistic, feminist, gay-friendly, and so on—that they had largely created in their own pluralistic image. (Hughes 2015: xii)

He describes the "good" or "authentic" Islam that these, and other, scholars manufacture as a set of "noble lies […] in the sense that they seek to provide Islam with a series of benevolent attributes in order to counter what amounts to real hostility against this religion in the West" (Hughes 2015: xiii). Understandable as this might be, "[i]n their desire to create a progressive Islam, scholars in secular university settings have [according to Hughes] done what they accuse their critics of: producing a one-sided version of the religion to score a political point" (ibid.: 3).

Using these scholars as exemplars, and drawing on the critiques of Talal Asad (e.g. 1993, 2003), Timothy Fitzgerald (e.g. 2000, 2007), Tomoko Masuzawa (2005), and others, Hughes argues that whether we like it or not, much of what passes for Religious Studies is predominantly a theological—or perhaps 'crypto-theological'—undertaking "in terms of its overwhelming desire to articulate as opposed to query truth claims on behalf of the various religions of the globe. The result is little more than a form of liberal ecumenicism in which all 'religions' are assumed to contribute to the betterment of human civilization" (Hughes 2015: 15). He concludes that, for the scholars he critiques

> Religion, or at least "good" religion, is something real and is supposed to be based on equality, justice, pluralism, and so on. In holding this position, however, scholars of Islamic religious studies inadvertently maintain a host of Christian assumptions that reflect the all too Christian heritage of the term "religion." (Hughes 2015: 120)

In another context, I would go into more detail here.[2] But this is enough to get my point across. Again, for others' expansions on this, see other essays in this volume.

The Same Rhetoric, with an Added 'Non-'

The past few decades have seen a marked rise in the number of individuals choosing to not identify as 'religious' across the globe, a related rise in academic studies of what it might mean to be other than 'religious,' and a burgeoning body of substantive studies mapping and theorizing the beliefs, practices, identifications, values, and social contexts of 'non-religious' populations (see J. M. Smith and Cragun 2019; Cotter 2020: ch. 1).

The case that is made for these studies is that there was until recently a dearth of research on non-religious populations, and that much of the early research that mentions the 'non-religious' included them for purposes of comparison, as statistical outliers, as afterthoughts, or as somehow problematic (Pasquale 2012; also Lee 2015: 52). Indeed, this seems to hold for a body of work, largely within the sociology of religion, which acknowledges the 'non-religious' but pays them little attention, or treats them as a monolithic minority religious position alongside other minority groups; as a residual category, or abnormality (as in, for example, Sherkat and Ellison 1999: 367; C. Smith et al. 2002: 600; Bryant 2006). In other words, until recently the majority of acknowledgments of the 'other than religious' occurred in a framework dominated by secularization theory, and focused upon 'religion' as something substantial and interesting, as opposed to the insubstantial, empty, baseline norm that remains when 'religion' is removed from the equation (cf. Lee 2015: 50). This amounts to what Hughes (2015: 1) and others would describe as a reification of "the 'religious' as if it somehow existed independently from more social or political (i.e. mundane) concerns," and problematically constructs the scholars who study this bounded phenomenon as unbiased, rational outsiders.

However, there now exist numerous large-scale social surveys which can be taken to show that 'the non-religious' are a numerically significant 'religious' group. If smaller groups are deemed worthy of attention, so the argument goes, then shouldn't the same attention be directed towards the 'non-religious' (cf. Lee 2015: 61; cf. Baker and Smith 2015: 1; Zuckerman, Galen, and Pasquale 2016: 4–6)? We thus find a growing body of work focusing on the 'nones' and/or aiming to substantiate what it 'means' to be other than religious.[3] Much of this work has a great deal to offer to our understanding of identity formation, ritual, parenting, politics, gender, material culture, and more. It can also be roundly critiqued for constructing a specific social group, repeating and reinforcing a World Religions model with all its attendant problems, and by imagining that either side of a constructed religion/non-religion binary can be addressed as a research topic (see Cotter 2020: ch. 2). But my focus in this essay is on how many of these studies implicitly or not-so-implicitly buy into the good/bad religion discourse.

These studies are, in many ways, a logical progression of a broader move away from secularization theory in the academic study of religion,[4] or even its reversal,[5] and the attendant radical particularism in the form of 'lived religion' and related concepts[6] that seems to have overtaken the discipline in recent years. This relatively recent move to acknowledge and theorize religion 'in the lives of individuals' as opposed to exclusively in the systematized theologies of male elites was certainly a welcome and necessary move for the field. All too often, however, this focus results in "the loss of a vantage-point 'from outside'" (Meyer 2015: 9) and the reification of one particular aspect of religion as somehow more authentic or more real than others such as history, tradition, theology, and institution (Cotter and Robertson 2016: 12). Given that the supposed 'evidence' for the currently prevalent view that religion has 'returned,' or that it 'never left,' seems to be largely based upon a combination of in-depth studies of what people are 'really' doing 'on the ground,' and redefining religion to fit this data—speaking of the "changing nature of religion," etc. (Davie 2015: xii)—it makes sense that some scholars would turn their attention to similarly in-depth studies of social actors who appear not to have this 'religion.'

Turning to the dust jacket of Lois Lee's important *Recognizing the Non-Religious* (2015) as an example, here we see Grace Davie commenting that the book "recognizes non-religious experience as a lived and above all social reality, rather than a reasoned and individualized epistemology." While this is all well and good, here we have the same dominant trope, evident throughout substantive studies of non-religion, which seems to privilege 'lived non-religion,' 'non-religious experience,' etc. as 'good' or 'authentic' non-religion, whilst rejecting or denigrating the textual, intellectual, discursive, individual, theoretical, etc. as bad or inauthentic. The rhetoric is the same, despite the added 'non-.'

Furthermore, much as with 'Islamic religious studies,' studies of the non-religious are frequently constructed as positive interventions to counteract negative stereotypes. Indeed, within the social science of religion constructions of the 'non-religious' have oftentimes been biased and derogatory (Cragun and Hammer 2011), and it is not uncommon to find "non-religious" people castigated for believing "anything rather than nothing" (Percy 2004: 39) or for holding nothing to be "sacred or holy" (Paden 1988: 48–49; cited in Thomas 2004: 51). Think, again, of the trope of the 'angry atheist' or the 'militant secularist' …

Thus we find scholars such as Phil Zuckerman arguing in *Society without God* (2010) that religion is not "a necessary ingredient for a healthy, peaceful, prosperous, and [...] deeply good society" and selling *Faith No More* (2011) as finding that apostates are not "the cliché of the angry, nihilistic atheist" but are "life-affirming, courageous, highly intelligent and inquisitive—and deeply moral." Zuckerman has also recently published a monograph—*What It Means to Be Moral: Why Religion Is Not Necessary for Living an Ethical Life* (2019)—which actively deconstructs god-based morality and argues for his own brand of secular morality—his good non-religion.

Another example is Callum G. Brown's *Becoming Atheist: Humanism and the Secular West* (2017). Brown sees this book as contributing to a shift "from culture and statistics to personal testimonies" and swinging "the secularization story of the late twentieth and early twenty-first centuries from one of subtraction to one of addition—to the millions of people of a new ethical Western world who have discovered themselves to be good without god" (ibid.: vii). He argues that "the sine qua non of this [i.e. his] study is that becoming atheist has all the potential of being a life-enhancing transformation" (ibid.: 17). He sees himself as embattled, against "faith-informed studies" and outlines how his "book studies atheism in itself, doesn't regard the loss of religion as a catastrophe for either the individual or for society [... and approaches atheism as] a positivity, as an enhancement of the individuals' sense of their self" (ibid.). Apparently "audiences of Christians can be incredulous when presented with evidence of the high moral standards of atheists," treating various examples with "sceptical guffaws" (ibid.: 161). I am not denying that this is the case. Yet the strength with which he defends the "moral cosmos of the non-believer" surrounding, for example, gay rights, feminism, and so on, which "has been under construction through individuals making decisions which, with surprising speed, have been, or are in the process of being, adopted in most Western nations" (ibid.) is telling. I agree with Brown that—when looking at the majority of "non-religious" who don't identify with labels—"being label-less is not being value-less" (ibid.: 168) but here we have the key conflation: (good) religion = values, and so too for (good) non-religion.

My point is that this persistent academic effort to demonstrate that atheism, agnosticism, non-religion, etc. are good, proper, and authentic, mirrors and tacitly endorses the similarly problematic academic discourse on good, proper, and authentic religion. Not only are the concepts in a "semantically parasitic" relationship (Fitzgerald 2007: 52), but so too are the problematic discourses surrounding them. We also find the reproduction of this discourse in studies that focus upon the beliefs and worldviews of the 'non-religious.'

A recent report from the large-scale *Understanding Unbelief: Across Disciplines and Across Cultures* project attempts to chart the substantive beliefs 'atheist' and 'agnostics' might hold in Brazil, China, Denmark, Japan, the UK and the United States. Three of the project's key findings are:

- "While atheists and agnostics are disproportionately likely to affirm that the universe is 'ultimately meaningless' [...], it still remains a minority view [...]" (Bullivant et al. 2019: 3).

- "With only a few exceptions, atheists and agnostics endorse the realities of objective moral values, human dignity and attendant rights, and the 'deep value' of nature, at similar rates to the general populations in their countries" (ibid.).

- "There is remarkably high agreement between unbelievers and general populations concerning the values most important for 'finding meaning in the world and your own life.' 'Family' and 'Freedom' ranked highly for all" (ibid.).

Here we have once again the (no doubt positively motivated) trope of countering 'negative' stereotypes about the non-religious. Bad non-religion, presumably, affirms a meaninglessness to the universe, subjective moral values, utilitarian approaches to life and nature, etc. The *Understanding Unbelief* project is constructing good non-religion (and, with it, good religion) in the face of this discourse. Furthermore, celebrating a shared emphasis on family and freedom among "believers" and "unbelievers" obscures the polysemy of these symbols which gather together an abundance of incompatible beliefs—for example, freedom for religion and freedom from religion, or 'traditional family values' and 'marriage equality.' These are powerful symbols which can mask very real differences. Obscuring these differences, or placing dissenting voices beyond the pale of analysis, amounts to a normative commitment to "liberal secular principles" to which good non-/religion conforms, and against which bad non-/religion "takes a critical stand [...] and is, therefore, fanatical" (Fitzgerald 2015: 306; also Casanova 2009: 139).

Finally, in a recent effort to find an overarching rubric for the study of religion and non-religion, Ann Taves opts for "worldviews" as a way forward (Taves 2018; Taves, Asprem, and Ihm 2018). With Asprem and Ihm, Taves uses concepts such as "ways of life" and "big questions" relating to ontology, epistemology, axiology, praxeology, and cosmology as ways of getting at these "worldviews" (Taves, Asprem, and Ihm 2018: 207–208). I argue that studies guided by questions on "what it means to be" (non-)religious or secular (e.g. Lee 2012), on what (non-)religious people believe (e.g. Day 2011), or which focus upon "big questions"—no matter what the critical, destabilizing intent—are doomed to play into the hands of vested interests. These interests wish to make non-/religion—at least *good non-/religion*—all about addressing the ineffable question of life, the universe, and everything pondered by 'Deep Thought,' the fictional mega computer in Douglas Adams's *The Hitchhiker's Guide to the Galaxy* (Adams 1982). Acknowledging and attempting to understand a prevalent discursive entanglement between the religion, non-religion, and the "big questions" is a worthy project for critical scholarship. Studying and mapping ways of life and responses to "big questions" is another. But allowing one's interest in the latter to tarnish the former—as so many within non-religion studies seem to do—by obscuring the contingent, socially constructed nature of the conflation between religion, non-religion, and the "big questions" is critically problematic, normative, and ideologically loaded.

Why Does This Matter?

Returning to one of the central arguments of this volume, Jennifer Eyl lays out the critical case that people "who do 'bad things' with God(s) on their side are not doing religion 'wrongly' since religion is neither more nor less moral than any other type of human activity" (2017: 52). Religion and non-religion are constituted by contestations "over authority, negotiations of power, identity formation, ideologies, and all other types of human activities" because these are, quite simply, human activities (ibid.). I have argued in this essay that there are similar processes occurring within non-religion studies surrounding the rhetoric of good/authentic-bad/inauthentic religion as Hughes has highlighted within Islamic religious studies. But why does this matter?

First, it matters because scholars in both sub-fields "inadvertently maintain a host of Christian assumptions that reflect the all too Christian heritage of the term 'religion'" (Hughes 2015: 120). Religion is a problematic and contested category which is implicated in a particular history and bound up in the discourses and power dynamics of modernity. Tendencies to conflate 'religion' with (Protestant) Christianity have been utilized to justify imperialism and colonialism, just as recent constructions of 'religion' as 'irrational' are "a convenient way to justify killing enemies we can successfully label as irrationally 'religious'" (Martin 2017: 12; cf. Cavanaugh 2009). Many studies of non-religion are thus bound up in the colonial encounter, the use of Christianity as the 'ideal type,' claims to in-group superiority, cultural chauvinism, and so on.

If this seems quite abstract, then the second reason is more concrete: the tacit participation of non-religion studies in the machinations of the neoliberal state. Linda Woodhead has described a situation in the contemporary UK where "religion is positioned, represented and actively constructed as a minority interest [...] in politics, the media, state services, education and professional bodies—the effect being to maintain religion's minority status by regulation, opposition, exclusion and silencing" (2012a: 25). Indeed, it seems that "only the liberal secular nation state and its agents have the right to decide what is and is not a genuine 'religion'" (Fitzgerald 2015: 306). Good religion can also be conceptualized as a resource that can be both co-opted by the state for its own ends and utilized by social actors in their interactions with the state—think of former UK Prime Minister David Cameron's short-lived 'Big Society' agenda, for example.

Recent decades have also seen the continued shift from the communal to the individual, with institutions being invested with less authority, 'religion' being viewed as field in which individuals engage in choice, and the more 'open' and 'individualized' language of 'spirituality' (i.e. 'good religion') being preferred over the rigidity and traditionalism of '(bad) religion.' Thus, demonizing the 'bad' can be seen as supporting the neo-liberal, individualized system. Just as the "liberals" and "(Christian) right" of Hermann and Priester's chapter find themselves constructed as allies versus the "bad religion" of "political correctness," so too do 'religious' and 'non-religious' moderates find themselves allied against anything that might challenge the legitimacy of the liberal, secular state and its principles.

As Daniel Pals notes on the contemporary relevance of Marx, just as the capitalist owners of modern industrial society needed a large pool of "moveable workers, people with few ties beyond their immediate family and no claim to social privilege or status," it should be little surprise that in the present era "the moral watch-words are individual freedom and social equality" (Pals 2006: 132). He continues, arguing that contemporary "philosophers and theologians promote these new moral values because they serve the new economy" (ibid.). Much is made in the contemporary study of non-/religion about the insider/outsider 'problem' (McCutcheon 1999; Chryssides and Gregg 2019), and whether scholars of non-/religion are necessarily, or should be, insiders or outsiders to the "traditions" they study, or to the broader "discipline of religion" (McCutcheon 2003). However, beyond the central category of non-/religion, there is often little critical reflection on the situatedness of the scholar. Based on my argument above, I suggest that many scholars of non-/religion are insiders to the neoliberal, secular tradition, and in promoting (explicitly or implicitly) these distinctions between good and bad non-/religion they are (intentionally or unintentionally) acting as cheerleaders for that system (Lincoln 2012: 3), promoting the "moral values [of modern society] because they serve the new economy" (Pals 2006: 132). I am not taking a position on whether this should be the case (although, personally, I think that critical scholarship has a duty to be critical of the hegemonic order). Nor am I suggesting that scholars would ever, or should ever, be expected to be cripplingly reflexive about all their socio-political entanglements. I am simply pointing out the ideological function of the distinction between good and bad non-/religion, and urging that scholars be humble and reflexive about their role in the promotion of this problematic binary. Lest, through the state of their resolve, they earn *Bad Religion*'s reprobation, and quickly devolve to a liberal, secular fundamentalist.

As my closing admonition, we can substitute any combination of religious or non-religious identifications for "religion," "Islam," "Islamic," or "Muslim" in the following:

> As scholars of religion it is our job to discuss the rhetoric of authenticity, not what or whose Islam is more authentic. Teaching in public universities [...] it is not up to us to create "good" religion and differentiate it from so-called "bad" religion, even though many students and others want us to. We need to contextualize and explain, not to adjudicate and deprive. The moment we, as scholars of religion, say what gets to count as an authentically Islamic act, practice, or belief, all those who do not ascribe to them cease to be objects of study. In so doing, we actually end up depriving Muslim actors, whether existing synchronically or diachronically, of their agency. (Hughes 2015: xv)

Christopher R. Cotter is Leverhulme Early Career Research Fellow in Religious Studies at the University of Edinburgh.

Notes

1. On 'strategies' and 'tactics' (Certeau 1984), see Woodhead (2012b) and (Cotter 2017, 2020).
2. Such that religion is centered on the primacy of belief and properly evinced by texts and institutions, and in the accounts of elites (see Cotter and Robertson 2016; Cotter 2020: ch. 2).
3. For an overview of existing studies see Cotter (2020) and J. M. Smith and Cragun (2019).
4. Towards, for example, notions of 'implicit religion' (Bailey 1998), believing without belonging (Davie 1994), or 'vicarious religion' (Davie 2007, 2008).
5. On the "resurgence of religion" (Blanes and Oustinova-Stjepanovic 2015) see, for example, Berger (1999) on "desecularization," Davie (2010) on "resacralization," or Gane (2002) on "re-enchantment."
6. See, for example, Hall (1997), Orsi (2005) or McGuire (2008).

References

Adams, Douglas. 1982. *Life, the Universe and Everything*. London: Pan Books.
Asad, Talal. 1993. *Genealogies of Religion: Discipline and Reasons of Power in Christianity and Islam*. Baltimore, MD: John Hopkins University Press.
Asad, Talal. 2003. *Formations of the Secular: Christianity, Islam, Modernity*. Stanford, CA: Stanford University Press.
Aslan, Reza. 2010. "Preface." in Amarnath Amarasingam (ed.), *Religion and the New Atheism: A Critical Appraisal*, xiii–xv. Leiden: Brill.
Bad Religion. 2010. "The Resist Stance." On the album *The Dissent of Man*. Hollywood, CA: Epitaph Records.
Bagg, Samuel, and David Voas. 2010. "The Triumph of Indifference: Irreligion in British Society." In Phil Zuckerman (ed.), *Atheism and Secularity. Volume 2: Global Expressions*, 91–111. Santa Barbara, CA: Praeger.
Bailey, Edward. 1998. *Implicit Religion: An Introduction*. London: Middlesex University Press.
Baker, Joseph O., and Buster G. Smith. 2015. *American Secularism: Cultural Contours of Nonreligious Belief Systems*. New York: New York University Press.
BBC News Online. 2018. "'Gay Cake' Row: Q&A." October 10, sec. Northern Ireland. Retrieved from www.bbc.com/news/uk-northern-ireland-32065233.
Beckford, James A. 1985. *Cult Controversies: The Societal Response to the New Religious Movements*. London: Tavistock.
Beckford, James A. 1999. "The Politics of Defining Religion in Secular Society: From a Taken for Granted Institution to a Contested Resource." In Jan G. Platvoet and Arie L. Molendijk (eds.), *The Pragmatics of Defining Religion: Contexts, Concepts and Contests*, 23–40. Leiden: Brill.
Berger, Peter (ed.). 1999. *The Desecularization of the World*. Grand Rapids: W. B. Eerdmans.
Blanes, Ruy Llera, and Galina Oustinova-Stjepanovic. 2015. "Introduction: Godless People, Doubt, and Atheism." *Social Analysis* 59(2): 1–19. https://doi.org/10.3167/sa.2015.590201
Brown, Callum G. 2017. *Becoming Atheist: Humanism and the Secular West*. London: Bloomsbury Academic.

Brown, Wendy, Jan Dobbernack, Tariq Modood, Glen Newey, Andrew F. March, Lars Tønder, and Rainer Forst. 2015. "What Is Important in Theorizing Tolerance Today?" *Contemporary Political Theory* 14(2): 159–196. https://doi.org/10.1057/cpt.2014.44

Bruce, Steve. 1995. *Religion in Modern Britain*. Oxford: Oxford University Press.

Bryant, Alyssa N. 2006. "Exploring Religious Pluralism in Higher Education: Non-Majority Religious Perspectives among Entering First-Year College Students." *Religion & Education* 33(1): 1–25. https://doi.org/10.1080/15507394.2006.10012364

Bullivant, Stephen, Miguel Farias, Jonathan Lanman, and Lois Lee. 2019. *Understanding Unbelief: Atheists and Agnostics around the World*. Twickenham: St Mary's University.

Casanova, José. 2009. "Immigration and the New Religious Pluralism: European Union-United States Comparison." In Geoffrey Brahm Levey and Tariq Modood (eds.), *Secularism, Religion and Multicultural Citizenship*, 139–163. Cambridge: Cambridge University Press.

Cavanaugh, William T. 2009. *The Myth of Religious Violence: Secular Ideology and the Roots of Modern Conflict*. New York: Oxford University Press. https://doi.org/10.1093/acprof:oso/9780195385045.001.0001

Certeau, Michel de. 1984. *The Practice of Everyday Life*. Translated by Steven F. Rendall. Berkeley, CA: University of California Press.

Chryssides, George D., and Stephen E. Gregg (eds.). 2019. *The Insider/Outsider Debate: New Perspectives in the Study of Religion*. Sheffield: Equinox. https://doi.org/10.1007/978-3-319-09602-5_11

Cotter, Christopher R. 2017. "A Discursive Approach to 'Religious Indifference:' Critical Reflections from Edinburgh's Southside." In Johannes Quack and Cora Schuh (eds.), *Religious Indifference: New Perspectives from Studies on Secularization and Non-religion*, 43–63. Dordrecht: Springer. https://doi.org/10.1007/978-3-319-48476-1_3

Cotter, Christopher R. 2020. *The Critical Study of Non-Religion: Discourse, Identification, and Locality*. London: Bloomsbury.

Cotter, Christopher R., and David G. Robertson. 2016. "Introduction: The World Religions Paradigm in Contemporary Religious Studies." In Christopher R. Cotter and David G. Robertson (eds.), *After World Religions: Reconstructing Religious Studies*, 1–20. Abingdon: Routledge.

Cragun, Ryan T., and J.H. Hammer. 2011. "'One Person's Apostate Is Another Person's Convert:' What Terminology Tells Us about Pro-Religious Hegemony in the Sociology of Religion." *Humanity and Society* 35(1–2): 159–175. https://doi.org/10.1177/016059761103500107

Davie, Grace. 1994. *Religion in Britain since 1945: Believing without Belonging*. Oxford: Blackwell.

Davie, Grace. 2007. "Vicarious Religion: A Methodological Challenge." In Nancy T. Ammerman (ed.), *Everyday Religion: Observing Modern Religious Lives*, 21–36. New York: Oxford University Press. https://doi.org/10.1093/acprof:oso/9780195305418.003.0001

Davie, Grace. 2008. "From Believing without Belonging to Vicarious Religion: Understanding the Patterns of Religion in Modern Europe." In Detlef Pollack, Daniel V.A. Olson (eds.), *The Role of Religion in Modern Societies*, 165–176. New York: Routledge.

Davie, Grace. 2010. "Resacralization." In Bryan S. Turner (ed.), *The New Blackwell Companion to the Sociology of Religion*, 160–177. Chichester: Wiley-Blackwell. https://doi.org/10.1002/9781444320787.ch7

Davie, Grace. 2015. *Religion in Britain: A Persistent Paradox*. 2nd Revised edition. Hoboken, NJ: Wiley-Blackwell.

Day, Abby. 2011. *Believing in Belonging: Belief and Social Identity in the Modern World*. Oxford: Oxford University Press. https://doi.org/10.1093/acprof:oso/9780199577873.001.0001

eNCA. 2014. "'They Are Not Muslims They are Monsters'—David Cameron on Islamic State." *eNCA*, September 14. Retrieved from www.youtube.com/watch?v=uADSWum5cKc.

Eyl, Jennifer. 2017. "Religion Makes People Moral." In Brad Stoddard and Craig Martin (eds.), *Stereotyping Religion: Critiquing Clichés*, 41–54. London: Bloomsbury.

Fergusson, David. 2009. *Faith and Its Critics*. Oxford: Oxford University Press. https://doi.org/10.1093/acprof:oso/9780199569380.001.0001

Fitzgerald, Timothy. 2000. *The Ideology of Religious Studies*. New York: Oxford University Press.

Fitzgerald, Timothy. 2007. *Discourse on Civility and Barbarity: A Critical History of Religion and Related Categories*. New York: Oxford University Press.

Fitzgerald, Timothy. 2015. "Critical Religion and Critical Research on Religion: Religion and Politics as Modern Fictions." *Critical Research on Religion* 3(3): 303–319. https://doi.org/10.1177/2050303215613123

Gane, Nicholas. 2002. *Max Weber and Postmodern Theory: Rationalization versus Re-Enchantment*. Basingstoke: Palgrave. https://doi.org/10.1057/9780230502512

GodWorksOut. 2015. "Atheists Stop Being So Damn Hostile." *GodWorksOut*, May 8. Retrieved from www.youtube.com/watch?v=E4yMhTozB8o.

Hall, David D. (ed.). 1997. *Lived Religion in America: Toward a History of Practice*. Princeton: Princeton University Press.

Harris, Sam. 2007. *Letter to a Christian Nation: A Challenge to Faith*. London: Bantam Press.

Hjelm, Titus. 2014. "Understanding the New Visibility of Religion." *Journal of Religion in Europe* 7(3–4): 203–222. https://doi.org/10.1163/18748929-00704002

HM Government. 2012. "Channel Duty Guidance: Protecting Vulnerable People from Being Drawn into Terrorism." London: Home Office. Retrieved from www.gov.uk/government/uploads/system/uploads/attachment_data/file/425189/Channel_Duty_Guidance_April_2015.pdf.

HM Government. 2015a. "Revised Prevent Duty Guidance: For Scotland." London: Home Office. Retrieved from www.gov.uk/government/uploads/system/uploads/attachment_data/file/445978/3799_Revised_Prevent_Duty_Guidance__Scotland_V2.pdf.

HM Government. 2015b. "Counter-Extremism Strategy." London: Home Office. Retrieved from www.gov.uk/government/uploads/system/uploads/attachment_data/file/470088/51859_Cm9148_Accessible.pdf.

Hughes, Aaron W. 2015. *Islam and the Tyranny of Authenticity: An Inquiry into Disciplinary Apologetics and Self-Deception*. Sheffield: Equinox.

James, Aaron. 2013. *Assholes: A Theory*. London: Nicholas Brealey Publishing.

Knott, Kim, Elizabeth Poole, and Teemu Taira. 2013. *Media Portrayals of Religion and the Secular Sacred: Representation and Change*. Farnham: Ashgate.

Lee, Lois. 2012. "Being Secular: Toward Separate Sociologies of Secularity, Nonreligion and Epistemological Culture." Unpublished PhD thesis, Cambridge: University of Cambridge.

Lee, Lois. 2015. *Recognizing the Nonreligious: Reimagining the Secular*. Oxford: Oxford University Press. https://doi.org/10.1093/acprof:oso/9780198736844.001.0001

Lee, Lois. 2017. "Vehicles of New Atheism: The Atheist Bus Campaign, Non-Religious Representations and Material Culture." In Christopher R. Cotter, Philip Andrew Quadrio, and Jonathan Tuckett (eds.), *New Atheism: Critical Perspectives and Contemporary Debates*, 69–86. Dordrecht: Springer. https://doi.org/10.1007/978-3-319-54964-4_5

Lincoln, Bruce. 2012. *Gods and Demons, Priests and Scholars: Critical Explorations in the History of Religions.* Chicago, IL: University of Chicago Press. https://doi.org/10.7208/chicago/9780226035161.001.0001

Martin, Craig. 2017. *A Critical Introduction to the Study of Religion.* 2nd ed. Abingdon: Routledge. https://doi.org/10.4324/9781315474410

Masuzawa, Tomoko. 2005. *The Invention of World Religions; or, How European Universalism Was Preserved in the Language of Pluralism.* Chicago, IL: University of Chicago Press. https://doi.org/10.7208/chicago/9780226922621.001.0001

McCutcheon, Russell T. (ed.). 1999. *The Insider/Outsider Problem in the Study of Religion.* London: Continuum.

McCutcheon, Russell T. 2003. *The Discipline of Religion: Structure, Meaning, Rhetoric.* New York: Routledge. https://doi.org/10.4324/9780203451793

McGuire, Meredith. 2008. *Lived Religion: Faith and Practice in Everyday Life.* Oxford: Oxford University Press.

Meyer, Birgit. 2015. "How to Capture the 'Wow:' R. R. Marett's Notion of Awe and the Study of Religion." *Journal of the Royal Anthropological Institute* 22(1): 7–26. https://doi.org/10.1111/1467-9655.12331

Mortimer, Tim, and Melanie Prideaux. 2018. "Exploring Identities between the Religious and the Secular through the Attendees of an Ostensibly 'Atheist Church'." *Religion* 48(1): 64–82. https://doi.org/10.1080/0048721X.2017.1386135

Orsi, R. 2005. *Between Heaven and Earth: The Religious Worlds People Make and the Scholars Who Study Them.* Oxford: Oxford University Press.

Paden, William E. 1988. *Religious Worlds: The Comparative Study of Religion.* Boston, MA: Beacon Press.

Pals, Daniel L. 2006. *Eight Theories of Religion*, 2nd edn. New York: Oxford University Press.

Pasquale, Frank L. 2012. "The Social Science of Secularity." *Free Inquiry* 33(2): 17–23.

Percy, M. 2004. "Losing Our Space, Finding Our Place." In S. Coleman and P. Collins (eds.), *Religion, Identity and Change: Perspectives on Global Transformations*, 26–41. Aldershot: Ashgate.

Plantinga, Alvin. 2007. "The Dawkins Confusion: Naturalism 'Ad Absurdum'." *Books & Culture*, March–April 2007, 21–24. Retrieved from www.booksandculture.com/articles/2007/marapr/1.21.html.

Poole, Steven. 2019. "The Four Horsemen Review—Whatever Happened to 'New Atheism'?" *The Guardian*, January 31. Retrieved from www.theguardian.com/books/2019/jan/31/four-horsemen-review-what-happened-to-new-atheism-dawkins-hitchens (archived at http://archive.today/Xk19u).

Potter, Jonathan, and Alexa Hepburn. 2008. "Discursive Constructionism." In James A. Holstein and Jaber F. Gubrium (eds.), *Handbook of Constructionist Research*, 275–293. New York: Guildford Press.

Quillen, Ethan G. 2015. "Assholes: A Theory of New Atheism." Everything Is Fiction (blog), January 20. Retrieved from https://everythingisfiction.org/2015/01/20/assholes-a-theory-of-new-atheism (archived at http://archive.today/OUNjc).

Sherkat, Darren E., and Christopher G. Ellison. 1999. "Recent Developments and Current Controversies in the Sociology of Religion." *Annual Review of Sociology* 25: 363–394. https://doi.org/10.1146/annurev.soc.25.1.363

Smith, Christian, Melinda Lundquist Denton, Robert Faris, and Mark Regnerus. 2002. "Mapping American Adolescent Religious Participation." *Journal for the Scientific Study of Religion* 41(4): 597–612. https://doi.org/10.1111/1468-5906.00148

Smith, Jesse M., and Ryan T. Cragun. 2019. "Mapping Religion's Other: A Review of the Study of Nonreligion and Secularity." *Journal for the Scientific Study of Religion* 58(2): 319-335. https://doi.org/10.1111/jssr.12597

Taves, Ann. 2018. "What Is Nonreligion? On the Virtues of a Meaning Systems Framework for Studying Nonreligious and Religious Worldviews in the Context of Everyday Life." *Secularism and Nonreligion* 7(9): 1-6. https://doi.org/10.5334/snr.104

Taves, Ann, Egil Asprem, and Elliott Ihm. 2018. "Psychology, Meaning Making, and the Study of Worldviews: Beyond Religion and Non-Religion." *Psychology of Religion and Spirituality* 10(3): 207-217. https://doi.org/10.1037/rel0000201

Thomas, Terence. 2004. "'The Sacred' as a Viable Concept in the Contemporary Study of Religions." In Steven J. Sutcliffe (ed.), *Religion: Empirical Studies*, 47-66. Aldershot: Ashgate.

Tomlins, Steven, and Spencer Culham Bullivant (eds.). 2016. *The Atheist Bus Campaign: Global Manifestations and Responses*. Leiden: Brill. https://doi.org/10.1163/9789004328532

Woodhead, Linda. 2012a. "Introduction." In Linda Woodhead and Rebecca Catto (eds.), *Religion and Change in Modern Britain*, 1-33. London: Routledge. https://doi.org/10.4324/9780203130643

Woodhead, Linda. 2012b. "Strategic and Tactical Religion." Paper presented at the Sacred Practices of Everyday Life Conference, Edinburgh.

Zuckerman, Phil. 2010. *Society Without God: What the Least Religious Nations Can Tell Us About Contentment*. New York: New York University Press.

Zuckerman, Phil. 2011. *Faith No More: Why People Reject Religion*. New York: Oxford University Press. https://doi.org/10.1093/acprof:oso/9780199740017.001.0001

Zuckerman, Phil. 2019. *What It Means to Be Moral: Why Religion Is Not Necessary for Living an Ethical Life*. Berkeley, CA: Counterpoint.

Zuckerman, Phil, Luke W. Galen, and Frank L. Pasquale. 2016. *The Nonreligious: Understanding Secular People and Societies*. New York: Oxford University Press. https://doi.org/10.1093/acprof:oso/9780199924950.001.0001

Chapter 16

The Campus as a 'Safe Space'? A Sociology of Knowledge Perspective on the New Student Protests

David Kaldewey

In their chapter, Adrian Hermann and Stefan Priester discuss how recent forms of student protests, particularly in the United States, are labelled as a "new campus religion" of "political correctness" by various commentators.[1] While Hermann and Priester do offer some preliminary contextualization of the debates and the mass media reaction to it, the protests themselves—or, as some say, the resurgent "campus wars" (Rosenberg 2014)—are not much analyzed and are rather taken as a starting point for rethinking the insider/outsider problem in the study of religion. In the following, I want to instead discuss a sociology of knowledge perspective on these new student protests. In a first step, I will highlight the ideal of the university that becomes apparent in them. The next sections will point to some research desiderata, address the theoretical underpinnings of the student protest movements and suggest that what is needed is a historical encyclopedia dealing with the new vocabularies and the traveling of the concepts employed by student protesters.

Ideals of the University and the Campus as a 'Safe Space'

While Hermann and Priester touch on the fact that the debate about the new protests include a controversy about which ideals of the university should guide us in the twenty-first century, they do not follow in detail the arguments made by the student protesters. It therefore seems helpful to further explore the explicit and implicit ideals of the university that are being presented in the recent 'campus wars' discourse. Books and manifestos discussing particular ideals for reforming or reconstructing the university have been an established genre of academic self-reflection for over two hundred years. This genre has its own cycles of popularity, also depending on the different national contexts, but several new publications each year are to be expected from major publishers at least in the English, German, and French speaking contexts (e.g., Collini 2017; Strohschneider 2015; Quintili et al. 2016). In this light it is noticeable that the programmatic ideal of the university which in recent years has probably been most often discussed among students in North American and British universities—the ideal of the university as a 'safe space'—cannot be found in any manifesto or book. The critics, on the other hand, who see the traditional, idealist, and liberal understandings of the university as endangered through this emerging ideal of the university as a 'safe space,' continue to write programmatic books, asking "What's happened to the university?" (Furedi 2017; see also the collection by Slater 2016). Other observers have recently published more nuanced essays, reconstructing the basic ideas behind the student protests while at the same time keeping a critical distance (Zimmerman 2016; Palfrey 2017). The actual protagonists of the new student protests, however, keep their statements short; their ideas are mostly formulated in social gatherings, discussions, or in ephemeral media of communication (social networks, blogs, local university magazines). Their theory, in other words, does not come in the form of treatises, manifestos or books, but in the form of events.

But what is this emerging, mostly implicit ideal of the university that is conveyed in the recent 'campus wars' and student protests? It is, basically, the idea of the campus as a 'safe space,' i.e. a space in which all students feel secure, regardless of their ethnic, religious, or sexual identities, their social origins and independent of possible psychic histories, like trauma. 'Safe' not only in the sense of protection from open discrimination or violence, but also—as a number of prominent critics of this ideal claim—from a questioning of their own cultural identity or from a retraumatization triggered by certain academic discussions or study materials.

Discussing this emerging and contested ideal of the university raises the question of how to establish one's own position in a heated rhetorical climate. What I want to suggest in the following is taking a step back and reflecting on some possibilities for future research on these topics.

Perspectives for Further Research

From a sociological perspective it is interesting that—apart from extensive mass media reporting since 2015—very little is known about the new student protest movement. This might be due to the fact that this phenomenon is too recent for the rather slow-moving operations of sociological research, and as such, more detailed studies might be available only a few years from now. Another question is whether it actually makes sense to talk about a 'new social movement' in the sense of social movement studies, and if so, whether this movement has developed out of earlier student activism.[2] It would also be good to have comparative, and especially quantitative, studies (beyond anecdotal evidence) that allow us to assess how wide-spread this movement actually is, at what universities and in which regions it is particularly prevalent, and what kinds of students support it (and which don't).[3] Are there specific social, cultural, and political milieus that stand behind the movement, or are we observing new coalitions forming across traditional lines? Aside from that, a focus on the students and their social backgrounds alone will not be sufficient to understand the phenomenon. We also need studies from an organizational sociology perspective to understand the role played by the widely expanded university administrations in the last decades. This transformation process has been described as "new managerialism" (Deem and Brehony 2005) and as the rise of the "administrative university" (Zimmerman 2016: 109). The wide institutionalization and bureaucratization of diversity management, for example, does mesh well with the demands of many student protests—and is at the same time evaluated skeptically by some of those observers who in general share the ideal of an inclusive university that is particularly open to minorities (e.g. Berrey 2011; Subotnik 2016; Nagai 2017).

An additional lacuna of the existing research is the theoretical and cognitive configuration, or—to use a simpler term without adopting its pejorative connotations—the ideology of the movement. What is needed, therefore, is a sociology of knowledge perspective that systematically investigates the co-constitutive relationship between knowledge, social collectives, and social structures.[4] In this sense I prefer to speak of a 'campus wars' or 'student protest' *discourse*, leaving the question open of whether this discourse is sustained by a coherent *social movement*. The following reflections from a sociology of knowledge perspective are focused on this lacuna and begin with the assumption that the contemporary discourse is based on particular academic sources.

Theoretical Foundations of the New Campus Protests

How can we begin the search for the theoretical foundations of the contemporary student protest discourse? The ideals and demands of the students are a popular topic of satirical comments and in a certain sense have also already been turned into a pop-cultural phenomenon.[5] In an indirect way this points us to a methodological problem: the discourse is primarily visible in the negative: its protagonists rarely document their activities, they produce few long texts and manifestos, and they express their ideas mostly ad hoc in concrete situations.[6] The medium for their ideas is not theory but the local interaction, and their demands are not expressed *discursively* but *performatively*. Because of this, not many explicit references to theory can be found, and names of scholars or intellectuals are also rarely mentioned.

It is remarkable that those critics who attempt to identify concrete intellectual sources often come to similar conclusions—independent from their own political position as left/right or liberal/conservative. On the conservative side, we sometimes find a call to not just ridicule the protests but to investigate the "intellectual foundations that breed such fanaticism" through a critique of "prevailing theories of social constructivism, post-colonialism, privilege theory, critical theory, and the like" (Canaan 2016). At the same time, there are also voices from the liberal left arguing that social constructivist and post-modern academics for decades have nurtured an intellectual culture that sees language as an instrument of power that has to be controlled and censored. The punchline of this argument is that it would be too simple to blame the students for the increasingly restricted freedom of speech at universities, since it was primarily the radical faculty—"influenced by academic trends such as critical theory, postmodernism and feminism" (Williams 2016)—that has built the foundations for today's censorship.[7] In particular, theories of "intersectionality" have now been identified as a scape goat (Bartlett 2017). The libertarian journalist Andrew Sullivan, for example, as discussed by Hermann and Priester (Chapter 13, this volume), characterizes "intersectionality" as a religious creed (Sullivan 2017). This way of speaking of a "new campus religion" stands, on the one hand, in the tradition of left-liberal ideology critique, while on the other hand it is surprisingly compatible with right-conservative critique of the student discourse (Blair 2016). It seems evident that the Right has now learned from the Left how to use such rhetoric of bad religion: "It's nothing new – it's a tactic as old as religion itself. Instead of holy texts, though, the millennial social justice advocate bows at the altar of the currently-in-vogue ideological Trinity: Marxism, Feminism, and Post-Colonialism" (Orginos 2015).

At first glance, these critiques appear to be holding up the ideal of a free academic discourse against the demands of the student protests. If we look at them in more detail, however, the critics' name-dropping of a number of heterogeneous theory traditions from the last decades does not at all represent a thorough engagement with the discourse and its theoretical foundations. Nevertheless, such critiques point to an important research question: do the ideals of the university that are advocated in the student protest discourse represent an original and independent discourse about the forms, function, and meaning of university education (ultimately, the ideal of the university as a 'safe space'), or are these ideals only an epiphenomenon, an expression of an infantilized generation of students, a side-effect of a prevailing ideology of 'identity politics'?

In the following I want to explore the hypothesis that these new forms of student protest can be understood as a radical and impressively successful application of theoretical work from the social sciences and humanities into daily life.[8] To put it differently: I want to attempt to understand the discourse and the movement that carries it as an effect (or side-effect) of theory, maybe even a transformation of what theory can be—combined with the suggestion that theory has been translated from the medium of academic discourse into the medium of performativity.

A Historical Encyclopedia of the New Campus Protests?

How can we further explore the assumption that recent theoretical developments in the social sciences and humanities are taking on a new practical, performative form in the recent campus wars? What we have to reconstruct in a first step are the genealogies of concepts, theories, and academic disciplines. We can then confront the seemingly well-established 'identity politics' vocabulary of the student protests with its own history and historicize more and more associated concepts. This approach reflexively turns the social sciences' and humanities' strategies of analysis towards their own research practices and developments. At the same time, such an approach is deliberately 'old school' since it builds on the well-worn idea of the social construction of all identities in order to make contingent developments visible and the non-negotiable negotiable (Hacking 1999). From a normative point of view, it represents another attempt at reviving the emancipatory potential connected with the metaphor of social construction in the 1970s and 1980s.

The starting point could be a historical encyclopedia of the new student protests, modelled after the famous conceptual history projects by Reinhart Koselleck and others.[9] Such an encyclopedia would include entries on current keywords like 'cultural appropriation,' 'intersectionality,' 'microaggression,' 'rape culture,' 'safe space,' 'trigger warning,' or 'white privilege.' In addition, we would need essays on political programs and objectives, which in turn are connected to certain concepts and flowers of speech. In all this we would have to take into account if and in what ways the key terms function as self-descriptions of protagonists in the field that carry positive connotations (as with 'affirmative action,' or 'diversity management') or as external descriptions with negative connotations (like 'political correctness,' or 'identity politics'). Not least, such an encyclopedia would have to include entries about the history and self-understanding of particular academic disciplines and research fields. While the history of the big influential academic theories of the student movements of the twentieth century (Feminism, Marxism, Critical Theory, Poststructuralism) has been explored in detail, the dynamics of the genesis, development, and differentiation of the more recent cultural studies disciplines have not been historicized and analyzed in a similar way. The historical encyclopedia I am imagining here would therefore have to feature historical and sociological essays on, among others, 'Black Studies,' 'Critical Whiteness Studies,' 'Disability Studies,' 'Gender Studies,' 'Postcolonial Studies,' and 'Queer Studies.'[10]

Of course we can already find some glossaries online that contain exactly those terms we associate with the student protests and campus wars, but those mostly are meant to inform and define these concepts,[11] or conversely, ridicule them in a polemical manner (see, e.g., Zeroth Position 2016; see also O'Neill 2015). In more established and reputable dictionary projects we can find only few of the terms listed above. The online *Stanford Encyclopedia of Philosophy*, for example, contains currently some 1600 entries and includes essays on 'affirmative action' and 'identity politics,' but not the other concepts I am interested in here. In standard dictionaries we find a faster reaction to recent developments: Merriam Webster, for example, has picked up the terms 'microaggression' and 'safe space' in February 2017 (Merriam-Webster 2017).[12]

There exist some studies on at least some of the concepts that are at the center of the new student protests. But these rarely approach the topic from a sociology of knowledge perspective, aiming to historicize the discourse. In the early 1990s, for example, a lot was written about what in retrospect may be labelled the first wave of 'political correctness' and 'identity politics.' Those texts were most often authored by conservative writers who claimed to be saving the university as a space of free investigation and science.[13] The largest number of existing historical studies deals with ideas and practices of affirmative action (e.g., Rubio 2001; Anderson 2004; Karabel 2005). The related concepts of diversity and diversity management are mostly treated in practically oriented management or organization research, but we find at least some historical and reflexive studies as well (e.g., Wood 2003; Berrey 2011; Vertovec 2012). In recent years, the concept of intersectionality has received special attention. On the one hand, it can be pinned down more precisely than others to a particular source (Crenshaw 1989, 1991).

On the other hand, the meaning of the term today has become so variable that the concept no longer has clear boundaries: "[intersectionality] shape-shifts so much as to no longer be recognizable as anything other than a meme gone viral" (Ange-Marie Hancock, quoted in Bartlett 2017; see also Hancock 2016).

The 'intersectionality' example is interesting because it makes especially visible how an academic concept does not just travel between academic disciplines, but also enters into everyday communication. According to *Google Scholar*, the number of articles that use this term increased tenfold between 2005 and 2015, and nearly doubled again until 2019. In *Web of Science* there are nearly 6,000 publications that use the term in title, abstract, or in keywords (see below). Even more interesting is that on Instagram over 100,000 photos are tagged with a variation of 'intersectional' (Bartlett 2017). The career of the concept therefore takes place in academic and non-academic contexts at the same time, without it being clear in what way the respective usage is linked.

The discussion of possible candidates for a historical encyclopedia of the new student protest and the hints to some existing research that goes in this direction could be extended. This, however, would go beyond the scope of this essay. I therefore want to close by exploring one more important phenomenon in more detail: the travel of concepts.

Traveling Concepts

The idea of traveling concepts originated in various discussions in and beyond cultural studies (Bal 2002; Neumann and Nünning 2012) and has, in the meantime, often been picked up in conceptual history approaches. It refers to the traveling between academic contexts and the connected shifts in meaning:

> concepts [...] travel: between disciplines, between individual scholars and between historical periods and geographically dispersed academic communities. Between disciplines, their meaning, reach and operational value need to be assessed after each "trip." [...] When concepts travel from period to period, their contexts travel along, sometimes to the embarrassment of later users. (Bal 2000: 5-6)

The travel of concepts beyond scientific disciplines and into everyday life, such as into the practice of social movements or other societal areas like politics, law, or religion, is not taken into account in this original formulation. But irrespective of which travels one is interested in, it can be said that travelling concepts on the one hand carry an existing operational value, and on the other hand—after various translation processes—also take on new meanings. In what ways the entanglement in earlier or geographically distant contexts is relevant for a concrete new situation cannot be decided in the abstract but requires a detailed and careful analysis of each individual case.

What does this mean for the student protest discourse? Observers from different political sides—as sketched above—seem mostly to agree that the current situation is characterized by the heritage of the big academic currents of cultural and social studies of the 1960s to the 1980s: critical theory, Marxism, feminism, poststructuralism and postmodernism, and, lastly, postcolonialism—the latter appearing much less, as one would probably expect.[14] This consensual view, however, is not only over-simplifying but also mostly wrong. Of course these traditions are influential, but their influence on the student protests is at best an indirect one. This leaves us with the question of whether the vocabulary that is being used stems from non-academic contexts (for example from the political sphere of from social movements), or if it has been developed in totally different academic contexts. This question cannot be answered as long as we do not know more about the whole discourse and all the concepts embedded within. However, in accordance with the idea of the historical encyclopedia presented above, I want to sketch how we can use simple search routines in the *Web of Science* database to get some first indications regarding those disciplines and research fields which many important terms seem to have been fostered in and exported from.[15]

To illustrate that research strategy, I chose four central concepts of the discourse, and searched for all indexed publications that contained these terms in title, abstract, or as a keyword: 'intersectional*' (5,834 hits), 'microaggression*' (859 hits), 'safe space*' (823 hits), and 'white privilege*' (517 hits). *Web of Science* allows us to display for this corpus the variety of research areas in which the search terms appear most frequently. A full list of this information cannot be reproduced here, but for a first impression I want to name only the three research areas in which the four terms appear most often: For 'intersectional*' this is Women's Studies (983), Psychology (747), and Sociology (665); for 'microaggression*' it is Psychology (378), Educational Research (203), and Social Work (79); for 'safe space*' it is Educational Research (150), Psychology (98), and Public Health (81); and for 'white privilege*' it is Educational Research (97), Psychology (94), and Sociology (73). By looking at the full data we can also see that both traditional humanities disciplines (like philosophy or literary studies) as well as the different cultural and area studies are mostly absent. This result suggests that the vocabulary of the student protest discourse is connected much less to the usual suspects named above (such as Marxism, Feminism, or Postcolonial Studies). Rather, a wholly different set of disciplines is of high importance: there is a dominance of Educational Research, Psychology, and Public Health—and, much behind, Sociology.

This data is of course highly abstract, but the literature selected through this process easily allows additional insight into the genesis, career, and diffusion of the selected concepts. If we take, for instance, the 'safe space' concept and look at the distribution of all indexed publications over time, an impressive dynamic becomes visible: the term first appears in 1993 but only becomes regularly used in the last decade (since 2006 we see more than 10 publications a year, since 2017 more than 100 publications a year). In looking at the earliest usage and its disciplinary context, a report by Robert Boostrom (1998) from the late 1990s is helpful. Unlike the concept of intersectionality, there is no original definition or concrete terminological suggestion for "safe space." Rather, Boostrom observes that terms like "safe space" or "safe place" are being used metaphorically by many scholars in Pedagogy to describe good learning environments. A particularly relevant case is the report of a teacher from 1987 that Boostrom discusses: It concerns Caleb, a deeply scared fourth grader, who only murmurs silently in the classroom. One day the teacher observes how Caleb puts a pencil in his little case and tells it how good it has it in its "safe space." Inspired by this, the teacher acquires a big cardboard box ("refrigerator box") that could encompass Caleb's desk and in which the boy could prepare a safe space for himself. In the following days Caleb brought a variety of things with him and made himself at home. In the course of time, he became able to leave his box and even communicate and play with his classmates. The success goes beyond this, however: other children began to furnish their desks and workspaces with personal effects following Caleb's lead. The conclusion of the teacher was: "With their spaces defined, they began to produce more and better work, and I realized that they too each needed a space to feel safe and comfortable" (Hawkins quoted after Boostrom 1998: 400).

What do these preliminary results mean for our investigation into the theoretical foundations of the student protest discourse? What does it mean if metaphors from pedagogy are translated into ideals of the university as a 'safe space' and are linked with social psychology theories about the harm done by microaggressions? It seems as if an established mode of thinking about the university—shaped by a long tradition of idealistic concepts and liberal values—is fundamentally being questioned, as it now becomes apparent that one can also think and speak about the university in different ways. Taking this into account, analyses about changing ideals of the university should pay attention to which academic disciplines and subfields are setting the tone for contemporary ideals of the university. We often attribute this role to the humanities and have been discussing for decades the ways in which the STEM fields have gained in importance and are increasingly constitutive for the idea of world class research universities. Unnoticed by these debates, disciplines at the periphery of the academy have taken up the conceptual work. It is possible that in the future scholars from pedagogy, social psychology, health science, and legal studies will set the tone, and the traditional social sciences and cultural studies—which often see themselves as particularly autonomous and entitled to set the tone when the future of the university is at issue—will increasingly import concepts and theories from those other academic fields.

David Kaldewey is professor for science studies and science policy at the University of Bonn. He holds a PhD in sociology from Bielefeld University. His research interests lie in the fields of science studies and in sociological theory. Recent publications deal with the changing relationship of science and politics, particularly with the contemporary pluralization of science policy discourses and how they transform the identity work of scholars, scientists and policy makers.

Notes

1   See Hermann and Priester, Chapter 13, this volume; The description of the "new campus religion" is taken from an essay by William Deresiewicz (2017).

2   The German press has described it as the "biggest student movement since 1968." See Novotny, Khuê and Schmidt (2016). While this is probably much exaggerated and not based on detailed sociological data, it nevertheless may be helpful to draw comparisons with earlier student movements (see e.g. Rochester 2016).
3   What we have are some opinion polls about the views of faculty and students in the USA in regard to free speech and related topics. See for a first discussion of this data Guernsey (2016: 45–48).
4   For the sake of brevity, I cannot provide a detailed discussion of the different sociology of knowledge positions that would either give primacy to the societal structures (being determines consciousness) or to knowledge (social structures are materializations of discourse).
5   See for example the video "Trump Voter Feels Betrayed by President after Reading 800 Pages of Queer Feminist Theory," at www.youtube.com/watch?v=lpzVc7s-_e8.
6   There are exceptions, of course; for example, the programmatic article by Harvard student Sandra Y. L. Korn (2014). In some cases, but rather rarely, the ideas of the protesting students are also defended systematically by older faculty members (e.g. Baer 2017; Gumbrecht 2016).
7   For an elaborated version of this argument see also Pluckrose (2017).
8   In a similar vein Helen Pluckrose and James A. Lindsay speak about an "applied postmodern conception of society" that becomes visible in some forms of campus activism. See Pluckrose and Lindsay (2019).
9   It seems like the history of concepts is shaking off the dust of the past. Ten years ago Hans Ulrich Gumbrecht (2006) wrote about the rise and fall of large conceptual history projects ("Pyramiden des Geistes"). Since then, the international reception of conceptual history, new journal projects, and the publication of handbooks and compendia demonstrate the vitality of the field. See e.g. Müller and Schmieder (2016); Pernau and Sachsenmaier (2016); Steinmetz et al. (2017).
10 All these lists are reproduced in alphabetic order without any claim for completeness.
11 See, for example, http://sjwiki.org (archived at archive.today/n8o2y); www.suffolk.edu/campuslife/27883.php (archived at archive.today/r0o30).
12 Microaggression is defined as "a comment or action that subtly and often unconsciously or unintentionally expresses a prejudiced attitude toward a member of a marginalized group (such as a racial minority)." Safe space is defined as "a place (as on a college campus) intended to be free of bias, conflict, criticism, or potentially threatening actions, ideas, or conversations."
13 One of the triggers of the debate about political correctness was Allan Bloom's bestseller *The Closing of the American Mind* (1987), followed by the conservative-critical books of Kimball (1990) and D'Souza (1991). Other volumes have a more documentary character, e.g. Arthur and Shapiro (1995) and Berman (1992). A more affirmative account of the identity politics movement is provided by Sidel (1994).
14 In regard to their normative and political positions, a close relationship between postcolonialism and the student protests seems obvious. My preliminary investigation into the conceptual history of the protest discourse does however not show many direct relationships, at least in regard to the USA and the UK. One of the few exceptions seems to be the concept of "cultural appropriation."
15 *Web of Science* (core collection) is one of the most important proprietary citation databases with over 64 million indexed publications from 1945 until today—from all disciplines. No full texts are available but core data like titles and (at least for entries after 1991) abstracts and keywords. The database is continuously updated, For the

query in this manuscript I accessed it on July 26, 2019. An earlier query for the same concepts was conducted on June 6, 2017. Within these two years, the hits for the four terms increased by 92% (for 'intersectional*'), 114% (for 'microaggression*'), 86% (for 'safe space*'), and 46% (for 'white privilege*'). This drastic increase further indicates the relevance of these concepts for the current intellectual discourse.

References

Anderson, Terry H. 2004. *The Pursuit of Fairness: A History of Affirmative Action*. Oxford: Oxford University Press.

Arthur, John and Amy Shapiro (eds.). 1995. *Campus Wars: Multiculturalism and the Politics of Difference*. Boulder, CO: Westview Press.

Baer, Ulrich. 2017. "What 'Snowflakes' Get Right about Free Speech." *New York Times*, April 24. Retrieved from www.nytimes.com/2017/04/24/opinion/what-liberal-snowflakes-get-right-about-free-speech.html (archived at archive.today/mnSe0)

Bal, Mieke. 2000. "Crossroad Theory and Travelling Concepts: From Cultural Studies to Cultural Analysis." In Jan Baetens and José Lambert (eds.), *The Future of Cultural Studies: Essays in Honour of Joris Vlasselaers*. Leuven: Leuven University Press.

Bal, Mieke. 2002. *Travelling Concepts in the Humanities: A Rough Guide*. Toronto: University of Toronto Press.

Bartlett, Tom. 2017. "When a Theory Goes Viral: Intersectionality is Now Everywhere. Is That a Good Thing?" *The Chronicle of Higher Education*, May 21. Retrieved from www.chronicle.com/article/The-Intersectionality-Wars/240095.

Berman. Paul (ed.). 1992. *Debating PC: The Controversy over Political Correctness on College Campuses*. New York: Delta.

Berrey, Ellen C. 2011. "Why Diversity Became Orthodox in Higher Education, and How it Changed the Meaning of Race on Campus." *Critical Sociology* 37(5): 573–596. https://doi.org/10.1177/0896920510380069

Blair, Leonardo. 2016. "This New Religion is Causing an Existential Crisis at American Colleges and Universities, NYU Prof Says." *The Christian Post*, May 25. Retrieved from www.christianpost.com/news/new-religion-causing-existential-crisis-american-colleges-nyu-prof-says.html (archived at archive.today/VFTIv); Deresiewicz, "On Political Correctness."

Bloom, Allan. 1987. *The Closing of the American Mind*. New York: Simon & Schuster.

Boostrom, Robert. 1998. "'Safe Spaces:' Reflections on an Educational Metaphor." *Journal of Curriculum Studies* 30(4): 397–408. https://doi.org/10.1080/002202798183549

Canaan, Gabriel R. 2016. "The Problem with 'Cultural Libertarianism'." *medium.com*, January 2. Retrieved from https://medium.com/@GabrielCanaan/the-insufficiency-of-culturallibertarianism-4e2d2e62022e.

Collini, Stefan. 2017. *Speaking of Universities*. London: Verso.

Crenshaw, Kimberle. 1989. "Demarginalizing the Intersection of Race and Sex: A Black Feminist Critique of Antidiscrimination Doctrine, Feminist Theory and Antiracist Politics." *University of Chicago Legal Forum* (1/8): 139–167.

Crenshaw, Kimberle. 1991. "Mapping the Margins: Intersectionality, Identity Politics, and Violence against Women of Color." *Stanford Law Review* 43(6): 1241–1299. https://doi.org/10.2307/1229039

Deem, Rosemary and Kevin J. Brehony. 2005. "Management as Ideology: The Case of 'New Managerialism' in Higher Education." *Oxford Review of Education* 31(2): 217–235. https://doi.org/10.1080/03054980500117827

Deresiewicz, William. 2017. "On Political Correctness: Power, Class, and the New Campus Religion." *The American Scholar*, March 6. Retrieved from https://theamerican scholar.org/on-political-correctness (archived at: archive.today/UhP6d)
D'Souza, Dinesh. 1991. *Illiberal Education: The Politics of Race and Sex on Campus*. New York: Free Press.
Furedi, Frank. 2017. *What's Happened to the University? A Sociological Exploration of Its Infantilisation*. Abingdon: Routledge. https://doi.org/10.4324/9781315449609
Guernsey, Andrew. 2016. "Classroom Warfare: How the Weaponization of Race, Class and Gender Sensitivity Threatens Free Speech and Academic Freedom at Colleges and Universities." Honors thesis, submitted to Johns Hopkins University, May 13.
Gumbrecht, Hans Ulrich. 2006. *Dimensionen und Grenzen der Begriffsgeschichte*. Munich: Wilhem Fink Verlag.
Gumbrecht, Hans Ulrich. 2016. "Political Correctness. Die Dialektik der Mikro-Aggression." *NZZ*, September 10. Retrieved from www.nzz.ch/feuilleton/zeitgeschehen/politicalcorrectness-die-dialektik-der-mikro-aggression-ld.115923 (archived at archive.today/bzNOM).
Hacking, Ian. 1999. *The Social Construction of What?* Cambridge, MA: Harvard University Press.
Hancock, Ange-Marie. 2016. *Intersectionality: An Intellectual History*. Oxford: Oxford University Press. https://doi.org/10.1093/acprof:oso/9780199370368.001.0001
Hawkins, Christine. 1987. "Caleb Was Afraid of Everything." *Learning* 16(2): 57–58.
Karabel, Jerome. 2005. *The Chosen: The Hidden History of Admission and Exclusion at Harvard, Yale, and Princeton*. Boston, MA: Mariner Books.
Kimball, Roger. 1990. *Tenured Radicals: How Politics Has Corrupted Our Higher Education*. New York: Harper & Row.
Korn, Sandra Y. L. 2014. "The Doctrine of Academic Freedom: Let's Give Up on Academic Freedom in Favor of Justice." *The Harvard Crimson*, February 18. Retrieved from www.thecrimson.com/column/the-red-line/article/2014/2/18/academic-freedom-justice (archived at http://archive.today/9VrlU)
Merriam-Webster. 2017. "We Just Added More Than 1,000 New Words to the Dictionary." Retrieved from www.merriam-webster.com/words-at-play/new-words-in-the-dictionary-feb-2017 (archived at archive.today/BwPXS).
Müller, Ernst and Falko Schmieder. 2016. *Begriffsgeschichte und historische Semantik: Ein kritisches Kompendium*. Berlin: Suhrkamp.
Nagai, Althea. 2017. "The Pseudo-Science of Microaggressions." *Academic Questions* 30(Spring): 47–57. https://doi.org/10.1007/s12129-016-9613-5
Neumann, Birgit and Ansgar Nünning (eds.). 2012. *Travelling Concepts for the Study of Culture*. Berlin: de Gruyter. https://doi.org/10.1515/9783110227628
Novotny, Rudi, Pham Khuê and Marie Schmidt. 2016. "Die neuen Radikalen." *Die Zeit*, July 14. Retrieved from www.zeit.de/2016/30/linke-bewegungen-studenten-usa-grossbritannien-deutschland/komplettansicht (archived at archive.today/cKvnf)
O'Neill, Brendan. 2015. "An A-to-Z Guide to the New PC." *The Spectator*, February 7. Retrieved from www.spectator.co.uk/2015/02/an-a-to-z-of-the-new-pc (archived at archive.today/YDDtR).
Orginos, Aristo. 2015. "Social Justice Bullies: The Authoritarianism of Millennial Social Justice." *medium.com*, April 8. Retrieved from https://medium.com/@aristoNYC/social-justicebullies-the-authoritarianism-of-millennial-social-justice-6bdb5ad3c9d3 (archived at archive.today/KWyxd).
Palfrey, John. 2017. *Save Spaces, Brave Spaces: Diversity and Free Expression in Education*. Cambridge, MA: MIT Press. https://doi.org/10.7551/mitpress/11245.001.0001

Pernau, Margrit and Dominic Sachsenmaier (eds.). 2016. *Global Conceptual History: A Reader*. London: Bloomsbury.

Pluckrose, Helen. 2017. "How French 'Intellectuals' Ruined the West: Postmodernism and its Impact, Explained." *Areo*, March 27. Retrieved from https://areomagazine.com/2017/03/27/how-french-intellectuals-ruined-the-west-postmodernism-and-its-impact-explained (archived at archive.today/8WrKd).

Pluckrose, Helen, and James A. Lindsay. 2019. "The Influence of Anti-Racist Scholarship-Activism on Evergreen College." *Areo*, January 20. Retrieved from https://areomagazine.com/2019/01/20/the-influence-of-anti-racist-scholarship-activism-on-evergreen-college (archived at http://archive.today/LBM0).

Quintili, Paolo, Carlo Cappa, and Donatella Palomba. 2016. *Université ou anti-université: Les humanités dans l'idée de formation supérieure*. Paris: L'Harmattan.

Rochester, J. Martin. 2016. "Too Much and Too Little. Campus Demonstrations in the 1960s and Today." *Academic Questions* 29(4): 422–427. https://doi.org/10.1007/s12129-016-9596-2

Rosenberg, Alyssa. 2014. "The Resurgence of Campus Wars and the Battle Against Discourse." *The Washington Post*, April 23. Retrieved from www.washingtonpost.com/news/act-four/wp/2014/04/23/the-resurgence-of-campus-wars-and-the-battle-against-discourse (archived at archive.today/TvCPG).

Rubio, Philip F. 2001. *A History of Affirmative Action, 1619–2000*. Jackson, MS: University Press of Mississippi.

Sidel, Ruth. 1994. *Battling Bias: The Struggle for Identity and Community on College Campuses*. New York: Viking Adult.

Slater, Tom (ed.). 2016. *Unsafe Space: The Crisis of Free Speech on Campus*, London: Palgrave Macmillan.

Steinmetz, Willibald, Michael Freeden, and Javier Fernández-Sebastián (eds.). 2017. *Conceptual History in the European Space*. New York: Berghahn Books. https://doi.org/10.2307/j.ctvw04kcs

Strohschneider, Peter. 2015. *Versuch über die Universität: Selbstbezug und Fremdbezug der Wissenschaften*. Konstanz: UVK Verlagsgesellschaft.

Subotnik, Dan. 2016. "How Diversity Training Hurts." *Academic Questions* 29(2): 198–204. https://doi.org/10.1007/s12129-016-9564-x

Sullivan, Andrew. 2017. "Is Intersectionality a Religion?" *NYMag*, March 10. Retrieved from http://nymag.com/daily/intelligencer/2017/03/is-intersectionality-a-religion.html (archived at http://archive.today/tE4cb).

Vertovec, Steven. 2012. "'Diversity' and the Social Imaginary." *Archives Européennes de Sociologie* 53(3): 287–312. https://doi.org/10.1017/S000397561200015X

Williams, Joanna. 2016. "Teaching Students to Censor: How Academics Betrayed Free Speech." In Tom Slater (ed.), *Unsafe Space: The Crisis of Free Speech on Campus*, 47–57. London: Palgrave Macmillan. https://doi.org/10.1007/978-1-137-58786-2_5

Wood, Peter. 2003. *Diversity: The Invention of a Concept*. San Francisco, CA: Encounter Books.

Zeroth Position. 2016. "A Glossary of Social Justice Warrior Terminology." Retrieved from www.zerothposition.com/2016/03/30/a-glossary-of-social-justice-warrior-terminology (archived at archive.today/cMGkr).

Zimmerman, Jonathan. 2016. *Campus Politics: What Everyone Needs to Know*. New York, NY: Oxford University Press.

Part V

Classroom

Introduction to Part V

Leslie Dorrough Smith, AVILA UNIVERSITY
Steffen Führding, LEIBNIZ UNIVERSITY
Adrian Hermann, UNIVERSITY OF BONN

Most cultures that exert bureaucratic control over educational curricula presume that part of the role of the classroom experience is not just classic skill-building (reading, writing, arithmetic, etc.), but *citizen-building*, as well. That is, we go to school to learn to be proper people. The problem, of course, is that what constitutes a "proper" person is an inherently political question—one that is certainly never static—because it is the product of the intersection of cultural preferences, the media, government politics, and a host of other globalist forces.

The essays in this section consider how the experience of teaching religion has been constructed and managed by the political and cultural climates of the classrooms in which such education occurs. Although the contributions are quite diverse in that they represent a variety of international perspectives that span the education of a large number of different populations, what they all share is the sense that engaging in questions of "good" or "bad" religion is virtually unavoidable. In other words, at least some of the participants in the educational process appear to come with the "good/bad" religion dichotomy already engaged, whether this is a function of a particular textbook writer's prose, a government's policy regarding the teaching of religion, or the attitude of students enrolled in a course.

The anchoring essay for Part V comes from *David G. Robertson* (Chapter 17), who reflects on his university classroom experience teaching about new religious movements (NRMs) at a British university. NRMs and "cult" groups are often considered outside of the religious mainstream by scholars of religion, and thus scholars of NRMs often spend substantial time discussing the politics of definition that frame their subjects in this way. Yet Robertson's observations argue that a particular folk-sensibility about religion was more common among his students, who were more likely to judge something a "real" religion based on its adherence to markers quite different than those upon which scholars rely. Robertson ultimately shows that the act of teaching critical thinking as it regards the construction of the category "religion" is just as much about understanding students' own colloquial definitions as it is about engaging scholars' categories.

In the context of the Japanese university, *Mitsutoshi Horii* (Chapter 18) demonstrates that colloquial definitions of religion that are common in Japan make it very difficult for his Japanese students to avoid categorizing religions as "good" and "bad," particularly when they are learning about classical sociological theories of religion. Horii argues that because such theories make Western presumptions about religion's nature that are quite different from traditional Japanese conceptualizations of the concept, the use of the term "religion" is virtually meaningless in this setting.

In Chapter 19, *Wanda Alberts* focuses on religion in the school classroom to reflect on "legitimate" and "illegitimate" religion as these concepts are discussed at different levels of educational systems in Europe. In most German federal states, religion is taught in what Alberts calls "*separative* contexts," dividing pupils according to their religious affiliation. Such confessional models are not based on teaching knowledge *about* these religions but are designed to instruct the pupils on how to live a good life as a Christian, or Muslim, etc. Traditional ideas about the "world religions" are therefore reproduced, leaving hardly any space to consider why and how this particular set of religions has been normalized as legitimate (and therefore worthy of educational attention). As her experience in Lower Saxony shows, the political processes involving the study of religions in the drafting of curricula for such school subjects as *values and norms* (the obligatory alternative for pupils who do not take part in confessional religious education") means having to navigate a complex hierarchy of existing understandings of the legitimacy and illegitimacy, as well as the good and bad nature, of particular religions.

Suzanne Owen (Chapter 20) discusses a small controversy in the 2010s about the acceptance of Druidry into the Inter Faith Network UK. The example shows how government commissions and organizations are in the business of domesticating religion, leading groups like the Druids to conform to "liberal Protestant" ideas of religion. In the classroom, the discussion of NRMs, Pagans, and other marginal groups often contrasts them to the "classical" world religions, making it hard to question underlying assumptions about how religion as a category is rendered. Instead of "religious literacy" in the "great traditions" built on a theological model, what is needed, according to Owen, is "religion literacy," or an understanding of the construction of "religion" as a category and the interests served by these processes.

Chapter 17

What Teaching New Religions Tells Us about the Discourse on 'Good' and 'Bad' Religion

David G. Robertson

Introduction

This chapter introduces the section on the Classroom, which I interpret as indicating a focus on pedagogy at an elementary or introductory level. Although this chapter concerns the university classroom, there are of course many different kinds of classroom, and the chapters which follow will explore some of these. This chapter concerns the introductory course in a British university, where the majority of students will be encountering the social-scientific study of religions for the first time.

What I'm going to reflect on in this chapter is that my experience in teaching new religious movements (hereafter, NRMs) as part of such an introductory course suggests that the things that we might expect to cause the students to react against a particular new religion are not in fact what we find. In other words, teaching NRMs suggests that the discourse on 'good' and 'bad' religion has some unexpected dynamics, which I suggest point to some less-obvious implicit assumptions about "what religion really is," and reveal some public inheritances from the Protestant heritage of the term.

I'll begin by looking briefly at the idea of 'cults' and NRMs, and their position within the contemporary undergraduate introductory course. I then describe how I teach this unit, and how I use the course to explicitly challenge the students' assumptions about religion. I then reflect upon how this has thrown up some unexpected issues, by here focusing upon the Church of Scientology as a case-study. I offer some suggestions as to why issues of sincerity, economic activity, and lack of perceived ethnicity may present such issues in accepting an NRM as 'good' religion, and conclude by reflecting upon what this might tell us about how we frame our discussions of religion in the classroom more broadly.

New Religious Movements and the Discourse on Good and Bad Religion

NRMs are a very good place to look for the discourse on 'good' and 'bad' religion. NRMs are almost always taken to be 'bad' religion, both in the public sphere and, troublingly, in scholarship. It is still the case that, for many—or perhaps most—NRMs are simply 'cults,' which brainwash innocent people into sex, drugs, and the occult. High profile media stories, such as the deaths at the Peoples Temple in Guyana in 1978, the sarin gas attacks on the Tokyo subway in 1995 carried out by Aum Shinrikyo, or the suicides by the members of Heaven's Gate in 1997, can also reinforce the impression that NRMs inevitably lead to abuse, violence, and even death.

For scholars trained in the 1960s and 1970s, NRMs—then still frequently referred to as 'cults' in academic writing—were together with secularization the key concern, particularly in the UK and Europe, as the post-war decline of mainstream churches became undeniable and a number of NRMs caught the attention of the media. The term 'cult' is drawn from Ernst Troeltsch's (1956 [1912]) tripartite division of religious groups into *church* (traditional, stable, open, and often embroiled with the state), *sect* (novel off-shoots of mainstream churches, often focused around a charismatic figure and tending towards strict or 'extreme' readings of texts), and *cult* (charismatic leadership, a focus on 'mysticism,' but lacking the connection to mainstream churches). In practice, however, 'cult' functions as a marker of illegitimacy—as Eileen Barker puts it, "a cult is a religion I don't like" (Barker et al. 2017). For this reason, the term has been almost universally replaced by NRM in contemporary religious studies (not that it is an unproblematic alternative, however—more on that later).

For my generation, training in the wake of 9/11 and the Rushdie Affair,[1] these issues have largely been superseded by a focus on Islam, with multiculturalism and identity-politics as key issues. Moreover, during this period religious studies departments have for a number of reasons become increasingly balkanized into different area studies, which has had the result of favoring insiders and marginalizing those who identify as scholars of religion in general (Davidsen 2012: 195). These factors have resulted in NRMs being squeezed out, as the organizational model of the Religious Studies department is almost always drawn from the World Religions paradigm (Owen 2011; Cotter and Robertson 2016). The World Religions paradigm is the dominant system in public and political discourse for categorizing religions, in which Christianity, Judaism, Hinduism, Islam, and Buddhism (and occasionally others) are not simply religions, but are granted the status of *world* religions due to their perceived importance. Implicitly, however, they are also being ranked on their economic importance to the nineteenth century colonial powers, and on their theological and structural similarity to Christianity—real or perceived. Problematically, this model has become firmly entrenched in the classroom, from elementary schools to the university. Edinburgh, where much of my teaching has taken place, is one of the few institutions that consistently includes NRMs and other forms of alternative and popular religion as part of its core undergraduate curriculum. I taught this section on the undergraduate "Global Religions"[2] course for three years, and during that time I also taught on an adult education course (two years) and the Sutton Summer School, which is aimed at academically gifted high school students from low-income families (two years). This makes me one of very few religious studies scholars of my generation whose teaching experience has focused primarily on NRMs.

Perhaps due to the dominance of the World Religions paradigm, there is frequently a clear apologetic rhetoric in academic work on NRMs. As Davidsen (2012: 194) notes (writing about Paganism in particular, but noting that this is a problem across the discipline), such scholarship "advances idealized notions of paganism's essence" and "insider interpretations of social processes." Pleas for NRMs to be taken seriously and counted as World Religions are common, and there are frequently other types of identity politics in play, including intersections with feminist or LGBT issues. Identity politics, as Hughes (2015: 22) notes,

> signifies a wide range of political activity and theorizing grounded in the shared experiences of injustice among members that perceive themselves to comprise certain social groups (e.g. women, blacks, Jews) [...]. Such processes can take place not only in political organisations and movements, but also in politically charged academic fields.

Perhaps because I identify as a critical historian rather than scholar of NRMs per se, I have always found this tendency troubling, and I have tried to avoid such essentialism in my teaching, instead using NRMs to destabilize the idea of World Religions. It is to this teaching that I now turn.

Teaching New Religious Movements

I have found NRMs to be an excellent way to get students to think about the theoretical issues of the study of religion in the introductory classroom. On a basic level, it is relatively easy to hold their attention, due to the novelty of the material and its wealth of entertaining and rich data, such as images of witches dancing naked around a fire in a wood, or science-fiction-derived cosmogonies. On a deeper level, however, NRMs challenge much of what students tend to implicitly understand to make something a religion. This also makes NRMs a very good place to look for how the discourse on 'good' and 'bad' religion is reproduced among students. The remainder of this section outlines the course and shows how it pushes students to address the question of the legitimacy of NRMs, as well as the World Religions.[3]

I begin by asking the students what a religion is. Students arrive at university with an implicit model: typically, that they are constructed as discrete traditions; based on an alleged revelation by a prophetic founding figure; they have a formal system of prescribed beliefs and a well-organized institutional structure; they are a private matter of belief; they confer moral teaching. I won't belabor the issues here, beyond directing readers to Brad Stoddard and Craig Martin's *Stereotyping Religion: Critiquing Clichés* (2017) for a number of critiques of these ideas, pitched at a level suitable for assignment to students on introductory courses.

Additionally, students increasingly also make a distinction between 'religion' and 'spirituality,' though these are seldom theorized beyond their popular usage. Nevertheless, it is generally the case that the question of how 'religion' is being used, and why these particular traditions have been selected, has not been raised on the course up until this point, nor frequently in the year or two years that they've been studying. The course is structured according to the World Religions paradigm, and by dividing it into five 'world religions' plus one (or both) of NRMs and Indigenous religions (depending on staff availability), there is a distinct, if implicit, hierarchical categorization being made. The students, whether they are aware or not, are being told that these are these five 'real' religions, and these others require further qualification. They are religions, *but not fully so*. NRMs has two such provisos, in fact—not only are they 'new', so failing the qualification of 'tradition,' but they are 'religious movements,' implying something that is similar to a religion, but nevertheless falls short in some way. What I am aiming to achieve over those three weeks then is to get the students to start thinking about what exactly it is that makes them incomplete, inauthentic, even 'bad' religions.

I organized my section of the course[4] to present examples of NRMs which challenge one or another of the common-sense definitions of religion. It begins with the history (or more accurately, *histories*) of Wicca. This serves to show that what religious people give as reasons for their present actions cannot necessarily be taken at face value, as the historical record is at odds with insider accounts. Conversely, it shows that the day-to-day practices of members of NRMs are not quite as popular culture presents them, for example that Wiccan practices are much more mundane (and therefore relatable) than typically presented in the media. Some students will be challenged by the use of Christian elements, especially the inversion of the traditionally heretical figure of the witch, and others may find the magical and sexual aspects at odds with their own morals. However, it is often the case that Wicca's stress on the 'divine feminine,' the sacrality of nature, and the importance of individual experience strikes the students as 'empowering,' and quite in keeping with contemporary 'spiritual' discourse.

In week two, I shift focus to New Age, 'spirituality,' and other more diffuse forms of contemporary religious praxis. New Age, having no formal structure or set practices, is typically presented in the public sphere (and often in academic writing also) as a Choose Your Own Adventure through the spiritual supermarket. To undermine this assumption, I hand the students a questionnaire (based upon the one used by the Kendal Project (Heelas and Woodhead 2005) which asks the students which of a range of alternative healthcare, esoteric, and other 'spiritual' practices they have tried or regularly take part in, as well as their religious self-identification. Unpacking the results of this makes the point that the New Age milieu is not an either/or situation, but rather that these practices and ideas are widespread in society. Yoga is a very clear current example: many, perhaps the majority, of female students are regular or occasional practitioners,[5] despite yoga having a complex relationship with the category 'religion,' with the question even reaching the California Appeals Court in 2013 (Graham 2013). The exercise helps challenge the idea of religion being an either/or identification, and starts them questioning why going to yoga classes, having acupuncture, or reading the horoscope are or are not identified as a religious act in different contexts. I then push the point to World Religions by asking them to consider the same issues in relation to praying and going to church.

In the third and final week, I look at Heaven's Gate to problematize the familiar discourse of 'brainwashing.' I begin by show them videos of the group's leader Marshall "Herff" Applewhite speaking, and they are typically amused by his wide-eyed manner and sci-fi stylings.[6] However, when I show them the "Exit Videos" made by the members shortly before their suicides, there is a noticeable shift as the students start to see the members of Heaven's Gate as people, and begin to question the degree to which there was coercion or violence involved.

Finally, I bring in 'invented religions'—that is, NRMs whose members *self-consciously* draw from fictional sources, including the highly satirical Discordianism, and Jediism, based upon the *Star Wars* films (Cusack 2010). These help to challenge the students' preconception of religion as an ancient tradition based upon 'divine revelation,' and bring questions of authenticity and sincerity into the conversation. Interestingly, while these aspects often challenge students, they are often ready to accept that invented religions are *functionally* legitimate— as the students typically consider religion to be 'a private matter of faith,' they accept that there is nothing wrong with a religion based on fiction 'if it works for you.'

The unit is not an attempt to legitimize NRMs as 'real' or 'good' religions, although it may seem that this is what I am doing at the time. Rather, I aim to enable and encourage the students to think through what makes something a 'good' or 'bad' religion for themselves. I constantly use comparisons with the World Religions they have encountered previously, on the course and in their everyday lives, not to legitimize NRMs by comparing them favorably to World Religions—making them 'good' religions—but to *delegitimize* or bring into question the World Religions by comparing them with NRMs. I aim to show the problems at the edge of the familiar categories, not to argue for a place within those categories for NRMs. To do so would be to reinforce the system of categorization which marginalizes minority religions in the first place.

This process has thrown up some unexpected implicit assumptions in the students, however, which I suggest reveal some less-obvious assumptions about the public discourse on good and bad religion. These are unpacked below.

Unexpected Implicit Assumptions

In this section, I will focus particularly on Scientology, as a result of the exercise (described below) which initially suggested these under-analyzed assumptions to me. The exercise follows from asking the students what a religion is in the first lecture. I present the class with a list of things we might conceivably classify as religions. The first slide lists Christianity, Judaism, Islam, Buddhism, and Hinduism. I ask them to put their hands up if they think these are religions; all hands go up. Then I add Wicca and Rastafarianism to the list; perhaps half the hands continue to be raised. I then add Jediism, Communism, and Atheism; at this point usually most of the hands have gone down, though a few remain aloft. Finally, I add Scientology to the list; the last time I did this, only one hand remained held up.

The list is revisited in the final lecture, to see if they have changed their mind over the three weeks. I go through the slides from week one again, and ask who now would count these as religions. By then they still have their hands raised for all of the World Religions, although perhaps a few who have been paying close attention might lower their hands for Buddhism. Noticeably more hands are raised for the NRMs presented, with most prepared to classify Wicca as a religion now. However, each time I have done this, only one or two hands remained raised for Scientology.

Of all of the examples given in my unit, including Jediism, New Age, and Heaven's Gate, Scientology is the one that students seem most reluctant to accept as a religion. It seems to be the *terminus post quem* for the students' acceptance of NRMs as 'real' religions. This seems to extend beyond the classroom, too: it is notable that popular criticism of Scientology often takes the form of open mockery of specific doctrines, something which we do not frequently see in other cases. Why is this? What is it that the students find particularly problematic? Scientology would seem to fit the common-sense implicit model of religion better than many of the other examples considered on the course, inasmuch as it has a prophetic founding figure, a formal system of prescribed beliefs, and a well-organized institutional structure. Moreover, it is legally recognized as a religion in several countries, including the US (Urban 2011).

Scientology's critics go to great lengths to make Scientology fit the standard model of charges of immorality and criminality against NRMs, even though in many ways it is an ill-fit. As identified by Stuart Wright and Susan Palmer (2016: 5), these charges are "child abuse, sexual abuse, polygamy, forced servitude, undue influence ('brainwashing'), and medical or financial fraud." Interestingly, no allegations of sexual abuse against Scientology have ever been pursued, and the few charges of child abuse are against individuals, rather than institutions or doctrinal mandates. There are allegations of violence, though these are relatively few and, again, largely specific to the Church's current leader, David Miscavige. Charges of 'brainwashing' are widespread, however, even though the concept has fallen from favor with psychologists as well as scholars of NRMs. There are accusations of fraud, including some, such as Operation Snow White, in which Scientologists systematically infiltrated the IRS (Robertson 2017: 306–308), which are undeniably legitimate. However, the three primary criticisms of Scientology are its financial operations, its particular aesthetic, and its perceived lack of sincerity. I unpack each of these below.

Scientology charges for various services, and this seems to be a barrier for many in accepting a classification of Scientology as a religion. Indeed, in public discourse (and surprisingly in academic work), Scientology is frequently presented in a dichotomy: religion or racket? (Doherty 2014: 44–45; Kent 1999; Beit-Hallahmi 2003; Palmer 2009: 304). Often, these claims are supported by the statement attributed to L. Ron Hubbard, "I'd like to start a religion. That's where the money is!" (Urban 2011: 58–59). The evidence that this was ever actually said is slim, however; several individuals have attested to it, but all at different times and places, none with multiple witnesses, and all years after the fact. Further, as

Urban (ibid.: 59) notes, it is hard to square this claim with the actual history of Scientology, which Hubbard resisted describing as a religion and only did so when the label became legally advantageous.

Nevertheless, the Church's financial activities seem to have been a factor in the decision by the United Kingdom Charity Commission's decision to reject Scientology's application for charitable status in 1999. The Commission's report states:

> The Commissioners considered that a further distinguishing characteristic from established religions is that Scientology's normal practices require prepayment in the form of requested donations for participation in its central practices of auditing and training. Although organised donations are a feature of some religions, it was not clear that such donations extended to access to the core or central religious practices of such religions. It is a feature which suggested to the Commissioners a possible marked difference to established religions. (Charity Commission 1999: 42)

For the presence of commercial activity to be seen as problematic relies on an either/or polarization where religion is held in contradistinction from commercial activity. It may seem counterintuitive that this is seen as delegitimising, given that we all live in and must play by the rules of a capitalist economy driven by the media. Nevertheless, this would seem to be a legacy of the Protestant heritage of religious studies, and indeed the category 'religion' itself (Masuzawa 2005). Money, as Weber (1930) famously argued, is important in Protestantism, but it is the accumulation which is encouraged, rather than the conspicuous spending thereof.

We do not have to look far for counter-examples, however. In Hinduism, for example, the manufacturing and selling of religious iconography is not seen as in any way violating religious duty, but rather fulfilling an essential role (Preston 1996). For a European example, we might point to the massive wealth of the Institute for the Works of Religion, popularly known as the Vatican Bank, which was heavily implicated in the P2 scandal that followed the death of Roberto Calvi in London in 1982 (Raw 1992), and more recently the laundering of Nazi gold (Pellegrini 1997).

A less obvious factor is the particular aesthetic of Scientology, which while not generally stated explicitly, is frequently mentioned, particularly in popular journalism. We might also relate this to critics' ongoing fascination with—and perhaps revulsion by—the Church's aggressive courting of celebrities, beginning in the 1970s. The Scientology aesthetic, like Hollywood, draws from a particular 1950s, middle-class, suburban version of the American dream which now seems somewhat old-fashioned, gaudy, tacky, or even crass to many. It is possible that the issue is in part that this aesthetic is not considered to be suitably 'reverent' for a religion. If religion is about 'authenticity' and 'reverence,' as the public tend to think, then Hollywood is indeed the antithesis.

However, it may also have to do with issues of ethnicity—or more accurately, the perceived lack thereof. The average Scientologist (in the public mind, at least) is white, wealthy, and successful. Perhaps such a group, as to some degree 'insiders' to the structures of power, are more of a threat that the typical idea of the member of an NRM as disenfranchised and lacking agency. This may be because we cannot orientalize it away, to construct it as the product of a suppressed minority—and implicitly, a primitive minority. At the same time, it can be openly criticized in a way that is not generally seen as acceptable for ethnic or nationalistic groups. In other words, it may not be exotic enough to neuter through orientalization.

What seems clear is that both these factors ultimately have to do with ideas of 'authenticity,' 'reverence,' or 'sincerity.' The importance put on sincerity is almost certainly an inheritance of Protestantism, in which personal faith and intention were paramount (Masuzawa 2005). This shows that simply expanding the introductory course—or indeed, the World Religions paradigm—to include NRMs is not enough to challenge the hegemony of Protestant theology, and indeed, may in fact entrench these norms even further. As Hughes (2015: xv) writes, "it is not up to us to create 'good' religion and differentiate it from so-called 'bad' religions, even though many students and others want us to."

Conclusion

To sum up, this chapter has argued that by observing how NRMs are used in the classroom to provoke students to problematize their implicit common-sense notions of religion, we bring to light some expected factors: financial operations, aesthetics and, ultimately, sincerity. These implicit assumptions about the role of religion, which we can easily identify with a Protestant theological position, suggest that for my students, at least, there is a desire for religion to be something other than the capitalist media-driven economy in which they exist. This suggests an assumption of religion itself as a kind of sacred space within the everyday world, as Hughes (2015: 16) puts it, existing "timelessly and as somehow immune from historical, cultural, and political forces." For the students, then, religion is something that should not be sullied with the mundane, pecuniary concerns of their everyday life, but should be something set apart. Therefore Wicca, while theologically very different from Protestantism, does not clash with this idea of religion as something set apart. Scientology, however, with its populism, money-making, and flash, certainly does. Yet religions outside the Western context seem to be excepted. This may be because we orientalize them, or it may be because of a problematic inherited data set—in effect, students "already know what [a] religion is" (Robertson 2014). This is problematic, because it requires us to teach against the students' desired outcomes for the course. How are we to impart the tools for critique without simply alienating students who have not come to the classroom with a desire for such tools?

Avoiding apologetics while using a critically comparative framework, my course does help students to rethink NRMs, yet they remain 'bad' religions in more subtle, implicit ways which are related to the genealogy of the discipline and the category 'religion' itself. Understanding why this should be suggests that the debate about 'good' and 'bad' religion in the public sphere is more complicated than we sometimes acknowledge. Yet it also raises further questions—among them, how do we challenge these implicit norms in ways which do not result in their further entrenchment?

David G. Robertson is Lecturer in Religious Studies at the Open University, co-founder of the Religious Studies Project, and co-editor of the journal *Implicit Religion*. His work applies critical theory to the study of alternative and emerging religions, and to "conspiracy theory" narratives. He is the author of *UFOs, the New Age and Conspiracy Theories: Millennial Conspiracism* (Bloomsbury 2016), co-editor of *After World Religions: Reconstructing Religious Studies* (Equinox 2016) and the *Handbook of Conspiracy Theories and Contemporary Religion* (Brill 2018). Twitter: @d_g_robertson.

Notes

1. The issuing of a fatwa against author Salman Rushdie in 1989 by Iranian leader Ayatollah Khomeini due to alleged blasphemy in his 1988 novel *The Satanic Verses*. Tariq Modood (2012) identifies this as the beginning of the current climate of distrust of Muslims in the Western media.
2. Note the not-so-subtle change from "World" to "Global."
3. The outline presented here is an idealized amalgam of the various different offerings of the three courses I taught, for the sake of narrative and rhetorical clarity.
4. I must here gratefully acknowledge the work of Steven Sutcliffe, who developed this course at Edinburgh and who gave me the opportunity to teach it. The overall structure of the course at Edinburgh is entirely his, though he has since adopted some of my additions (such as the material on Invented Religions), and our teaching style is very different. The shorter courses were written entirely by me.
5. Female yoga practitioners outnumber males by more than two to one (IPSOS 2016). The New Age milieu is around 70% female (Heelas and Woodhead 2005). Female students at undergraduate level RS in Edinburgh outnumber male around eight to one (an estimate based on experience and anecdotal evidence).
6. Originally, Applewhite was co-leader with Bonnie-Lou Nettles, who died in 1985. Applewhite was sole leader at the time of the group's suicides in 1997 (see Zeller 2014).

References

Barker, Eileen, Moojan Momen, Joseph Webster, and Tristan Sturm. 2017. "Millennialism and Violence?" The Religious Studies Project (Podcast), May 22. Retrieved from www.religiousstudiesproject.com/podcast/millennialism-and-violence/ (archived at archive.today/KXfCV).
Beit-Hallahmi, Benjamin 2003. "Scientology: Religion or Racket?" *Marburg Journal of Religion* 8(1): 1–56.
Charity Commission. 1999. "Decision of the Charity Commissioners for England and Wales Made On 17th November 1999. Application for Registration as a Charity by the Church of Scientology (England and Wales)." Retrieved from www.gov.uk/government/uploads/system/uploads/attachment_data/file/324212/cosfulldoc.pdf.
Cotter, Christopher R. and David G. Robertson. 2016. "Introduction: The World Religions Paradigm in Contemporary Religious Studies." In Christopher R. Cotter and David

G. Robertson (eds.), *After World Religions: Reconstructing Religious Studies*, 1–20. London: Routledge.

Cusack, Carole M. 2010. *Invented Religions: Imagination, Fiction and Faith*. Farnham: Ashgate Press.

Davidsen, Markus A. 2012. "Review Essay: What is Wrong with Pagan Studies?" *Method and Theory in the Study of Religion* 24(2), 183–199.

Doherty, Bernard 2014. "Sensational Scientology! The Church of Scientology and Australian Tabloid Television." *Nova Religio* 17(3), 38–63. https://doi.org/10.1525/nr.2014.17.3.38

Graham, Marty. 2013. "Yoga in School Not Same as Teaching Religion, California Judge Rules." Reuters, July 2. Retrieved from www.reuters.com/article/us-usa-yoga-california/yoga-in-school-not-same-as-teaching-religion-california-judge-rules-idUSBRE96016Y20130702 (archived at www.webcitation.org/78aFqRHnc).

Heelas, Paul and Linda Woodhead. 2005. *The Spiritual Revolution: Why Religion Is Giving Way to Spirituality*. Malden, MA: Blackwell.

Hughes, Aaron. 2015. *Islam and the Tyranny of Authenticity: An Inquiry into Disciplinary Apologetics and Self-Deception*. Sheffield: Equinox.

IPSOS. 2016. "Yoga in America Study." Retrieved from www.yogaalliance.org/Portals/0/2016%20Yoga%20in%20America%20Study%20RESULTS.pdf.

Kent, Stephen A. 1999. "Scientology – Is this a Religion?" *Marburg Journal of Religion* 4(1). https://doi.org/10.17192/mjr.1999.4.3754

Masuzawa, Tomoko. 2005. *The Invention of World Religions, Or, How European Universalism Was Preserved in the Language of Pluralism*. Chicago, IL: University of Chicago Press. https://doi.org/10.7208/chicago/9780226922621.001.0001

Modood, Tariq. 2012. "The Crisis of European Secularism." The Religious Studies Project (Podcast), May 28. Retrieved from www.religiousstudiesproject.com/podcast/podcast-tariq-modood-on-the-crisis-of-european-secularism (archived at archive.today/ljVdz).

Owen, Suzanne 2011. "The World Religions Paradigm: Time for a Change." *Arts and Humanities in Higher Education* 10(3): 253–268. https://doi.org/10.1177/1474022211408038

Palmer, Susan J. 2009. "The Church of Scientology in France: Legal and Activist Counter-attacks in the 'War on Sectes'." In James R. Lewis (ed.), *Scientology*, 295–325. Oxford: Oxford University Press. https://doi.org/10.1093/acprof:oso/9780195331493.003.0016

Pellegrini, Frank. 1997. "The Vatican Pipeline." *Time Magazine*, July 22. Retrieved from http://content.time.com/time/magazine/article/0,9171,8505,00.html.

Preston, James J. 1996. "Creation of the Sacred Image: Apotheosis and Destruction in Hinduism." In Joanne Punzo Waghorne and Norman Cutler (eds.), *Gods of Flesh, Gods of Stone: The Embodiment of Divinity in India*, 9–30. New York: Columbia University Press. https://doi.org/10.7312/wagh91314-004

Raw, Charles. 1992. *The Moneychangers: How the Vatican Bank Enabled Roberto Calvi to Steal 250 Million Dollars for the Heads of the P2 Masonic Lodge*. London: Harvill Press.

Robertson, David G. 2014. "World Religions Paradigm: Comparing Like with Like." Religion Bulletin, June 11. Retrieved from http://bulletin.equinoxpub.com/2014/06/world-religions-paradigm-comparing-like-with-like (archived at archive.today/ND1M1).

Robertson, David G. 2017. "Hermeneutics of Suspicion: Scientology and Conspiracism." In James R. Lewis and Kjersti Hellesoy (eds.), *Handbook of Scientology*, 300–318. Leiden: Brill. https://doi.org/10.1163/9789004330542_013

Stoddard, Brad, and Craig Martin. 2017. *Stereotyping Religion: Critiquing Clichés.* London: Bloomsbury.
Troeltsch, Ernst. 1956 [1912]. *The Social Teaching of the Christian Churches.* London: Allen & Unwin.
Urban, Hugh. 2011. *The Church of Scientology: A History of a New Religion.* Princeton, NJ: Princeton University Press. https://doi.org/10.1515/9781400839438
Weber, Max. 1930. *The Protestant Ethic and the Spirit of Capitalism.* London: George Allen & Unwin.
Wright, Stuart A., and Susan J. Palmer. 2016. *Storming Zion: Government Raids on Religious Communities.* New York: Oxford University Press. https://doi.org/10.1093/acprof:oso/9780195398892.001.0001
Zeller, Benjamin E. 2014. *Heaven's Gate: America's UFO Religion.* New York: New York University Press.

Chapter 18

Unintentionally Constructing 'Good' and 'Bad' Religions in Teaching Classical European Social Theories at a Japanese University

Mitsutoshi Horii

I live in the UK working for a private college, which is set up as an overseas campus of a Japanese university. At the time of this writing, I am employed by this Japanese university, and once a year, I travel to Japan to teach first year undergraduate students a short intensive course called 'Introduction to Sociology.' I usually have 40–50 students enrolled in my course. These students are first year undergraduate students who belong to the Social Studies major at the Faculty of Teacher Education. They are being trained to be social studies teachers for Japanese primary or secondary schools. They do not have any academic background in either sociology of religion or religious studies.

My sociology course includes an introduction to the classical social theories of Marx, Weber, and Durkheim. In this part of the course, 'religion' is a key category. Famously, Marx equated 'religion' to opium. Weber studied the relationship between 'religion' and 'economy.' Durkheim defines 'religion,' by associating it with the notion of the 'sacred.' The category 'religion' is employed in classical social theories, as if it is a universal and transhistorical phenomena. Marx and Weber for example do not define the term 'religion,' but they utilize the category as if they know what it is. We can assume that what they mean by 'religion' is the taxonomy of the so-called 'world religions.' In contrast, the Durkheimian definition of 'religion' includes all sorts of collective rituals and representations. In Durkheim's discourse, the boundaries between 'religious' and 'secular' forms of rituals and symbolism are extremely ambiguous.

More importantly, I have found that the term 'religion' is problematic in order to achieve the leaning objective of introducing European classical social theories to Japanese first year undergraduate students with no previous exposure to either the sociology of religion nor religious studies. It is problematic because the term 'religion' in this specific context unintentionally constructs a binary between ostensibly *good* religions' and *bad* religions.' This essay explains how and why this happens utilizing some examples from introductory Sociology textbooks published in English for first year undergraduate students.

The language in my course at the Japanese University is Japanese. However, since I was trained as a sociologist in the UK, I usually refer to English textbooks for my preparation. Thus the Japanese discourse which I deliver in my course usually follows the semantic pattern of these English textbooks. In addition, since this article is written in English, English texts are more useful to demonstrate the semantic transformation which produces the distinction of good/bad religions.

'Religion' in contemporary Japan

The Japanese encountered the English term 'religion' for the first time in the mid-nineteenth century, and the word '*shūkyō*' has been the definitive translation of 'religion' since the late nineteenth century until today. In their co-authored book, Reader and Tanabe (1998: 5) state that the Japanese concept of *shūkyō* is "imbued with multiple meanings and historical accretions that provoke different interpretations and suggest different and frequently elastic meanings to different people in different contexts." A number of scholars of Japanese religion, including Reader and Tanabe, have noticed that Japanese people often use the term in a particular way, although it has been almost always at the periphery of their studies of so-called Japanese religion. For example, according to Reader (1991: 11):

> In fact many Japanese people I have talked to about *hatsumode* [the New Year's visit to shines and temples] hardly consider it a religious festival at all, and are reluctant to view their participation in religious terms. [...] Again, many Japanese state that this [*o-bon*, and visiting the graves of the ancestors at this time] is a cultural and social event, revolving around family obligations and tradition.

Furthermore, Dorman (2007) discusses that, within the context of popular discourse, the practice of divination and the element of 'ancestor worship' are referred to as 'non-religious.' His study deals with how a particular person with a large following distances oneself from the term 'religion.' In this case, ancestor-related activities are portrayed as 'non-religious,' partly because the concept 'religion' had been darkened due to Aum Shinrikyō, whose leaders were responsible for the Tokyo subway sarin gas attack in 1995. It is also noted that the more general identification of ancestor-related activities as 'non-religious' is not necessarily related to the impact of Aum Shinrikyō, but it is a very common description of these kinds of social practices. Davis (1992: 234–235), for example, comments that the "feelings [of 'revering one's ancestors' and 'filial piety']—which one naturally associates with 'ancestor worship'—seem to be divorced from 'religion' (*shūkyō*) by the Japanese."

Within the popular discourse on *shūkyō* in Japan, what ordinary Japanese people generally mean by *shūkyō* tends to be confined to what Ama (2005) calls 'revealed religion,' whose examples "include Christianity, Buddhism, Islam, and Japanese new religions, which are revealed through texts, preached by certain people, and managed by profitable organizations" (ibid.: 3), while associations with other forms of belief and practices, which are also referred to as religion or *shūkyō* by scholars, are generally described as 'non-religious.' It also has to be pointed out that the term *shūkyō* has more specific associations with the practices and philosophies of so-called new religions, whose general image was very poor for most of the post-war period and worsened with the Aum Shinrikyo affair of the 1990s (Hardacre 2003).

In a similar line of argument, Shimada (2009) claims that most Japanese people associate the term *shūkyō* with Christianity and Islam as well as the so-called new religions. The stereotypical image of these describes adherents who show their commitment to daily practices of their faith, including participation in activities to propagate their beliefs to others. Thus, Reader (1991: 14) explains: "In *shūkyō* and hence in the idea of 'religion' there is a hint of something committing, restrictive and even intrusive." For this reason, according to Shimada (2009), the Japanese are likely to identify themselves as 'non-religious' (*mushūkyō*) when they are asked the question: 'Do you believe in any religion?' In the words of Kawano (2005: 36):

> The word [*mushūkyō*] implies that a person does not belong to any religion that emphasizes personal faith, such as Christianity or the so-called new religions. *Mushūkyō* persons often follow social convention by participating in life-cycle and calendrical rites at Shinto shrines and Buddhist temples.

The claim of *mushūkyō* could be seen as an expression of the dominant ideology, to which the emphasis on personal faith in Christianity and new religions, for example, is fundamentally alien. The social norm of *mushūkyō* symbolically eliminates *shūkyō* as a source of conflict, or "pollution" (Douglas 1966), from the structure of social relations in order to maintain the existing social order.

In this context, many social practices, which are described as 'religion' by scholars of Japanese religion are unlikely to be seen as *shūkyō* by the Japanese. More specifically, although Reader and Tanabe (1998: 5–6) define religion as 'a matter not only of doctrine and belief but of participation, custom, ritual, action, practice, and belonging,' these are all likely to be described by the majority of the population as 'non-religious,' characterized instead by terms such as 'cultural,' 'traditional,' and the like.

In the colloquial discourse in Japan, the term 'religion' has more specific associations with the practices and teachings of the so-called new religions, whose general image has been very poor for most of the post-war period. In particular, it was worsened with the 1995 Aum Shinrikyo subway attack. Thereafter, the term 'religion' in Japan continued to be darkened by the controversies provoked by particular organizations. One such organization is Life Space, which insisted in 2000 that the corpse of one of its members was still alive, whereas the media sensationally reported in 2003 that members of another organization, Pana Wave, wore completely white uniforms and insisted electro-magnetic waves were causing great harm. It seems that the term 'religion' in this context carries a very similar nuance to 'cults.' Whatever is called 'religion' is seen as delusional. Therefore, my Japanese students tend to assume: "Religion is bad."

The following sections outline the ways in which introductory sociology textbooks articulate the notion of 'religion' in the writings of Marx, Weber, and Durkheim, and then consider the ways in which each of these semantics of 'religion' interacts with the Japanese colloquial notion of 'religion' in a university classroom in Japan. To sum up, the nuances and meanings of the term 'religion' in social theories are rather counter-intuitive for my Japanese students.

Marx's 'Religion' in a Classroom

> Religion is the sigh of the oppressed creature, the heart of a heartless world and the soul of soulless conditions. It is the opium of the people.

Above is the famous quotation from Karl Marx's "Towards a Critique of Hegel's Philosophy of Right" (Marx [1844] 2002: 171). It was written in 1843, when Marx was in his mid-twenties, and was published in 1844 in *Deutsch-Französische Jahrbücher*. What did young Marx mean by this? Some textbook answers to this question go as follows.

Robin Cohen and Paul Kennedy (2007: 384) explain: "For Karl Marx, religion was similarly consigned to the category of 'false consciousness' and 'ideology'." What Marx meant by 'religion' in his mid-nineteenth-century German context is highly ambiguous (Horii 2017). However, the discourse on 'religion' in sociology text books proceeds as if what is meant by 'religion' is self-evident.

Anthony Giddens (2009: 680) also clarifies what Marx meant by his 'religion as opium' equation in his introductory textbook:

> Religion defers happiness and rewards to the afterlife, teaching the resigned acceptance of the existing conditions of this life. Attention is thus diverted away from inequalities and injustices in this world by the promise of what is to come in the next. Religion has a strong ideological element: religious beliefs and values often provide justifications of inequalities of wealth and power.

When the Marxist equation of 'religion as opium' is introduced in my Japanese university classroom, it resonates with students' understanding of 'religion' as 'delusional cults.' At this level of understanding, students are likely to think about such controversial organizations as Aum Shinrikyo, Pana Wave, Life Space, and the like as examples of 'religions.' Then, when the Marxist critique equates 'religion' to the form of a 'drug' which alleviates the immediate 'pain' of social inequality, students may imagine the members of the aforementioned organizations as the victims of capitalist exploitation. They may also imagine that their doctrines somehow alleviate the pain of social injustice but discourage people from challenging the social structure which causes such pain. 'Religion' in this sense is hallucinogenic, causing delusion, and functioning to maintain the existing state of social inequality. In this conceptual framework, the students' assumption that 'Religion (= delusional cults) is bad' seems to be authorized by Marx.

However, another textbook explanation of Marx's critique of religion tacitly subverts this kind of understanding. James Fulcher and John Scott (2007), for example, explain: "Marx saw *theistic* and *metaphysical religions* as expressions of the deepening alienation that people experienced in a modern capitalist society" (Fulcher and Scott 2007: 410, italics added). They also use the terms "traditional religious thought" and "traditional religion" on the same page. They appear to be avoiding generalization about religion by rescuing ostensibly 'non-theistic,' 'non-metaphysical,' and 'non-traditional' religions from Marx's critique against religion as "simply a distorted reflection of the real class relations" (ibid.).

When the target of Marx's critique is said to be limited to 'traditional religions,' the organizations such as Aum Shinrikyo, Pana Wave, and Life Space are excluded from the critique. Other 'new religions' such as Soka Gakkai would also escape Marxist critique. By the term 'traditional religion,' Japanese students are likely to assume Temple Buddhism and Shrine Shinto. However, they could not be attacked in the Marxist sense because they do not appear to be *theistic* and *metaphysical*. These institutions are generally associated with the category of 'cultural practices' for the majority of the Japanese. Given this, students may conclude that what Marx meant by religion in his critique must be Christian and Jewish traditions in his own time. This conclusion may lead students to assume that '(traditional) religion' in Japan is probably not 'bad,' while traditional religions in the West were probably 'bad' in the Marxist sense.

In addition, to counter-balance the uncritical version of the religion–opium equation, it seems to be the norm in sociological teaching to explain to students about the specific historical cases in which 'religion' motivated people to challenge social injustice. For example, John J. Macionis and Ken Plummer (2008: 613) state:

> Social conflict analysis reveals the power of religion to legitimise social inequality. Yet critics of religion's conservative face, Marx included, minimise ways in which religion has promoted changes as well as equality. Nineteenth-century religious groups in the United Kingdom, for example, were at the forefront of the movement to abolish slavery. In the United States, religious organisations and their leaders (including the Reverend Martin Luther King, Jr) were at the core of the civil rights movement and today serve as one of the main lobbies for the needs of poor immigrants from Latin America. There has been a long-standing 'radical' Catholic movement in supporting revolutionary change in Latin America and elsewhere.

This kind of example challenges students' views against 'religion' ("Religion is bad"). Recognizing the positive impact of Dr. King's 'religion,' for example, the students may admit: "Religion can be good." In the light of this, their assumption "Religion is bad" becomes "Religion can be 'good' or 'bad,' but religions I know in Japan are 'bad' ones." Here, the assumption "Religion is essentially bad" is transformed into the '*good* religion'/'*bad* religion' dichotomy.

Weberian 'Religion' in a Classroom

As just explained, to counter-argue the Marxist charge that 'religion' promotes social inequality, sociologists often make the case that "religious ideals have both supported and motivated people to seek greater equality" (Macionis and Plummer 2008: 633). This type of discourse often directs the course of sociological teaching towards the introduction to Max Weber's sociology of religion. According to Giddens (2009: 680–683): "Weber argues that religion is not necessarily a conservative force; on the contrary, religiously inspired movements have often produced dramatic social transformations." For example, Weber's *The Protestant Ethic and the Spirit of Capitalism* is considered an "analysis of Calvinism's contribution to the rise of industrial capitalism" which "demonstrates religion's power to promote social change" (Macionis and Plummer 2008: 633).

With regard to Weber's notion of religion, he famously refuses to define the term in his *Sociology of Religion*:

> To define "religion," to say what it is, is not possible at the start of a presentation such as this. Definition can be attempted, if at all, only at the end of the study. The essence of religion is not even our concern, as we make it our own task to study the conditions and effects of a particular type of social behaviour. (Weber [1922] 1993: 1)

Nonetheless, throughout his writings, it is also apparent that Weber conceptualized 'religion' as something almost universally found in all cultures throughout history. He identifies the multiplicity of 'religions' in the world, and later in his life, he endeavors extensive studies of 'world religions' [Weltreligionen], which according to him include "Confucianism" [Konfuzianismus], "Hinduism" [Hinduismus], "Buddhism" [Buddhismus], "Islamism" [Islam], "Judaism" [Judentum], and "Christianity" [Christentum] (Weber [1915] 1997: 268–269).

According to Giddens (2009: 680), "Most of his [Weber's] attention was concentrated on what he called the world religions—those that have attracted large numbers of believers and decisively affected the course of global history." Another textbook (Fulcher and Scott 2007: 411) explains that Weber's particular concern was about "the relationship between religious values and economic action," which is also characterized by Cohen and Kennedy (2007: 390) as "religion and capitalism." More specifically, "Weber suggested that pursuit of material gain could be supported by particular convictions" (ibid.). Weber carried out comparative studies of the so-called 'Eastern religions,' namely, 'religions' of China, India, and ancient Israel, but Fulcher and Scott (2007: 411) believe that "his most important study was set out in a book on *The Protestant Ethic and the Spirit of Capitalism*." This is because Weber concluded that while those 'Eastern religions' "cultivate an attitude of passivity in the believer towards the existing order, Christianity involves a constant struggle against sin, and hence can stimulate revolt against the existing order of things" (Giddens 2009: 684). This means that the religions of the East "provided insuperable barriers to the development of industrial capitalism, such as took place in the West" (ibid.: 683).

Given this kind of introduction to Weber's sociology of religion, Japanese university students tend to construct the 'good religion'/'bad religion' dichotomy in three ways. These relate to Weber's utilization of the typology of 'world religions.' In the process of understanding this typology, students tend to further construct the idea of 'good/bad religions.'

Firstly, out of Weber's 'world religions' paradigm, when 'Christianity' and 'Islam' are mentioned as 'religion,' students generally do not have a problem understanding these as 'religions.' However, each of them tends to be divided into two forms:

'good' and 'bad' ones. At one level, students tend to associate these 'religions' with so-called 'fundamentalism,' which is understood as 'bad' religion. At the same time, Christianity and Islam are also understood as the cultural heritage of specific parts of the world, and in this case, they are seen as 'good' religions.

Secondly, Weber's typology of 'world religions' can be counter-intuitive when 'Buddhism' and 'Confucianism' are classified as 'religions.' For example, for my Japanese students, when 'Buddhism' is represented in the form of traditional temples and various practices associated with them, it tends to be regarded as 'cultural tradition' rather than 'religion.' However, when traditional Buddhism is labelled as a 'religion,' students have to alter their preconceived idea about 'religion' as a 'cult,' and add a more positive element of 'cultural tradition' into the category. Therefore, students are encouraged to think: "Not all religions are cults." This thinking constructs the 'good/bad religions' dichotomy. They may think that while traditional Buddhism is a 'good' religion, other less traditional ones, for example, new religions, are 'bad' religions.

Finally, it appears for students that Weber is pointing out the Western Protestant 'religious' origin of the spirit of capitalism. This implies that the current industrial capitalist economy of Japan could have been originally 'invented' by the imported Protestant ethic from the West after the Meiji Restoration of 1868.[1] Students may ask: "Is it the ideological colonization of Japan by the Western powers?" Having studied capitalism in the session on Marx and having conceptualized it in terms of exploitation and alienation, Protestantism appears to be a 'bad religion' for having created such an inhumane economic system. At the same time, as quoted above, Weber claims that an "attitude of passivity" in 'Eastern religions' acted as a barrier against capitalist development (Giddens 2009: 684). This encourages the students to wonder whether 'Buddhism' and 'Shinto,' which can be regarded as the 'national religions' of Japan, could be 'good religions' that could counterbalance the negative social consequence of modern capitalism.

Durkheimian 'Religion' in a Classroom

Émile Durkheim's *The Elementary Forms of Religious Life* provides the famous definition of 'religion': "A religion is a unified system of beliefs and practices relative to sacred things [...]" (Durkheim [1912] 1995: 44).

Like Weber, Durkheim assumed that there are many 'religions' across the world. Unlike Weber, however, he tried to seek the essence which all these 'religions' have in common. For this purpose, Durkheim "argues that totemism represents religion in its most 'elementary' forms," while he "defines religion in terms of a distinction between the sacred and the profane" (Giddens 2009: 681). Why is the totem sacred? Answering this question explains what the essence of all religions is:

> [W]hy is the totem sacred? According to Durkheim, it is because it is the symbol of the group itself; it stands for the values central to the group or community. The reverence with which people feel for the totem derives from the respect they hold

for central social values. In religion, the object of worship is actually society itself." (Giddens 2009: 681)

Fulcher and Scott (2007: 410) explain: "The origin of the idea of the sacred was to be found in society itself." As the sacred is the essence of religion, "Religion is also central to the production of a sense of moral community." In other words: "It is through religion that the symbols and ideas that sustain social life and that underpin the social order are sustained." Given this, Giddens's description of the Durkheimian idea of religion stresses that "religions are never just a matter of belief" (Giddens 2009: 681). More specifically, "All religions involve regular ceremonial and ritual activities in which a group of believers meets together" (ibid.). Macionis and Plummer (2008: 633) summarize: "Émile Durkheim argued that individuals experience the power of their society through religion."

When the Durkheimian notion of 'religion' is introduced in my classroom at a Japanese university, it seems to reinforce students' understanding of 'religion' as 'cult' in its association with collective rituals and sacred symbolisms. It provokes an image of a mass ritual devoted to a fetish object or a charismatic guru, where individuals are totally subordinated to the group. This goes against the value orientation of individualism, which is generally subscribed to by undergraduate students in the course. Thus this echoes their initial preconception about religion: 'Religion is bad.' Religion in this context denotes new religions which tend to be regarded as 'cults' in the Japanese context.

In addition, when the function of 'religion' is defined in terms of social cohesion, it tends to be understood rather normatively as if one can know a true 'religion' precisely because it performs this social function. In this light, I have the impression from my students that they might end up thinking that 'religions,' in the sense of socially controversial 'new religions,' are all 'bad' religions, 'fake' religions, or non-religions. This is because students assume that ostensibly *bad* 'religions' are the ones which make controversy, whereas the true and *good* 'religions' should function as a source of social cohesion.

At the same time, Durkheimian notions of religion force students to identify what they generally regard as non-religion as something essentially religious. In Durkheimian discourse on religion, any form of group and community are conceptualized as 'religious' by default as they generate and maintain their cohesion through collective rituals and symbolism. In this light, Japanese nationalism and identity can be seen as the religion of the Japanese.[2] In this context, the conventional religions such as Buddhism, Shintoism, New religions, and the like may be evaluated as 'good' or 'bad' according to their contribution to national integration and obedience to its social order.

The Durkheimian concept of religion is probably the most counterintuitive idea of religion, compared with ones of Marx and Weber. It potentially opens up students' minds to conventional 'religions' in contemporary Japan, which are generally regarded as delusional cults. This is because, in Durkheimian conceptual work, everyone is essentially 'religious' as long as one is integrated into a collective entity. In this sense, the Durkheimian conceptualization of religion could naturalize the 'religiousness' of new religions as a universal aspect of human lives. Nevertheless, this would be too optimistic. The colloquial notion of religion would not disappear easily. The Durkheimian idea of religion can be utilized by students to evaluate conventional 'religions,' according to the degree of their commitment to the national culture and social norms.

Concluding Remarks: Be More Specific than 'Religion'

There are discrepancies between the meaning of the term 'religion' in classical social theories and its use in Japanese colloquial discourse. The meaning of the term 'religion' in social theories was constructed within the European context in the nineteenth and early twentieth centuries, while the meaning of 'religion' in the colloquial Japanese discourse has been constructed within the culturally specific context of Japan in the late-twentieth and early-twenty-first centuries. Therefore, an uncritical utilization of 'religion' for teaching social theory to these Japanese undergraduates, in my view, risks misunderstanding. For example, when the ideas such as 'religion as opium,' 'religion and economy,' and 'religion as sacred,' are presented to my Japanese students, 'religion' here means controversial new religions, which are often regarded as 'cults.' By the word 'religion,' my students do not presume Christian (and Jewish) teachings and institutions in Western Europe in the nineteenth and early twentieth centuries.

In my view, the generic notion of religion is useless in my teaching for Japanese undergraduate students. The strategy which I have been taking is to avoid the term 'religion' altogether and replace it with more specific terms. This echoes Naomi Goldenberg (2015: 280) when she suggests: "Scholars who are expert in particular periods of history in varied regions of the globe would have to evaluate the idea to judge its use as a hermeneutic in specific contexts."

For example, when Marx equates 'religion' as 'opium,' the category 'religion' here means Christian and Jewish theologies and faiths in the mid-nineteen century German context. In the case of Weber, rather than describing Weber's study as examinations of influence of 'religion' upon economic ethos, I explain that Weber studied how specific teachings and worldviews generated particular forms of economic activities, without the generic term 'religion.' Finally, the main point of Durkheim's social theory can be articulated without using the term 'religion.' In my view, his sociology is an attempt to theorize the function of rituals and symbolisms for communities to generate and maintain their respective order.

In the classroom where I teach at a Japanese university, even though my students often think of 'religion' as bad, the same term can be used more positively in different discursive contexts. Japanese academics in religious studies and sociology of religion, for example, use the term in more neutral ways. Some other intellectuals often employ the term positively, associating it with the inner realm of individuals. In addition, those who are involved in 'religion' (for example, members of new religions) employ the term affirmatively to categorize their own beliefs and practices, claiming 'religion' as a universal aspect of human life. However, these positive and affirmative semantics of 'religion' are not the norm in the classroom where I teach. As students are exposed to sociological ideas of 'religion,' the result is that they mentally construct the good/bad religion paradigm, which is not helpful, either.

Using the term 'religion' in the teaching of classical social theories in the context of the Japanese university classroom has to be negotiated with culturally specific semantics of the same term. Such negotiation unintentionally constructs the 'good'/'bad' religions paradigm. In my experience, the term 'religion' is not helpful, and it should be abandoned. It must be replaced with the denotations of specific institutions, beliefs, and practices, which were actually meant by the term 'religion' by Marx, Weber, and Durkheim in Western Europe in the nineteenth and early twentieth centuries.

Mitsutoshi Horii is Professor at Shumei University, Japan. He works at Chaucer College, UK, as Shumei's representative. His recent research focuses on the function of modern Western categories, such as 'religion,' and examines the ways in which these categories authorise and naturalise specific norms and imperatives in a variety of socio-cultural contexts, including Japan and Euro-American social theories. His most recent publications include the monograph *The Category of 'Religion' in Contemporary Japan: Shūkyō and Temple Buddhism* (Palgrave Macmillan, 2018). His forthcoming monograph is entitled *Social Theory and the Ideas of 'Religion' and 'the Secular': Postcolonial Reflections on Sociology* (Palgrave Macmillan).

Notes

1 It should be mentioned at this point that Robert Bellah's *Tokugawa Religion* ([1957] 1985) famously locates the origin of the spirit of Japanese capitalism in the 'religion' of Tokugawa-period Japan, namely, the native doctrine of Buddhism, Confucianism, and Shinto. However, this book was not introduced in my course in order to focus on Max Weber's social theory, not the ones influenced by Weber.
2 This echoes Izaya Ben-Dasan (1975) who famously saw a 'religion' itself in the characteristics of the Japanese and coined the term *nihonkyō*.

References

Ama, Toshimaro. 2005. *Why Are the Japanese Non-Religious? Japanese Spirituality: Being Non-Religious in a Religious Culture*. Lanham, MD: University Press of America.
Bellah, Robert. [1957] 1985. *Tokugawa Religion: The Cultural Roots of Modern Japan*. London: Collier Macmillan Publishers.
Ben-Dasan, Izaya. 1975. *Nihonkyō ni tsuite*. Tokyo: Bungei Shunjū.
Cohen, Robin and Paul Kennedy. 2007. *Global Sociology*, 2nd edn. London: Palgrave Macmillan.
Davis, Winston. 1992. *Japanese Religion and Society: Paradigms of Structure and Change*. New York: State University of New York Press.
Dorman, Benjamin. 2007. "Representing Ancestor Worship as 'Non-Religious': Hosoki Kazuko's Divination in the Post-Aum Era." *Nova Religio* 10(3): 32–53. https://doi.org/10.1525/nr.2007.10.3.32
Douglas, Mary. 1966. *Purity and Danger: An Analysis of Concepts of Pollution and Taboo*. New York: Routledge.
Durkheim, Émile. [1912] 1995. *The Elementary Forms of Religious Life*. London: Free Press.

Fulcher, James and John Scott. 2007. *Sociology*, 3rd edn. Oxford: Oxford University Press.
Giddens, Anthony. 2009. *Sociology*, 6th edn. Cambridge: Polity Press.
Goldenberg, Naomi. 2015. "The Category of Religion in the Technology of Governance: An Argument for Understanding Religions as Vestigial States." In Trevor Stack, Naomi Goldenberg, and Timothy Fitzgerald (eds.), *Religion as the Category of Governance and Sovereignty*, 280–292. Leiden: Brill. https://doi.org/10.1163/9789004290594_013
Hardacre, Helen. 2003. "After Aum: Religion and Civil Society in Japan." In Frank J. Schwartz and Susan J. Pharr (eds.), *The State of Civil Society in Japan*, 135–153. Cambridge: Cambridge University Press. https://doi.org/10.1017/CBO9780511550195.008
Horii, Mitsutoshi. 2017. "Contexualizing 'Religion' of Young Karl Max: A Preliminary Analysis." *Critical Research on Religion* 5(2): 170–186. https://doi.org/10.1177/2050303217690897
Kawano, Satsuki. 2005. *Ritual Practice in Modern Japan*. Honolulu, HI: University of Hawai'i Press.
Macionis, John J. and Ken Plummer. 2008. *Sociology: A Global Introduction*, 4th edn. Harlow: Pearson Education.
Marx, Karl. [1844] 2002. "Critique of Hegel's Philosophy of Right." In John Raines (ed.), *Marx on Religion*, 170–182. Philadelphia, PA: Temple University Press.
Reader, Ian. 1991. *Religion in Contemporary Japan*. Honolulu, HI: University of Hawai'i Press.
Reader, Ian, and George Tanabe, Jr. 1998. *Practically Religious: Worldly Benefits and the Common Religion of Japan*. Honolulu, HI: University of Hawaii Press. https://doi.org/10.1057/9780230375840
Shimada, Hiromi. 2009. *Mushūkyō koso nihonjin no shūkyō dearu*. Tokyo: Kadokawa shoten.
Weber, Max. [1915] 1997. "The Social Psychology of World Religions." In H. H. Gerth and C. Wright Mills (eds.), *From Max Weber: Essays in Sociology*, 267–301. London: Routledge.
Weber, Max. [1922] 1993. *The Sociology of Religion*. Boston, MA: Beacon Press.

Chapter 19

Good and Bad, Legitimate and Illegitimate Religion in Education

Wanda Alberts

David Robertson (Chapter 17, this volume) shows how different levels of concepts of good and bad religion influence teaching the study of religions at universities, even if one tries to find a more analytical approach. By an analytic comparison of aspects of "world religions" that students are somewhat familiar with and aspects of new religious movements, some popular views of new religious movements (NRMs) may be questioned, encouraging the students to reflect on their own notion of religion. Thus, stereotypes such as dangerous brainwashing "cults" can be successfully challenged. However, the genealogy of the study of religions and of the category "religion" itself effectively contributes to the fact that NRMs remain "bad" religions in more subtle and implicit ways.

I would like to take this observation as a starting point for a more general reflection on what counts as "good" or "bad," or perhaps more specifically "legitimate" and "illegitimate" religion at different levels of educational systems. Not least with regard to the question of what a legitimate or an illegitimate *object of study* is in particular educational contexts. Robertson focused on a very specific context: the undergraduate classroom of the religious studies program at the University of Edinburgh. I will broaden the focus of my reflection to both, university programs in the study of religions, school education about religion, and an interface between the two: teacher training programs in the study of religions.

Legitimate and Illegitimate Religion in the Academic Study of Religions

In the current study of religions (*Religionswissenschaft*) as a university discipline, there is a huge gap between theoretical and methodological reflection, not least about the categories *religion, religions,* and *world religions,* and the selection of aims and contents of introductory "history of religions" modules. Taking seriously the criticism of traditional concepts of religion and its implications for the study of religions would, in many cases, involve a complete revision of study programs. However, it almost seems as if many scholars in the study of religions see theoretical reflection about concepts of religion as something that should not seriously affect the classical way of conceptualizing the history of religions, not least because it may threaten exactly this classical (sub-)discipline, as it may involve a complete reconceptualization of the subject matter. This relates to the more subtle or implicit aspects of the question of what good or bad, legitimate or illegitimate religion is.

Despite frequent problematizations of an uncritical use of pre-academic concepts like religion or world religion, or the conceptualization of individual religions as discrete "-isms," I suppose that hardly anybody would question introductions to "Buddhism," "Christianity," "Islam," or "Hinduism" as legitimate parts of a current study program in the study of religions. This is an obvious contradiction, yet it makes sense, given the world religions paradigm's (WRP) "hegemonic status of ahistorical, universal 'common sense'" (Cotter and Robertson 2016: 10). A certain selection of a number of world religions (be it five, six, or seven) which each in itself forms an entity, with some kind of essence or "key aspects," is simply intuitively a legitimate subject matter for the study of religions, not only for outsiders such as politicians or scholars of other disciplines, but also for most scholars of religion. The canon of the world religions, including some core aspects of each of them, is too precious to be given up—also in the twenty-first-century research university. This leads to almost absurd arguments about the character and possible or impossible future of the study of religions.[1] Ironically, the fear of losing some kind of unique status (like theology?) of the study of religions—being able to study religions in a way that cannot be reproduced in any other academic setting—least of all in the sociology of religion (which, thus, apparently forms the most serious threat) is often used as an argument against truly making it a part of the social and cultural sciences, as opposed to any kind of theology. Letting go of pre-academic conceptions of a separate "sphere of the religious," which, in one way or another, often for better or worse, is expressed in the "world religions," and to be studied with special methods, is regarded as "academic suicide."[2] I think this links up to the question of good and bad, legitimate and illegitimate religion. Christianity (always legitimate) and the "-isms" (normally legitimate, depending on the contexts) and Islam (important, but often also the "significant other," intuitively related to "the abuse" of religion or "bad religion") are almost natural categories around which teaching in the Study of Religions is structured. Like animals and plants in biology. Trying to stay within the comparison, which always bears the danger of making simple mistakes: has the turn towards genetics been academic suicide for biology?

Building on the traditional concepts of religion and world religions, Scientology will always be "bad religion" or not really legitimate religion. Not because of the suspicion of brainwashing and other negative stereotypes ascribed to what is commonly conceptualized as "cult" (cf. Prophet 2014), but simply because it does not fit the pattern. It has not been in the focus, actually not even been around, when the concept was created. It is not part of the list that allows only for minimal variation.

Even studying aspects of the "big five," six, or seven that are part of the list *in alternative ways* that do not match the idea of some kind of essentials of the history, worldview, etc. of this "tradition" is suspicious. It somehow misses the very point: the holy subject matter of the history of religions.

Good and Bad Religion in School

With perhaps a few exceptions,[3] a study-of-religions approach to religion in school is virtually inexistent. I think, it is even almost safe to say that this is the case worldwide. Learning about religion from a critical, unbiased point of view is rarely part of school curricula. On the contrary, school systems in general tend to promote the instrumentalization of religion rather than its critical study. The frameworks in which religion is studied in school shows its peculiar status. It is part of most school curricula, but hardly ever by the same standards as other subjects.

This is most obvious in what I have called *separative* contexts, where pupils are divided into different groups when it comes to studying religion, as, for example, in most German federal states: religion is taught by or "in cooperation" with religious communities, always reflecting the general approach of that particular community. This may be liberal and somewhat critical—or it may not be. In the separative model,[4] the world religions paradigm figures prominently. In most European countries following that model, Christian RE (mostly divided in different denominations) is the unquestioned paradigm, by which "the rest" should be modelled or model itself. Due to historical sensitivity, if the wish arises, room is easily made for Jewish RE. Despite the large number of Muslims in many European countries, the introduction of Islamic RE has been a difficult process. In Germany, often simply because Islam is not structured like the Protestant or Catholic Churches. The model, when it was introduced, was made for the intuitively good and legitimate religion (Christianity) and can, in a way, only be introduced for a group that resembles this kind of *prototype* of religion in many important aspects. The rationale behind these kinds of confessional models in separative frameworks is, however, not to *teach about* those religions, but to educate the pupils to become good Christians or good Muslims and thereby good citizens. The whole debate about Islamic Religious Education shows that very clearly, including the role of Islam as the "significant other" that always has to face the hermeneutics of suspicion. Only when the fear of the phantom of Islamic terrorism grew stronger, the need for Islamic RE was acknowledged, with the clear aim of teaching "good" Islam in order to prevent radicalization. Other and, above all, smaller religions fit this structure even worse, thus the variety of confessional RE rarely stretches to other religious traditions, let alone new religious movements.

One recent development in separative contexts shows the instrumentalization of religion in school very clearly: the establishment of compulsory alternative subjects for children who do not take part in confessional RE. Why is confessional RE not just an optional subject for those who want to get orientation in "their" religious tradition from an insider's point of view? Apparently, confessional RE (irrespective of the fact that this may look very different in different traditions) is regarded as communicating something important that needs to be replaced by something else if it is absent. The names of the alternative subjects in German federal states, such as "ethics" or "values and norms" clearly show what those children who don't participate in confessional RE miss: to learn how to be a good and ethical person. Read from the bottom to the top, this is, apparently, the main aim of confessional RE, as this is the only common aspect to all the "alternatives" in the separative approach. You may learn that from a priest or teacher that belongs to a certain religious institution, who, in some way, relates the teachings of this tradition to leading an ethical life today. Any acknowledged religion is fine for providing this.

If you do not take part in confessional RE, however, you need to learn to be ethical in another way. But how? A closer look at the curricula for the so-called alternative subjects reveals the implicit agenda of this model. Often, they combine studying non-religious philosophical views on ethics and a study of ethical positions in different religions. At first sight, this seems to be less prone to instrumentalizing religion and to normatively dividing "good" from "bad" religion. After all, it is a framework that, unlike confessional RE, does not assign a particular religion a special position from the very beginning. However, in this context, judging religious traditions appears in a different shape, again heavily (perhaps even more so than in confessional RE) depending on the WRP.

In the current curriculum for the obligatory alternative subject *values and norms* ("*Werte und Normen*") in Lower Saxony, for example, religion is regarded mainly as a source of ethics.[5] Regardless of the actual complexity of the discourse about religion and very different ways of constructing, interpreting, and living religion/s, religion in general and the "world religions" in particular are regarded as sources of orientation, in some or another way now altogether providing a similar framework of orientation as individual traditions do in the neighboring classrooms, where the other children of the class attend confessional RE at the same time. Does it come as a surprise that also in this technically and legally non-confessional context Christianity has a very special status among the otherwise also acknowledged "world religions"? Perhaps not, if one looks further into the processes and responsibilities regarding curriculum development for those subjects. Ironically, theology and representatives of church institutions are often involved in teacher training and curriculum development for these non-confessional alternative subjects as well. Sometimes in an official function, often in a less visible way, as representatives of education authorities or schools who happen to have a background in theology or some other function in a church-related institution.

For example, the official guidelines and the curriculum for the subject *values and norms* in Lower Saxony relate it to philosophy, the study of religions (*Religionswissenschaft*) and other social sciences as responsible disciplines. In the last revision of the curriculum, however, there was no scholar of the study of religions involved. On the contrary, the official response of the Ministry to my comments—in my official function as the only professor for the study of religions and didactics of *values and norms*—to the draft curriculum, which I regard as crypto-theological and not at all in line with didactics of the study of religions, was that my reservations are not convincing, following a note that the revision committee had no need for support from the academic study of religions and its didactics. The Ministry just knows better than scholars in the study of religions what "Religionskunde" (knowledge about religion) is and what partial and impartial approaches to religious diversity are. The person responsible for the values and norms curriculum in the Ministry was trained in Protestant theology. Not an untypical situation, I suppose. At the moment, my conclusion about *values and norms* is, that declaring the study of religions one of the three responsible academic disciplines for *values and norms* is mere lip service and it will be only a question of time until this subject will be discussed in the courts again—the last court case against it made it up to the federal constitutional court, but took so long that it just ended when the respective child finished school.

In integrative contexts, where all children of a class together learn about religion/s—as for example in Sweden, Denmark, or Norway—similar issues arise in a different shape. Technically, integrative obligatory subjects have to represent religion in a "critical, objective and pluralistic"[6] way. Closer analyses show, however, that this also frequently is lip-service rather than reality. The adjustments to the curriculum of the obligatory subject KRL (later RLE, now KRLE),[7] after the judgement of the European Court of Human Rights (ECHR 2007) against it,[8] show that very clearly. Apparently, education about religion/s in school is inevitably an arena where the role of religion in society—and relationships between majority- and minority religion—is being negotiated controversially between different interest groups, in Europe with the well-established Christian Churches in a particularly privileged position in almost every model. This contributes to the creation of a hierarchy of legitimate and less legitimate, and thereby often also good and bad, religion.

Didactics of the Study of Religions in Evaluative Contexts

The situation sketched above, with respect to both school and university contexts, makes it very difficult to develop didactics of the study of religions, critically dealing with the various discourses in which good and bad religion are constructed. What should teachers trained in the study of religions know and be able to do? We have a problem already on the academic level, but, as I perhaps have shown above, even more so when it comes to school.

Sometimes, it seems to me that teaching in an academically responsible way is almost impossible in many given contexts. The authors of the chapters in *After World Religions: Reconstructing Religious Studies* (Cotter and Robertson 2016) develop critical, subversive, and innovative pedagogies for teaching introductory courses in the study of religions at universities. From my point of view, this is, without any doubt, a step in the right direction. However, relating that to teacher training for school subjects with much more restrictive legal frameworks (which, however, often contradict fundamental civil and human rights, as the cases against different models of religious education—not least the Norwegian one—have shown), is an even greater challenge.

On the one hand, it is an important educational success that the study of religions has become involved in teacher education at all. On the other hand, the frameworks for which the study of religions trains teachers often leaves it in a kind of catch-22 situation, having to make compromises that contradict its fundamental principles. In the present situation, where almost all teaching about religion in school is heavily influenced by religious interest groups, I don't see any alternative to extending the canon of critical, subversive, and innovative pedagogies also to teacher training. From an academic educational point of view, I think, it is more important to enable the students to develop critical analytical skills that allow them to analyze different contexts and the developments and power relations that have contributed to the status quo, rather than trying to stretch ourselves to, in one way or another, accommodating all these problematic presuppositions about religion that are inherent in most curricula. I think, this is a question of academic integrity. It is our duty as scholars to make visible the highly normative aspects of the dominant discourse about religion, religions, and world religions—and to show who actually benefits from and who loses by these dominant ways of conceptualizing religion/s. If we fail to do that, we become ourselves helpful instruments in the justification of the existing power structures, where intuitive evaluations of what is good or bad, legitimate or illegitimate religion are much more influential than actual facts.

Wanda Alberts professor in the study of religions at Leibniz Universität Hannover and chair of the working group "Religion in Public Education" of the European Association for the Study of Religions (EASR).

Notes

1. For example, recurrently, on the EASR-mailing list for the German speaking countries, Yggdrasill.
2. The formulation "academic suicide" was used by Perry Schmidt Leukel in his email to Yggdrasill on December 31, 2017, that sparked a new verbal exchange on that matter, with contributions from large number currently active scholars in the Study of Religions in Germany and other countries.
3. The subject "religion" in the Danish upper secondary school may be regarded as one of these rare exceptions. The syllabus even states that "it goes without saying" that this subject is based on the academic discipline of the study of religions (Undervisningsministeriet 2017: 2).
4. For my distinction between *separative* and *integrative* religious education, see Alberts (2007: 1).
5. See, for example, Niedersächsisches Kultusministerium (2017).
6. This is the formulation used by the European Court of Human Rights, for example, in a judgement against Norway (ECHR 2007).
7. The name of Norwegian integrative RE was changed several times, including *Kristendoms-, religions-, og livssynskunnskap* (KRL, *knowledge about Christianity, religions and views of life*), *Religion, livssyn og etikk* (RLE, *religion, views of life and ethics*, 2008-2015) and *Kristendom, religion, livssyn og etikk* (KRLE; *Christianity, religion, views of life and ethics*, from 2015).
8. The Norwegian model was found in conflict with human rights by two international institutions, the UN Human Rights Committee and the European Court of Human Rights (HRC 2004; ECHR 2007). Main points of criticism were the inclusion of religious practice in an obligatory subject and the qualitatively different representation of Christianity.

References

Alberts, Wanda. 2007. *Integrative Religious Education in Europe: A Study-of-Religions Approach*. Berlin: De Gruyter. https://doi.org/10.1515/9783110971347

Cotter, Christopher R., and David G. Robertson (eds.). 2016. *After World Religions: Reconstructing Religious Studies*. London: Routledge. https://doi.org/10.4324/9781315688046

ECHR (European Court of Human Rights). 2007. *Case of Folgerø and Others vs. Norway (Application no. 15472/02)*. Strasbourg: Council of Europe.

HRC (Human Rights Committee). 2004. "Communication No. 1155/2003, Adopted on 3 November 2004 (CCPR/C/82/D/1155/2003): *Leirvåg and Others v. Norway*." Retrieved from www.worldcourts.com/hrc/eng/decisions/2004.11.03_Leirvag_v_Norway.htm.

Niedersächsisches Kultusministerium 2017. *Werte und Normen Kerncurriculum für das Gymnasium - Schuljahrgänge 5-10*. Hannover: Land Niedersachsen.

Prophet, Erin. 2014. "Deconstructing the Scientology 'Monster' of Popular Imagination." *Alternative Spirituality and Religion Review* 5(2): 239–260. https://doi.org/10.5840/asrr20152183

Undervisningsministeriet. Styrelsen for Undervisning og Kvalitet. 2017. *Religion B/C, hf-enkeltfag, stx, valgfag - Vejledning*. Copenhagen: Undervisningsministeriet.

Chapter 20

Benign Religion as Normal Religion

Suzanne Owen

In many ways, I come from the same mold as David Robertson, as we had both completed our degrees in Religious Studies to PhD level at the University of Edinburgh. And, like Robertson, we departed from the dominant 'world religion' paradigm in our research. Mine began with investigating what makes an 'indigenous religion,' especially as the Mi'kmaq in Newfoundland were struggling for recognition as First Nations. Robertson went on to investigate 'conspiracy theory.' Thus, with encouragement from our respective PhD supervisors, James L. Cox and Steven Sutcliffe, both Robertson and I came to question the categories we were studying. While Robertson's area of research relates from the start to ideas of 'good' and 'bad religion,' it was when I began to research contemporary Druidry that this binary came to the fore in my own research with the prejudices against Paganism as 'religion.'

Druidry as 'Good' Religion

In a chapter Teemu Taira and I wrote on the Druid Network charity registration (Owen and Taira 2015), we included a discussion of the media discourse that followed, which implied a distinction between 'good' and 'bad' religion. Sensationalist headlines included the *Daily Mail*'s "Pagans Are on the March—but Are they Harmless Eccentrics or a Dangerous Cult?" (Brennan 2010) and the *Telegraph*'s "Druids: Worshippers of Nature Who Were Said to Sacrifice Humans" (Beckford 2010). A few years later, when the Druid Network applied to become a member of the Inter Faith Network UK, there was a similar distinction being made when they were initially rejected. The reason why the Druid Network sought membership to the IFN was because Druids were active in local interfaith groups but had been excluded by some because no Druid organization was a member of IFN. The IFN had sought exemption from admitting Druids "to avoid causing offence" to the other faiths in the network, which, according to an article in *The Times* (Gledhill 2012), prompted a Muslim representative to say, "allowing Druids to join would not offend Muslims." However, the "IFN defended its exclusion of the Druids by claiming that to allow them in would damage the charity's work to the extent that it could no longer carry out its charitable aim of 'promoting religious harmony among faith communities in Britain'" (ibid.).

When their application was rejected, several local interfaith groups did come out to support them, such as Hull and East Riding, who wrote in their letter to IFN: "It seemed puzzling and paradoxical to all who spoke [at their meeting] that the [...] IFN, should be opposed particularly to so benign a movement devoted to nature and the countryside" and that they "had no problem with Pagans, once some education was given about their modern form not the centuries-old fearsome one." They added that a policeman said Pagans were now accepted in a "normal way." At the end of the letter they pointed out that they find contemporary Pagan spiritual expressions interesting and sincere. In other words, a benign, non-threatening, sincere religion is the 'normal' religion (Hull and East Riding Interfaith 2012).

The IFN eventually revised their membership policy to be more inclusive whilst still holding the right to determine membership. In light of this change the Druid Network re-applied for membership and were admitted on 29th September 2014 along with the Church of Jesus Christ of the Latter Day Saints, the Spiritualists National Union, and the Pagan Federation. In addition, Prudence Jones of the Pagan Federation, was appointed to the Executive Committee of the Inter Faith Network (Druid Network 2014).

Gaining recognition as a religion helps to emphasize a distinction between good and bad religion. Thus, government-sponsored commissions and organizations serve to domesticate religion, keeping it out of the political sphere, and pushing groups to conform to a liberal Protestant Christian definition of religion: the supreme being is transcendent, requiring worship practices; there is a creed; religion is good and works for public benefit; religious people are good and do good works. If they don't, they're not *really* religious or that form of religion isn't really a religion.

The Problem of Teaching 'Religion'

Religious Studies scholars, if they are not primarily 'areas studies' specialists, tend to gravitate toward the study of 'contemporary religion' (as opposed to 'traditional religion,' for the purposes of this chapter) and by doing so come across discourses about religion as a category. Inevitably, they turn to those cases where current issues play out most strongly: if not an analysis of media or 'popular culture,' then a focus on minority religions that do not fit conventional definitions of the category based on Protestant ethical concerns with the 'good.' Hence, many scholars that present papers at the annual conference of the British Association for the Study of Religions research NRMs, Pagans, other marginal groups, and so-called secular religions or practices.

However, when it comes to teaching religion, we find a tension, an anxiety about whether our courses should be filled with references to Jedi, Druidry, Scientology, and spiritualism or to teach the basics of Hinduism, Buddhism, and the like. At first, I put studies of contemporary religion in the method and theory module, as that was where theories of 'religion' and the problems of categorization are easily illustrated by these boundary cases. My follow-on module, which has a section on sociology of religion, also includes such cases. Eventually, my final year module also included them. One problem, perhaps, is that by focusing on these cases, we are over-emphasizing their 'abnormality.' To counteract this, I have included examples from Catholicism, which I have come to know quite well, mainly through students' interests, after years of being in a Catholic-foundation institution. As Graham Harvey has argued, because we take it for granted, we do not recognize the "abnormality" of Christianity with its focus on "belief" (Harvey 2013: 43). He expanded on this later saying Christianity has been mis-defined as "belief" (ibid.: 187), as what Christians do is not so different from what other people do.

That aside, discussing NRMs in the classroom can be useful for several reasons, such as for exploring the notion of "invented religion" (Cusack 2010), and the interrelation between fiction and religion, as in obvious cases like Jedi and Scientology. Some members of the public, including students, at first regard some NRMs as "not real," such as Discordianism (ibid.: 2). I've heard this in relation to Druidry—that Druids are 'making it up' as they go along. In some scholarship, such groups might be referred to as 'quasi-religions,' which positions them as inferior to 'proper' religions modelled on Christianity with identifiable creeds, texts, and places of worship. Robertson, in his essay, refers to the assumption raised by the study of NRMs to consider "what religion really is."

Likewise, in essays, students often come to discuss the nature of 'true' Islam or Christianity as non-violent, etc., and do not realize they are making a distinction based on social preferences for 'good' religion. In the university classroom, it is worthwhile exploring students' own preferences about religion in open discussion, perhaps using Eileen Barker's short *Guardian* piece, "One Person's Cult Is Another's True Religion," as a starting point (Barker 2009). This would work as well in either a high school or a university classroom.

If students understand how religions are invented, then it should not be too much of a leap to re-evaluate long-established groups, such as the Catholic Church. However, as pointed out by Carole M. Cusack (2010: 1) at the start of her book on *Invented Religions*, the notion "contradicts the traditional understanding of religion as a phenomenon that traces its origins to divine revelation." Although the origins of Hinduism, included as one of the 'world religions,' are varied and contested (as all religions should be), there is the idea that seven rishis 'heard' the Vedas. As such, what might be regarded as 'tradition' has been shaped through selection, rejection, and invention. Cusack's book, though, focusses on those that explicitly state their inventedness.

Another reason to teach NRMs in the classroom is the religion/cult distinction in discourse. Eileen Barker's view that a cult is a religion you don't like (especially as many groups exhibit similar characteristics) relates directly to the question of 'good' and 'bad' religion (Barker 2009). Barker includes in a chapter she wrote in a volume on cults and violence a section called "Constructing the 'Other'" on cult awareness groups: "The predominant concern is to warn others of dangers and to control the activities of the movements" (Barker 2002: 128).

Barker points out how much of the language we use to discuss New Religious Movements emerged out of "cult awareness groups" (CAGs):

> Through the media, CAGs have not only supplied good stories, they have also provided the concepts and the grammar with which the general public (including officials) can frame their understanding of NRMs. Nouns such as "cult" and "pseudo-religion"; verbs such as "brainwash," "manipulate," and "exploit"; adjectives such as "bizarre," "fanatic," and "violent"; and the use of passive voice for "victims" who *had been* duped and *had to be* rescued effectively diminish the likelihood that members of NRMs could have made choices and/or be capable of leaving (although, in fact, most do of their own free will). Cultists become reduced to another species, incapable of the normal reasoning and morality of real people, and, thus, not to be treated as if they were like us. (Barker 2002: 143)

This is why including NRMs in the classroom can be essential for unpacking the interests of those who employ these distinctions such as good and bad religion. Although Barker does not mention precisely that scholars sometimes also repeat this rhetoric, she says that "what is presented as abnormal from a cult-awareness perspective might be seen as far more normal from a research-oriented perspective" (ibid.: 147). Certainly, it is worthwhile looking at the similarities between 'abnormal' cults and 'normal' religions, and thus dissolving that binary, but one could take this further to uncover what gets regarded as 'religion' in the first place.

Overhauling Religious Studies

I argue that it is time to stop doing what is traditionally expected in religious studies (RS), which is for students to gain 'knowledge and understanding' of two or more 'traditional' religions under the essentializing labels of Christianity, Islam, Hinduism, and the like. This version of RS is dead or dying as cut-backs have led to decreases in staff or the end of RS as a separate subject altogether. Initially, I lamented its passing, because I thought I had gained a 'solid' undergraduate education studying four years of mainly historical and textual religions, which served me well for the first few years of my teaching career, until the divergence between my research and what I taught became too great to sustain.

Students today in a UK university will have to attend a specialist area studies department now to get that kind of focus, but these programs are not really the best places for the study of 'religion.' Thus now we must decide what it is we are doing and what do we want students to gain out of it. Some speak about 'religious literacy' (e.g. Wright 2015, from the view of philosophical theology). Well, I think that's part of the old way of doing RS. What I would like to see instead is 'religion' literacy: knowledge and understanding of how 'religion' is constructed (by scholars, media, popular culture, etc.), the interests being served (issues of power, etc.) and the implications of this construction. I don't want to teach what students can find for themselves in Wikipedia and I don't want them to replicate this in their assessments. In short, I want students to become critical scholars. It doesn't matter what 'of,' but being a critical scholar of 'religion' is as good as any other Humanities focus and it easily adapts to other Humanities subjects (writing Master's-level essays on English literature taught me this). I once taught history in a school—again, being a critical scholar served me well. I knew I didn't need to 'know history,' I needed to know how to study it. This sounds like I'm saying content is irrelevant and in some ways I am saying that. Content is everywhere, hence the 'information age' we find ourselves in. But, being human, we look for the 'new,' and what is new in all that information? New insights, new theories, methods, perspectives. These are what we can bring with us to cast onto any topic. I only limit my research activities for the sake of convention, because, even though interdisciplinarity is considered a 'good thing,' at the end of the day grant funding wants two specialists in one subject each to collaborate rather than one scholar looking at different topics because they look like a dilettante if they study too many, as it appears on the surface. In my case, these were: indigenous religions and Paganism and method and theory in the study of religion, which theologians and scholars in area studies do not regard as a "real" subject. Yet the way I look at 'indigeneity' is the way I look at 'religion,' 'sacred,' 'spirituality,' and 'Pagan': as constructed categories expressing an individual's or group's preferences.

Suzanne Owen is Reader in Religious Studies at Leeds Trinity University (UK).

References

Barker, Eileen. 2002. "Watching for Violence: A Comparative Analysis of the Roles of Five Types of Cult Watching Groups." In David G. Bromley and J. Gordon Melton (eds.), *Cults, Religion, and Violence*, 123–148. Cambridge: Cambridge University Press. https://doi.org/10.1017/CBO9780511499326.008

Barker, Eileen. 2009. "One Person's Cult Is Another's True Religion." *The Guardian*, 29 May. Retrieved from www.theguardian.com/commentisfree/belief/2009/may/29/cults-new-religious-movements (archived at www.webcitation.org/6z18EDwpp).

Beckford, Martin. 2010. "Druids: Worshippers of Nature Who Were Said to Sacrifice Humans." *The Telegraph*, October 2. Retrieved from www.telegraph.co.uk/news/religion/8037258/Druids-Worshippers-of-nature-who-were-said-to-sacrifice-humans.html (archived at www.webcitation.org/6z18QHsOS)

Brennan, Zoe. 2010. "Pagans Are on the March—but Are They Harmless Eccentrics or a Dangerous Cult?" *The Daily Mail*, November 12. Retrieved from www.dailymail.co.uk/femail/article-1328968/Pagans-march--harmless-eccentrics-dangerous-cult.html (archived at www.webcitation.org/6z18UeGsl)

Cusack. Carole M. 2010. *Invented Religions: Imagination, Fiction and Faith*. Farnham: Ashgate Press.

Druid Network. 2014. "TDN to join Inter Faith Network." The Druid Network, October 1. Retrieved from https://druidnetwork.org/tdn-joins-inter-faith-network/ (archived at www.webcitation.org/6z1Buef9h).

Gledhill, Ruth. 2012. "Interfaith Group's Refusal to Admit Druids Sparks Row." *The Times*, December 1. Retrieved from www.thetimes.co.uk/article/interfaith-groups-refusal-to-admit-druids-sparks-row-nxf7mj3qswk (archived at www.webcitation.org/78aGznw4Q).

Harvey, Graham. 2013. *Food, Sex and Strangers: Understanding Religion as Everyday Life*. Durham: Acumen. https://doi.org/10.4324/9781315729572

Hull and East Riding Interfaith. 2012. "Missing Documents for Interfaith Network Annual General Meeting." June 28. Retrieved from www.theinterfaithnetwork.org.uk/missing_documents.pdf (archived at www.webcitation.org/78aGznw4Q).

Owen, Suzanne and Teemu Taira. 2015. "The Category of 'Religion' in Public Classification: Charity Registration of the Druid Network in England and Wales." In Trevor Stack, Naomi Goldenberg, and Timothy Fitzgerald (eds.) *Religion as a Category of Governance and Sovereignty*, 90–117, Leiden: Brill. https://doi.org/10.1163/9789004290594_006

Wright, Andrew. 2015. *Religious Education and Critical Realism: Knowledge, Reality and Religious Literacy*. Abingdon: Routledge. https://doi.org/10.4324/9780203866306

Index

African religions, 85
Adorno, Theodor W., 24, 32
agency, 16, 19–20, 41, 43, 47, 163, 190
Alberts, Wanda, 123, 182
Althusser, Louis, 70, 109, 111, 116
Altman, Michael, 82, 86
American Academy of Religion (AAR), 12–14, 21, 47
American Society for the Study of Religion (ASSR), 17
apologetics, 23, 25, 32, 43, 55, 60, 63, 67, 75, 82, 85, 124, 166, 192
Armstrong, Karen, 21
Arthur, John, 177–78
Asad, Talal, 41, 164
Aslan, Reza, 57, 69–87, 89–92, 94–96, 99–100, 103–6, 108–9, 111–16, 118–19, 156, 164
Asprem, Egil, 161, 168
atheism, 27, 66, 135, 148, 154, 156–57, 160–61, 164, 165, 167, 187
authentic religion, 19, 24, 63, 65, 71, 80–81, 102, 113, 118–23, 125, 160
authority, 9, 18–21, 23–24, 42, 64–65, 79, 82, 88–89, 110, 151, 162

Baer, Ulrich, 139, 146, 177–78
Bailey, Edward, 164
Bal, Mieke, 174, 178
Baldas, Tresa, 45–46
Barker, Eileen, 184, 191, 214–16
Barthes, Roland, 37, 46, 90
Bartlett, Tom, 171, 174, 178
Battaglio, Stephen, 85
Becker, Carmen, 69, 119
Beckford, James A., 63, 67, 155–56, 164
Beckford, Martin, 212, 216
Believer (TV show), 57, 69–78, 80–91, 94, 99–100, 102–3, 105–9, 111–12, 114–16, 118–20, 122, 161, 199, 201

Bellah, Robert, 203
Berger, Peter, 164
Berlant, Lauren, 65, 67
Blair, Leonardo, 172, 178
Boko Haram, 19–20
Boostrom, Robert, 175–76, 178
Bourdieu, Pierre, 88–89, 95–96
Brehony, Kevin J., 170, 178
Brown, Wendy, 155, 165
Brubaker, Rogers, 24–25, 32
Bruce, Steve, 156, 165
Buddhism, 28–30, 32, 85, 184, 187–88, 195, 199–201, 203, 206, 213
Butler, Judith, 41, 46–47, 56, 58, 60
Butler Bass, Diana, 74, 84

Cadwalladr, Carole, 152
campus religion, 127, 129, 131–32, 134–35, 141, 147, 169, 172, 176, 179
Canada, 46, 61–62, 64, 66
capitalism, 110, 114, 193, 199–200
Carroll, Michael P., 146
Carroll, William K., 110
caste, 79, 111
Catholicism, 80, 84, 112, 116, 124, 134, 148, 214
Cavanaugh, William T., 37, 46, 56, 60, 66–67, 162, 165
Christianity, 3, 5, 29–30, 51, 72, 131–32, 135, 138, 146, 162, 164, 184, 187, 195–96, 199–200, 206–7, 210, 214–15
Cohen, Robin, 197, 199, 203
Collins, Peter J., 142, 147
Cook, Michael, 13, 21
Cotter, Christopher R., 128, 184, 191, 206, 209, 211
Cragun, Ryan T., 158, 160, 164–65, 168
Crank, James A., 59
Crenshaw, Kimberle, 173, 178
critical theory, 46, 171, 173–74, 191

Crone, Patricia, 13, 21
cults, ix, 79, 106, 114, 148, 155, 181, 183–84, 196, 200–202, 205–6, 214–16
Cusack, Carole M., 187, 192, 214, 216

Darm, Ricarda, 122, 124
Davidsen, Markus A., 184–85, 192
Davie, Grace, 156, 159, 164–65
Davydov, Alexander, 130, 147
Dennett, Daniel, 152–53
Deresiewicz, William, 127, 129, 131–32, 147, 176, 178–79
desecularization, 164
Dobbernack, Jan, 165
Dorrough Smith, Leslie, 69
Drucker, Peter, 109–10, 116
druids, 182, 212–14, 216
Dugan, Lisa, 66–67
Durkheim, Émile, 194, 196, 200, 202–3
Dye, Guillaume, 21

El-Badawi, Emran, 21
Ellison, Christopher G., 158, 167
ethics, 129, 207–8, 210
European Association for the Study of Religions (EASR), 210
Eyl, Jennifer, 155, 162, 166
Eyre, Ronald, 75, 85

Farias, Miguel, 165
Faris, Robert, 167
Feiler, Bruce, 75, 84
Felsenthal, Julia, 85
feminism, 8, 25–26, 32, 41–42, 46, 127, 129, 133, 141, 157, 160, 171–73, 175, 178, 185
Fergusson, David, 156, 166
Fernández-Sebastián, Javier, 180
Fernando, Mayanthi L., 37–38, 46, 62, 66–67
Fessenden, Tracy, 42, 46–47
Fillitz, Thomas, 87, 96
fire-walking (Anastenaria), 48–55
Fisk, Robert, 64, 67, 69, 84, 119
Fitzgerald, Timothy, 46–47, 121, 124, 155, 158, 160–62, 166, 204, 217
Foucault, Michel, 132
France, 46, 109, 111, 192

free speech, 134–35, 140–41, 146, 149, 177–78, 180
Freeden, Michael, 180
Führding, Steffen, 70
Fulcher, James, 197, 199, 201, 204
Fuller, Thomas, 130, 147
fundamentalism, viii, 30, 80, 120, 154, 157

Galen, Luke W., 159, 168
gender, 7, 25, 36, 43, 46, 56–57, 59, 99, 106, 130, 132–33, 135, 159, 173
Germany, 10, 31, 66, 92–95, 118, 130, 145, 152, 207, 210
Giddens, Anthony, 197–201, 204
Gieryn, Thomas F., 127, 151, 153
globalization, 110, 114
Goldenberg, Naomi R., 35–36, 56, 62–63, 65, 202, 204, 217
good/bad religion discourse, viii–ix, 1, 49, 56, 62–65, 69, 155, 159, 195, 199–200, 203
Greece, ix, 48–55
Gregg, Stephen E., 163, 165
Gripentrog, Stephanie, 127
Guernsey, Andrew, 177
Gumbrecht, Hans Ulrich, 177

Hacking, Ian, 172, 179
Haidt, Jonathan, 98, 107, 134, 147
Hardacre, Helen, 196, 204
Harris, Marvin, 147
Harris, Sam, 155, 166
Harvey, Graham, 214, 216
Hawkins, Christine, 176, 179
Headland, Thomas N., 146–47
heresy, 28, 131–32
Hermann, Adrian, 127, 156, 163, 169, 171, 176
hijab, 64–65, 130
Hinduism, 71, 78–80, 82, 84, 105, 184, 187, 189, 192, 199, 206, 213–15
Hjelm, Titus, 155–56, 166
Horii, Mitsutoshi, 182
Hourmouziadis, Anastasios, 50–51, 54–55
Hughes, Aaron W., 1, 5, 11, 23–25, 27–29, 31–32, 47, 53, 55, 59–60, 62–63, 66–67, 81, 85, 122, 124, 154, 157–59, 162–63, 166, 190, 192
Huntwork, David, 130, 147

identities, 4–5, 7–9, 16, 19, 24, 47, 50–52, 55, 57, 60, 87–88, 99, 102, 118, 120, 124, 132–33, 136, 167, 172
identity politics, 24, 59, 131–34, 136, 139, 141, 143, 148, 157, 172–73, 177–78, 184–85
ideology, 16, 22, 39, 41, 44, 109, 112, 120, 124, 133, 135, 162, 166, 171–72, 178, 197
idolatry, 52, 54
Ihm, Elliott, 168
inclusion, 40, 62, 132, 156, 210
India, 73, 78, 81–82, 112–13, 116, 192, 199
Indigenous religions, 186, 212, 216
individualism, 24, 66, 112, 114, 201
interreligious dialogue, 120
intersectionality, 131, 133–34, 136, 146–48, 171–75, 178–79
Islamicists, 15, 95
Islamophobia, 64, 66–68
Islamic religious studies, 1, 12, 63, 81, 128, 158, 160, 162
Insider/Outsider Problem, 1, 32, 85, 122, 124, 127, 129, 136–48, 163, 165, 167, 169
International Quranic Studies Association (IQSA), 14, 21
Irak, 10, 19, 155
ISIS, vii, 3, 6–8, 10–11, 19–21, 121–22, 155, 157
Islam, vii, 1, 3, 8, 10, 12–16, 18–21, 23, 28–29, 32, 41, 43, 59–60, 66–67, 83, 85, 89, 92–94, 120–24, 155–58, 163–64, 184, 195–96, 199–200, 206–7, 214–15
Israel, 15, 39, 78, 112, 114

Japan, 31–32, 75, 161, 182, 194–98, 200, 202–4
Jesus, 8, 85, 96, 98
Johnston, Ian, 130, 147
Josephson-Storm, Jason Ānanda, 1
Judaism, 14–16, 31–32, 35, 45, 71, 80–82, 85, 112, 119, 124, 184–85, 187, 198–99, 202

Kaldewey, David, 128
Kehler, Marie Lisa, 130, 147
Kennedy, Paul, 197, 199, 203

Knott, Kim, 122, 124, 142, 146–47, 155–57, 166
Koch, Anne, 136, 147

Lange, Dirk, 122, 124
Lanman, Jonathan, 165
law, viii, 35, 39, 45–46, 57, 61, 63, 122, 174
Lee, Lois, 157–59, 161, 165–66
Levinovitz, Alan J., 137–38, 140, 147
Lincoln, Bruce, 14, 16, 18, 21–22, 29, 32, 66–67, 140, 143, 147, 163, 167
Lindholm, Charles, 87, 96
Lindsay, James A., 132–33, 135–36, 146–48, 177, 180
Lopez Jr, Donald S., 29–30, 32
Lukianoff, Greg, 134, 147
Lundquist Denton, Melinda, 167

Macionis, John J., 198–99, 201, 204
Mahmood, Saba, 41, 43–44, 47, 63
March, Andrew F., 165
Marcus, George E., 90, 96
marginalization, 127, 129, 139, 141, 144, 151
Marouan, Maha, 59
Martin, Craig, 59, 121, 124, 162, 166–67, 193
Marx, Karl, 32, 109, 156, 163, 194, 196–98, 200–204
Marxism, 172–75, 197–98
Mayblin, Maya, 148
McCutcheon, Russell T., 1, 16–17, 21, 32, 49–50, 52–55, 120–22, 124, 127, 138, 140, 147–48, 150–51, 153, 163, 167
McFarland, Melanie, 114–16
McMahan, David L., 29–30, 33
McPhillips, Kathleen, 46
media, vii–ix, 9, 15, 45, 50–51, 69, 72, 78, 81, 88, 99–100, 162, 181, 184, 186, 189, 196, 213, 215
Merton, Robert K., 146, 148
Meyer, Birgit, 146, 148, 159, 167
Michael-Dede, Maria, 50, 55
Middle East, 19, 42–43, 95
minorities, 42, 64, 155, 161, 171, 209, 213
Modood, Tariq, 165, 191–92
Muesse, Mark, 85
Muhanna, Elias, 85–86
Mulvey, Laura, 69, 100–101, 105, 107
Murray, Charles, 130–31

Nayna, Mike, 132–33, 135–36, 145, 147
Nelson, Lauren, 133, 148
New Age, 85, 186, 188, 191
New Atheism, 146, 156, 164, 166–67
New Religious Movements, 155, 164, 181–88, 190, 205, 207, 214–15
Newey, Glen, 165
niqab, 36, 61–68
non-religion, 128, 154–68, 201
normativity, 24, 26, 28–30, 65, 150–52

orientalism, 12, 14, 19–20, 30, 81–82, 190
orthodoxy, 28, 66, 91, 129, 131–32, 134
outsiders, 1, 23–26, 28, 32, 62, 103, 122, 138–39, 141, 146, 148, 163, 206
Owen, Suzanne, 182, 184, 192

paganism, 48, 50, 182, 212–13, 216
Palmer, Susan J., 188, 192–93
Pasquale, Frank L., 158–59, 167–68
perennialism, 76–77, 83, 89–91, 105
Pike, Kenneth L., 147
Pilgrim, Richard B., 85
Plantinga, Alvin, 156, 167
Pluckrose, Helen, 133, 146–48, 177, 180
Plummer, Ken, 198–99, 201, 204
political correctness, 14, 127, 129–32, 134–36, 139, 141, 146–47, 150, 155–56, 163, 169, 173, 177, 179
Poole, Elizabeth, 166
Poole, Steven, 155–57, 167
post-colonialism, 171–72
postsecularism, 37–47, 62, 67, 148
Powers, David S., 13, 22
Prentiss, Craig, 70
Preston, James J., 189, 192
Prideaux, Melanie, 156, 167
Priester, Stefan, 127, 156, 163, 169, 171, 176
Protestantism, 20, 66, 80, 84, 146, 162, 183, 189–90, 200, 207, 213
pseudo-religion, 215
public sphere, 36, 46, 66, 88, 92, 121, 130, 134–35, 140, 183, 186, 190
Putnam, Hilary, 27, 31, 33

race, 25, 59, 99, 103, 130, 132–33, 178–79
Reader, Ian, 195, 204
Regnerus, Mark, 167
Reifler, Jason, 152–53

religion
 bad, viii, 1, 52, 62, 71, 74–77, 79–83, 91, 128–49, 154–56, 163–64, 131, 135, 141, 172, 183, 187, 194, 198–200, 206, 209, 212–13, 215
 contemporary, 191, 213
 false, 134–35
 good, viii, 28, 62–63, 73–77, 79–81, 87, 91, 119, 154–55, 161–63, 194, 198–200
 illegitimate, 182, 205–6, 210
 in public education, 210
 new, 129, 132–33, 178, 193, 196, 198, 200–202
 traditional, 46, 133, 197–98, 213, 215
 true, 78, 135, 214, 216
religiosity, 42, 119
religious diversity, 69, 87–97, 209
religious education, 123, 209, 217
religious experience, 71–72, 76–77, 113, 118, 122, 145
religious freedom, viii, 44–45, 61–65, 67
religious pluralism, 83, 120, 165
religious studies, viii, 1, 10, 12–14, 16, 18–19, 21, 23–33, 46–47, 49, 59, 77, 81, 83, 85, 122, 137–39, 143–45, 154–55, 157–58, 164, 166, 189, 191, 194, 211–12, 215–16
 Islamic, 1, 12, 63, 81, 128, 158, 160, 162
religious violence, 37, 46, 60, 67, 165
Riordan, Michael, 151, 153
Roberts, Martha Smith 69, 87, 118–19
Robertson, David G., 159, 164–65, 181, 205–6, 209, 211–12, 214
Robinson, William I., 110–11, 117

Sachsenmaier, Dominic, 177, 180
Samuel, Sigal, 86
Saris, Jamie, 87, 96
Schmidt, Marie, 177, 179
Schnall, Marianne, 84
Schreiber, Constantin, 89, 92–97, 119
Scientology, 71, 73, 80, 91, 111, 114, 116, 183, 187–93, 206, 211, 213–14
Scott, Joan, 42, 47, 63
Scott, John, 197, 204
secularism, 30–31, 38, 41–43, 63, 67–68, 80, 82, 132–33, 136, 146, 157, 163, 165, 168

Shapiro, Amy, 177–78
Sheedy, Matt, 36
Sheehi, Stephan, 64, 68
Simmons, Merinda, 36
Simpson, Robert M., 141, 149
Singal, Jesse, 85
Sklair, Leslie, 110, 117
Slater, Tom, 134, 149, 170, 180
Smith, Buster G., 164
Smith, Jonathan Z., 5, 11, 16, 50, 54, 70, 76, 106–7, 158
Smith Roberts, Martha, 69, 71–87, 118
sociology of religion, 53, 158, 165, 167, 194, 199, 202, 204, 206, 214
spirituality, 37, 40, 78, 84, 103, 112, 114, 163, 168, 185–86, 192, 216
Stack, Trevor, 46, 204, 217
Stoddard, Brad, 47, 166, 185
Sturm, Tristan, 191
Sudan, 38, 62
Sullivan, Andrew, 131–34, 146, 148–49, 172, 180
Sutcliffe, Steven J., 168, 191, 212

Taira, Teemu, 155–57, 166, 212, 217
Tanabe, George, 195–96, 204
Taves, Ann, 161, 168
Teuwsen, Jan, 118–20, 123, 125
theology, 26, 29, 50, 83, 91, 138–39, 142, 159, 206, 208
Thomas, Terence, 160, 168
Tiffin, Helen, 153
Tønder, Lars, 165
Touna, Vaia, 36, 40, 47
Troeltsch, Ernst, 184, 193
Turkey, 48

United Kingdom, 40, 67, 130, 156–57, 161, 177, 184, 194, 198, 203, 212, 215–16
United States, 3, 6, 10, 14, 25, 45, 57, 75, 83, 91, 112, 130, 134–35, 151, 161, 169, 188, 198
Urban, Hugh, 188–89, 193

value-neutrality, 1, 24, 26, 28, 31
Van der Pijl, Kees, 110, 117
Van Maanen, John, 90, 97
Victoria, Brian Daizen, 25, 33
Voas, David, 156, 164
voodoo, 73–74

Wacquant, Loïc, 88–89, 96–97
Walls, Andrew F., 24, 33
Warner, Michael, 64–65, 67–68
Weber, Max, 27, 33, 40, 47, 139, 166, 189, 193–94, 196, 198–204
Webster, Joseph, 191
Wicca, 186–88, 190
Woodhead, Linda, 156, 162, 164, 168, 186, 191–92
world religions, 127–28, 132, 134, 159, 165, 167, 182, 184–92, 194, 199–214
women, ix, 8, 13, 25, 35, 39, 41–43, 61, 63, 66–67, 70, 94–95, 100–101, 106, 124, 133, 178, 185
Wright, Andrew, 215, 217
Wright, Stuart, 188, 193
Wylie, Alison, 25–26, 33, 143–44, 149

Xygalatas, Dimitris, 50, 53–55

yoga, 186, 192

Zuckerman, Phil, 159–60, 164, 168

www.ingramcontent.com/pod-product-compliance
Lightning Source LLC
Chambersburg PA
CBHW062023220426
43662CB00010B/1445